THE WEALTH GAME

THE WEALTH GAME

An Ordinary Person's Companion

Peter Alcaraz

Published by Hutchinson Reed

First edition published 2016 (print and electronic)

© Peter Alcaraz 2016 (print and electronic)

The right of Peter Alcaraz to be identified as the author of this work has been asserted by him in accordance with the Copyright, Designs, and Patents Act 1988.

Hutchinson Reed is not responsible for the content of third-party Internet sites.

ISBN: print   9780993197802
e-book—PDF   978-0-9931978-1-9
ISBN: 0993197809

British Library Cataloguing-in-Publication Data
A catalogue record for the print edition is available from the British Library.

www.hutchinsonreed.com

'What a refreshing book. *The Wealth Game* is an entertaining and practical guide to building wealth that goes beyond the usual what, when and how of personal finance. It also asks the much more interesting questions: why, who for and how much is enough?'
Tom Stevenson, investment director, Fidelity International and Sunday Telegraph columnist

'It's not often that a top city dealmaker passes on their top tips for success, which is one of several reasons that Peter Alcaraz's *The Wealth Game* is a compelling read. More surprisingly, though, Alcaraz identifies a delicate balance that so many in his profession have failed to even consider: how much is enough, how wealth and happiness must go hand-in-hand.'
Mark Leftly, deputy political editor, The Independent on Sunday and business commentator, The Independent

'*The Wealth Game* is the light at the end of the tunnel to a financial dummy like me. Not only has Peter Alcaraz managed to create an easy read about sorting out one's finances, but I actually feel I can now put this previously taboo subject into practice.'
Trish Sims, Daily Express Newspapers

'An excellent guide to creating and managing your own financial plan for those with the inclination and self-discipline to do so and the fact that the author has actually done it gives particular credibility. It addresses the important psychological aspects as well as the financial nuts and bolts and practicalities.'
Robert Lockie, Chartered Wealth Manager, Certified Financial Planner and branch principal, Bloomsbury Wealth

'If the Yuppies had Gordon Gekko and his double-breasted suits in the 1980's, then *The Wealth Game* author Peter Alcaraz has written the ultimate how-to-quit-the-rat-race for the Hipster Generation.

Goodbye to "greed is good" and hello to "think and act poor", "neediness is an obstacle" and "embrace the rebel within." Alcaraz knows the power of a good catchphrase in this thoroughly approachable read, which claims you don't need a degree in sums and weird financial symbols to achieve financial success.

Having fulfilled his dream to retire at forty five years old, this former city high-flyer shows us the "path to O" – a place where any ordinary solvent person with a bit of drive and one of those big whizzy calculators can over-haul their finances, maximise their surplus cash, and build a nest egg big enough to set them free.

This is no how-to-get-rich-quick book: it's part personal story of how one man played an inherently unfair system at its own game and won, and part spiritual guide on how to turn yourself into a lean, mean, non-spending machine using a sprinkling of Spartan and Buddhist philosophies and dull but necessary book-keeping skills.

There are many guides on how to play the markets, but this is one of the few that actually explains simply how to tear up the rule book, develop a bit of commercial nous and not let so-called financial experts siphon off half your pension in hidden charges.

Using easy to understand case studies to explain brain-numbing high fi-nance, the author opens up a whole new world to the average reader, in-cluding compounding, which Einstein called "the eighth wonder of the world; he who understands it, earns it, he who doesn't, pays it." Having read *The Wealth Game*, the fact that I now understand compounding must surely be the ninth wonder of the world."
Siobhan McNally, columnist and lifestyle journalist, The Daily Mirror

ACKNOWLEDGMENTS

Thank you to Derek Joseph, Darren Redmayne and Robert Lockie for their editing input, Sophie Lederer for her design help, and Richard Dale, David Bridgford, Tim Guy, Kevin and Zirrinia Austin Dean and Lucy Sayer for their ongoing support.

I dedicate the book to my wife, Jessie, and our daughters, Rebecca and Maddy, who patiently put up with my struggles to organize and refine the ideas and text and were ever-willing test subjects.

CONTENTS

PREFACE

Provision is a basic human instinct. It stems from our need to eat, drink, and stay warm. Money transforms the picture. Instead of having to make a shelter, grow your own food, and search for water, you can pay someone else to do these things. It offers a different kind of self-sufficiency. And, even better, you can build a pot of money to provide long after you are too feeble or old to earn it by your own labour.

This presents a dilemma: How do you balance the rewards from a finite working life between today's and future needs? Do you (1) work to afford daily demands but no more until you die or become dependent; at the mercy of charity or state, or (2) set aside money to achieve financial independence so that you can pay your way without working for money?

The dual premise of this book is that (1) financial self-sufficiency is a worthwhile goal, and (2) it is achievable far quicker than you might think.

Why worthwhile? It's a seminal moment: release from the obligation to work for money that has probably defined your existence since early adulthood. A door opens, and, like stepping up a level in a computer game, you enter a higher phase of play, with time and space to pursue other interests and goals. You can tick the box marked "enough" and move on. The value of this depends on how much you buy in to the idea that what you do in life is more important than what you have, if you believe in it at all.

Presenting a case for the second contention is more involved and forms the meat of the book.

I am driven by the knowledge that financial mismanagement causes suffering, yet frustration is easily avoidable. Why is it such a common problem?

The first difficulty is that people, particularly older generations, don't like talking about money. There's plenty of moaning, blaming, and superficial banter but not much of any substance. The topic touches a nerve and stays shut in an elephant-sized closet, unavoidable yet largely ignored. This reticence is compounded by a general failure to educate people, both young and old, about finance and an apparent acceptance by government and society that financial illiteracy or a lack of capability around money is quite normal and too hard to cure. Thrown into a noisy and confusing marketplace, many people fail to grasp basic financial concepts or any notion of medium-to long-term strategy, and they make lifestyle decisions in a vacuum, with no commercial framework or bigger picture, only to be surprised or disappointed with where they end up.

A further problem is that no one sets out to make you wealthy, but many set out to define your needs—if you let them. Every player in the wealth game will take your share if directly given the chance, but clever ones go further and encourage you to give them what you are able to gather. Closer to home, family, friends, and acquaintances—in fact, much of society—urges you to join a competitive spending conspiracy. Do you give in or stand firm and define your own requirements in isolation, letting the pressure groups whistle for their profit or support?

Stand up and fight—not for your right, because no one has a right to financial security, but for your share, because the money is out there if you want it. The game is a Darwinian exercise in survival, although the battle is not just against outsiders. When the *Times* newspaper asked G. K. Chesterton what was wrong with the world, he said "I am." Provision and needs are opposite sides of a weighted coin. You can flip it randomly and let the house collect, or fix the odds in your favour by loading the coin to land provision-side up more often than the other way around. In other words, you can be sure that you generate more than you need. You can manage your needs to win. In pursuit of self-sufficiency, why would you do otherwise?

This should be fertile ground for self-help, but it has not been. Is it still the case that few self-respecting individuals would buy or be seen with a personal finance guide? Is it still the case that, at least in the United Kingdom, the genre has failed?

The financial self-help industry has not helped its cause. What little product is available veers between academic and elementary step-by-step guides with not much in between. A number of the evangelical classics are showing their age, and many how-to books are hard to implement in practice. The trickery is often well disguised but follows familiar patterns.

Get Rich Quick

Buy property, shares, or other assets cheaply at a discount to their real value.
Sell before you buy, so pre-agree to a sale before you commit to pay, eliminating risk and guaranteeing a baked in profit.
Use a vendor loan as equity funding for your new debt package so that you don't need to put up any cash of your own.
Fund your purchase with cheap external credit or on a buy-now, pay-later basis.

Start a Business Empire

Obtain start-up funding without giving away any (or much) equity.
Be extraordinary, one in a million.
Be young and energetic.
Have nothing to lose.

Audit Your Way to Success

Record every financial transaction in your life; perform a rolling
audit, and become a full-time accountant.
Calculate a cost or value for all activities, and act accordingly.

Get-rich-quick and be-an-entrepreneur books, like muscle-men manuals,
tend to eschew any activity that might be seen as prosaic or pedestrian,
like employment, saving, and mortgages, and in doing so, they rule out the
vast majority of the population. Money-management guides frequently
combine tortuous codes of practice with endless, time-consuming administration, delivering spurious science of little use to anyone that's more
likely to frustrate and confuse.

There are, of course, some excellent textbooks and study aids, but for
people who don't yet appreciate that they should have an interest in the
subject, let alone know what they are looking for, these might as well be
stored in the ancient-foreign-language section.

Perhaps there is hope yet. Not long ago, few would admit to meeting
their partners with outside help, but Internet dating is now a commonplace and accepted practice. Solutions for sexual problems are available
at the press of a button and make popular television and radio material.
There is an index for happiness and gurus galore while the merits and
demerits of religion have been so much debated publicly that the whole

subject seems to have passed its sell-by date. Even death is creeping onto the forum.

To make progress in finance, individuals must open up, education must step up, and the self-help industry must grow up in a collective push for higher standards of financial capability. This little book is a call to action for the independent minded and aims to stimulate frank and open debate about money; a hunger to investigate and learn more about personal finance; and better thinking, better decisions, and energetic implementation.

It doesn't have all the answers—no book could—and it certainly isn't a step-by-step guide to anything. It's a travelling companion, a friend to inform, challenge, and annoy but always support and inspire you. Throw away off-the-shelf route maps, because in the wealth game, you cut your own path. There is no congestion, and you can journey far without meeting another person.

The book is a personal offering inasmuch as it originates from my own direct experience and knowledge rather than academic research, someone else's views, or received wisdoms. My working life was one large implementation exercise; there was no time to read about the subject or reflect, nor was there any obvious need to, since the plan consistently worked.

Only in the course of gathering my thoughts and writing have I begun to explore what others have said and done, and I've found that I was never quite as alone as I felt, that minds far greater than mine have wrestled with many of the same issues and described them beautifully. A light came on, the sense of isolation disappeared, and I found a family of thinkers spanning thousands of years. The few quotes and passages included are no more than a taste, and I am aware that I have only scratched the surface. They are here not to impress but to interest you.

None of the underlying philosophy is original; it is tried, tested, and proven. Just as importantly, it is universal, is not selective or exclusive, and belongs to no particular club or another. There is no magic, mysticism, or moralizing; no dogma or politics; and no right or wrong answers, just cause and effect—natural consequences to actions. The psychology, on the other hand, is largely homespun, although there are selected references to established ideas and research, again dug out to support my own existing theories rather than to inform them. As an impartial amateur in both areas, I feel free to speak plainly and roam anywhere. I have no reputation to maintain or side to support. I am interested only in practical results and the avoidance of waste, fuss, and any kind of deception or dishonesty.

As to finance, the book starts from a position one step up from elementary—so don't expect basic cash-flow and budgeting mechanics—and moves to the quite advanced. I take some of the foundational principles of finance and explore them in practice.

Part one previews the game and introduces many of the central themes, including the all-important prize. In part two, the book becomes interactive and invites you to check your current position and prospects. Where do you stand? Before moving on, your temperament, self-discipline, and commercial nous are challenged in part three as part of early skill building. Here, concepts borrowed from philosophy and corporate finance are explained and illustrated to show how they directly bear on your life decisions and how the financial consequences of your actions are largely foreseeable. It also includes a framework and techniques for maximizing your available cash and toughening up.

Part four, "Building the Pot," addresses a vast subject and can only be an introduction to it, although my intent has been to add meat (or at least protein) while recognizing different reader appetites. In a wealth companion, it's impossible to avoid the questions of where to put your cash and how to evaluate common asset classes. For some, this will be a stretch; for others, a recap.

Throughout, I have tried to add fresh perspectives and viewpoints, recognizing that there are reference books available that cover the facts and theories in detail and that the landscape is constantly shifting.

Two wealth creators and destroyers are debt and compounding, and there is a separate chapter for each. Debt, seen as public enemy number one, is rocket fuel if handled correctly while compounding, its quiet, independent-minded accomplice is a force of nature to be harnessed, yet nowhere near properly understood by most outside the world of money. If you only read one chapter, let it be this one.

Part four continues by making the case for attribution (matching your assets to different needs in order to build a pot fit for purpose), and while the book is peppered with techniques for achieving financial self-sufficiency, it also outlines a few proven wealth-building strategies. It concludes with thoughts on managing your assets.

Part five takes on the bloody subject of obstacles and calamities and asks, "Where's the catch?" Surely there must be one, if not many; otherwise, we'd all be financially self-sufficient! Pitfalls abound, but they are not all as troublesome as they seem.

Finally, part six helps you answer the question "Have I won?" and, if you haven't, "How far do I have to go?" I invite you to run the "NAN test," a new DIY diagnostic whose instruments will by now be familiar.

At the editor's suggestion, I have included a glossary of terms used in the book, some pre-existing and some new. The extent of this in itself underlines the linguistic and technical challenges facing the ordinary person in the game, and a cursory glance is not a bad way to begin.

To get the most out of this book, you need access to a computer and Microsoft Excel software to make spreadsheets. I'd also recommend that you buy a financial calculator and use it as you go. My favourite is the HP 17 bII +; its instruction book alone is an education in practical finance.

Finally, what authority do I claim? Thirty years in and around finance and a "particular set of skills," as Liam Neeson would say, but more importantly, I won a tick in the box marked "enough" at the age of forty-six. Equipped with an education, an overdraft, and a certain will, I set out to reach financial independence, and, twenty-four years later, I arrived. Wherever you are on the journey, this book will help.

PART ONE

PREGAME BRIEFING

I

INTRODUCTION

The wealth game is an exercise for one, where you are the only player, and the competition is yourself, not others. This "one" extends to family if you are the householder. In a crowded and noisy environment, it's easy to feel that other people are your rivals and that it is you against the world, but this is the first of many traps that can throw you off course.

The term *wealth* implies more than enough of something, in this case, money and assets. If you have more than you need, you are wealthy; if you don't, you are not. The test is relative and very personal. On one hand, you work to earn money and accumulate assets, and on the other hand, you consume them. You can earn only as much as your capabilities and opportunities allow, and you can spend only as little as your tastes and needs demand, but the scope to tip the scales in your favour is greater than you may think. In fact, it's compelling. Like an outdoor-survival specialist, you can toughen up by learning skills, developing resourcefulness, and training your needs so that you can take control, enjoy the moment, and relish the future.

What someone else has or doesn't have is irrelevant. People may say that you are wealthy only once you reach a certain number or are featured in this or that list, but this is misguided. The only yardstick that matters is your own needs. To follow others is a waste of time and energy.

A CAUSE

My father, who died of cancer when I was fifteen, was an immigrant adventurer steered by his Spanish mother, Madeleine, into no less likely a place than the Lloyd's insurance market of the 1960s—white, racist, sexist, class ridden, and brutally hierarchical. He learned his trade and left, moving us all to Bembridge on the Isle of Wight (near to boats), and setting up a reinsurance brokerage in the back of our garage. Business thrived, and despite 83% upper-rate tax and 98% on the very top slice of investment earnings, so did we. I never was quite sure how he made his money. It didn't matter. All that mattered was that he was around to enjoy it with us. Our family trips to collect him from Heathrow after his many trips to Spain, South America (primarily Paraguay and Colombia), and the Philippines were joyous—crystallized fruit, jewellery, Lladro ornaments, or perfume by Balenciaga for my mother; stuffed baby alligators and piranha or shrunken heads for the boys; and china-headed dolls and dresses for the girls. Life was different and unusual, and we absorbed it.

From these early experiences, certain characteristics and notions developed—a singular pleasure in being alternative and not following the pack or even really associating with it; an understanding that life is short and should be lived well and enjoyed; and a deep appreciation for luxuries, sharpened by the knowledge that nothing lasts and memories alone don't sustain.

After he died, the tax man caught up with us, and his erstwhile London partners found loopholes in the legal agreement through which he'd transferred his share of the businesses to them in return for a ten-year annuity, and they stopped paying. Properties we thought we owned turned out to be business assets, and to cap it all, poor advice and panic selling of the share portfolio in the crash of 1987 left us virtually destitute. It was back to work for my mother and state schools for my brother and two sisters. I left school at seventeen, just squeezing in final exams before the money ran out. Thank goodness for free university and maintenance grants!

Who knows whether I was born a rebel and an outsider, but certainly by the age of eighteen, I was both, and the mission was obvious. Loud and clear were the messages that form is no more than outer wrapping, that substance alone matters, and that in every department of life, it is unwise to depend on others. Self-sufficiency became my mantra—not the grow-it-yourself, good-life type that I respect or the stubborn, chip-on-the-shoulder, accept-no-help-from-anyone type, but rather the sort that says, as a matter of pride as well as practical sense, "I must take charge of becoming financially and emotionally independent and as physically fit and healthy as my particular carcass allows, because nobody else will." To ignore this is to sign up to a life of dependency, compromise, and missed opportunity.

Waiting for help from others must surely rank as one of the great follies of human existence. We wait and hope and dream, and all the while, our muscles weaken and time ebbs away.

And what worthwhile assistance can we be, either to ourselves or others, in the realms of sustenance and survival, psychological well-being, and relationships, if we are financially dependent, emotionally needy, or physically incapable? Where's the solid ground? The most generous pauper in the world can't put food on another's table, clothe a family, help with driving lessons and college fees, assist with a first step onto the housing ladder, or give to charity. Like fitting our own oxygen mask on the plane before helping others, we need to be functioning first.

As well as recognizing the importance of self-sufficiency and building solid foundations, I was propelled by the need to avenge the prejudice my father had suffered in the city, the avarice of his partners, the incompetence of the doctors who had failed to diagnose the cancer until he was riddled with it, and the lawyers who had so badly let us down through their slack drafting and commercial naïveté. These bastions of the establishment had been exposed as frauds, yet instead of taking a flyer in the opposite direction, I chose to leap headlong into their world—that establishment, the system—and operate from within like a tiny, profit-seeking Trojan horse.

There is something exhilarating about railing against the system that one lands in, challenging and rejecting actions and views, and replacing them with our own creations, however naïve and misguided. It stimulates the mind and stirs the passions drawing in fellow conspirators into societies of the new and better. The more comfortable, cosseted, privileged, and secure we are, the smaller our incentive to fight the system. Why react and reject when all is wonderful? We'll manufacture our own causes, of course, perhaps our own trivial and self-oriented insecurities and obsessions, like how we look, how others perceive us, our sexuality, and so on, or latch onto the pitiable circumstances of others, but where's the grandness in these?

It doesn't matter what the problem is. There simply needs to be one, and the bigger, the better. How about boredom and mediocrity at home, neglect, poverty, discrimination, woeful schooling, or a dysfunctional family? My school friend Andy Nicholas told us he came from a broken home. "I smashed it up," he said proudly. The problem or calamity is the spark that ignites us. Without a spark, there is no ignition, and without an ignition, there are no combustion and drive. Rich and poor alike worry about their children, and many work tirelessly to "make them happy," but in overdosing on comfort and insulating against unpleasantness, they can inadvertently deny their children the precious chance to learn resilience, resourcefulness, and self-reliance, the ingredients for self-confidence and stature.

A "something for nothing" ethos is corrosive, even if the "nothing" is mislabelled and in fact comes with strings or hidden obligations. It distorts cause and effect and throws players off course. A friend has spent the last twenty years dodging and dancing around taxes to manage and ultimately unwind a small family trust for him and his sister that, when divided, might keep them each in food and lodgings for three years.

The prospect of inheritance is another example. Exactly what or how much is coming might be unclear, but there will be something. We can ignore the prospect completely, assume it's already ours, and plan around it, or we can adopt a halfway position; whatever our stance, the knowledge alone corrupts. We've been tainted and must fight to overcome the desire and complacency that it fosters. Two other friends have suffered by planning their lives around an expected inheritance. One never bought a property, renting instead and living to the extent of her means; the other, like Richard Carstone, the ward in Charles Dickens's *Bleak House*, has not settled in a career but chased dreams. Neither has honed a commercial instinct or made meaningful efforts towards financial self-sufficiency. The first fell out with her father when he decided to spend his money rather than handing it out. The second is still waiting to collect, some ten years after the prospect of inheritance came into view.

Once at work, I cultivated an otherness from the people around, a detachment from the cares and worries of the institution, and a hunger to feed from the knowledge and experience available. I had no time for concerns and gripes, personality clashes, power plays, and politics. These ate up valuable time and distracted from the task at hand. Everything was possible, and my energy seemed unlimited. I chased jobs and was quietly hurt when choice projects were given to others, even if I was really too busy to take them on. The day started at 8:00 a.m.; ten hours later, when the phones stopped ringing, the pizzas arrived for the late shift, and the next phase of learning began. All that mattered was the learning.

WHO CAN PLAY?

For many people, being wealthy is something that others are. We know that there's money out there and that there are plenty of people with far more of it than they need to live comfortably—but we don't think we are these people.

These individuals are viewed as somehow different and in possession of extraordinary skills, wealth-enhancing circumstances, or plain good fortune. It's not so much wealth envy— more a weary resignation that we simply aren't going to be wealthy. It's like saying, "I won't have a good physique whatever I do, so I might as well eat what I like and give up exercise." Surprise, surprise, people who say this are fat.

In a financial sense, certain people *are* extraordinary—or their circumstances are. Money finds them like water collecting in a puddle. First are those with inherited or given wealth sufficient to meet their future needs and for whom paid work is optional. Think "trustafarians" or dynasty members. In a second, much larger group are individuals able to earn money and accumulate wealth so quickly or in such quantity that normal rules don't seem to apply. So much cash floods into their system that any motivation towards discipline and prudence is diluted and lost, and until the cash source dries up, the party goes on. Anyone, whether an early or late bloomer, who rises to the top of a place where there is money to be earned, can occupy this territory. Just look at the "rich lists" to see the huge range of activities that can deliver exceptional rewards.

The rest of us, however well paid, are still, at least for now, in the ordinary category—a place where the normal rules do apply.

To play the game, you must be able to generate more cash than you spend. To stand a realistic chance of winning, you need to have enough money to pay a deposit on a home and service the rent or mortgage on it with something left over each month. If you aren't at this point, do what you can to reach it without delay. If you are beyond it, the more cash you generate, the faster and further you can progress. In either position, small actions matter and add up surprisingly quickly. No action that generates surplus cash flow is too small.

If you are over the start line, the debate doesn't end with quantum; cash-flow profile also matters. Is it steady and predictable, ebbing and flowing by the month but constant, growing year on year, or is it lumpy and unpredictable? Each has its advantages.

Consistent, reliable cash flow allows medium-term strategic planning and is perfect for supporting debt, whilst irregular lumps of surplus cash begin earning a return and compounding value as soon as they are invested, so the earlier they are put to work, the better, regardless of whether there is a long period before the next one.

This book assumes that you have a primary source of income and cash flow to fuel wealth building and is not concerned what it is. That's up to you. Your task in the game is to generate and use surplus cash flow to build your net worth and manage the gap between this and your needs to achieve financial independence.

THE CHALLENGE OF WHAT TO KNOW

Finance, you say, is complicated, dry, full of jargon, and difficult to understand. Simply trying to work out what you need to know or where to start seems impossible. Some never begin to learn the skills; others try but get lost somewhere along the way.

If ever there was a case for expert help, this is it. In medicine, we rarely operate on ourselves or each other, carry out in-depth testing and diagnosis, or prescribe medicines and treatments. We turn to the experts of the medical profession. Whether conventional or alternative, specialists or generalists, these experts are all there to help, and by and large, we trust them. Their training is long and well regulated and includes instruction in ethics. Of course, health workers and expensive facilities, kit, consumables, and drugs need to be paid for, but most people accept that a medic's first duty is to the patient, and societies recognize the need to help and redirect an element of taxpayers' money to this cause.

The notion of expert financial help is less well established and tends to be ad hoc. Governments treat it as a luxury rather than an essential, and, on the whole, it is left to the private sector to deliver. A consequence is that outside of universities and business schools, financial know-how and expertise have developed as the preserve of banks and other firms promoting financial products and services for profit. As long as markets of any kind have existed, there have been insiders and outsiders, and the former have worked hard to protect their privileged position and the profits that flow from it. And why not? While ethics may not be on the syllabus for financial training, one could be a "gentleman in the market" and still make oodles of money simply by exploiting knowledge gaps, or "market imperfections" as they are termed. The financial expert's role in life was not to help people; it was to profit.

Society has been much slower to recognize any need to help the ordinary person (who, by definition, is an outsider) beyond teaching basic mathematics or citizenship at school. Only in 2013–14 did the United Kingdom force "independent" financial advisers (IFAs) to operate truly independently and transparently. Until then, they advised their clients—ordinary people—but were paid through hidden commissions by product providers, making them little more than sales channels. However ethical and client centric they were, it was impossible to escape the fact that their compensation was determined by what products they sold and for whom, not whether they were in the best interests of their clients—a horrible temptation, even for those with the steeliest virtue.

In practical terms, it has been and still is really hard to find help around finance that is genuinely expert *and* impartial. There's a large pool of brightly coloured but hungry fish waiting for tasty morsels. The biggest are the product providers: banks, building societies, and insurance companies, all of which offer "advice" but exist only to maximize profit within the current regulatory framework. Financial advisers and accounting and actuarial firms may or may not have the necessary and up-to-date skills and knowledge and are too often beyond the reach of the ordinary person, seen as impenetrable and expensive.

In the world of finance—the wealth game—you're on your own. It's best to realize that early.

Where does this leave you? Is it not a Hobson's choice of equally unappealing options? You can pay for poor or biased financial advice and take your chances, spend years learning entry-level financial skills, or steer clear of all but the most elementary financial transactions. Perhaps it's a combination of all three. Either way, it takes you straight back to the starting question: What do you need to know?

My suggestion is to keep matters as simple as possible. First, understand the idea of the game—what it is about and why you are playing it. Second, work out a few basic principles (no more than a handful) to guide your play, and third, make sure you grasp the small number of foundational finance concepts. Put this package in a protective eco-dome where you can always see and access it. You can build as much paraphernalia outside the dome as you like, but these jewels must never be contaminated or forgotten; they are your only constant allies.

When learning to drive, the desire for freedom, to travel independently and get somewhere, combines with the survival instinct to generate a powerful will. Specific skill requirements that can be learned, practiced, and improved over time begin with understanding the equipment and its functions. In this case, this refers to the vehicle—pedals, gears, mirrors, steering, indicators, lights, washers, air conditioning, navigation, entertainment, and internal configuration, plus routine maintenance, like oil and water, tyres, and so on. Next are elementary manoeuvres, such as safely pulling away, braking, cornering, hill starting, emergency stopping, reversing, overtaking, and parking, followed by roundabouts, motorways, and other situations. Advanced skills include driving abroad, defensive driving, snow and ice, off-road driving, skidpans, and handbrake turns. The whole exercise is neatly self-contained, with clear boundaries.

In the wealth game, the equipment is straightforward: a financial calculator and a PC with spreadsheet software. Your starter pack of skills should include basic mathematics, including BIDMAS (brackets, indices, division, multiplication, adding, and subtracting), basic algebra, percentages, tables, and graphs. Learning the language of finance and grappling with new concepts happens naturally over time, and these skills come more easily on the job than in the classroom.

An excellent starting place for practical money skills is the one-inch thick instruction manual for a Hewlett Packard financial calculator, together with the device itself. This illustrates everyday finance problems and shows how to calculate answers. You can make do without these specialist capabilities, but there is no reason why you should, as they will improve your decision making.

Knowledge of law is also invaluable, although outside the scope of this book. Legal training teaches critical thinking and problem solving and breeds confidence and fearlessness. At the very least, you should try to understand the basic rules of contract law, consumer rights, and property conveyancing.

Focus on the process of learning and on steady improvement, and be prepared to make mistakes without fear or anxiety. It is a normal and healthy part of self-improvement. When learning to ski, a child who isn't afraid of falling over and getting hurt will learn faster than an adult who is worried about injury or looking bad. A student who asks questions and seeks help from others will progress more than by not doing so. Most importantly, remember that in finance, there is no end to the skills and knowledge available; it's a lifelong practice.

Ability is won by effort and practice. All the skills you need in the wealth game are available and accessible to you, whatever your starting point. From the minute you play, you start to accumulate the hours necessary to become a virtuoso. Expect to improve, and you will. Never give in to disappointment and adversity or give up your quest for self-improvement.

Your growing ability and sustained action feed each other. The more time and effort you bank, the more skilled you become. This leads to successes and greater achievement, which feeds your confidence and self-belief, encouraging you to work harder. The initial call to action arises from your own ambition, a cause to rally for, and a worthwhile goal. Perseverance requires grit and determination. You need stamina and staying power and a willingness to put up with unpleasantness and discomfort. Once you realize that there is no pain-free way for the ordinary person to become wealthy, you will treat challenges and difficulties as routine obstacles to be overcome without fuss.

II

THE THEORY OF O

Every game needs a "how to win" section in the instructions. Without one, what's the point in playing?

There is a direct relationship between how hard you pursue something and the nature of the goal. The harder you pursue, the more you will achieve. To achieve, it is therefore important to have a strong goal. And without a goal of any kind, why would you act at all? To do so would be mindless, action by autopilot. Goals like surviving, finding a mate, and reproducing are instinctive, but in many areas, we need to create our own.

In martial arts, the objective is to physically demolish one's opponent, either to crush or immobilize him or her. A direct approach is best, and there is no room for halfheartedness or uncertainty. A person who wavers and hesitates, moves around without clear purpose, or stays rooted to the spot will lose. To achieve the goal, one needs to train body and mind and learn many skills. It also helps to pick the right opponent.

More everyday examples are found in dieting and eating regimes. A goal of "I want to lose weight" is weak and woolly compared with "I want to lose two stone and keep it off," "I want to fit into a size-ten party dress for my next birthday," or "I'm going to give up meat, go gluten free, or food combine."

To be most effective, a goal must be the following:

- Worthwhile—the starting point is that it must have great value to *you*. You must want to reach it very much and feel that its value exceeds the likely cost in terms of your time, effort, and self-sacrifice. If its pull isn't strong enough, you may lose heart and give up.
- Measurable—you know exactly what is required to achieve it. A precise, binary goal that can be proved by maths or science is more potent than a vague or abstract one. Not only is the target clear so that you'll know beyond doubt when you reach it, but you can also measure your progress against it at any time, most importantly, the gap still remaining.
- Realistically believable—an objective that isn't credible is no more than a dream or fantasy that will quickly vapourise in the Earth's atmosphere. And not only must it be believable but you must believe it without question or a shadow of a doubt. To do this honestly, rather than fooling yourself, challenge the assumption. You have no automatic entitlement to achieve your goal, so how are you going to do it, what steps are necessary, and what obstacles exist? Only when you have worked through this thought process and still convinced yourself that the target is achievable does your self-belief count. It will now be tempered with realism, and you will be better equipped to move ahead, understanding that success requires effort, determination, and sound actions rather than just blind hope and expectation.

WHERE'S THE FINISH LINE?

In the sphere of personal wealth, too many people have no set objective at all or jump back and forth and sideways. Here are some of the approaches I have seen.

Reach a number by a certain age
In my youth, the ambition of the money conscious was "to reach £1 million by thirty." Thirty years later, at 5% per annum, the target would now be £4 million. There's no doubt that people yearn to achieve this, and it passes the measurable test, but it falls down on credibility. It is so rigid and demanding that without early tangible evidence of being on track, a player will give up like a climber who knows that the mountain summit is out of reach.

Get rich
This goal is like "lose weight" or "become a celebrity" in that it lacks a definitive target and can too easily be fudged. Alternatively, some people try to make accumulation of money and assets an instinctive aim and spend their life pursuing greater wealth. Unlike survival that you achieve every moment you stay alive, this task is unending.

Shopping list
This gets a lot closer to a goal that is workable and useful. This goal sounds like this: "I want to have this house, that car, these possessions, and that kind of life." It is the basis for further consideration but in itself is no more helpful than a wish list.

Early retirement
How to Retire by Forty-Five could have been the subtitle for this book. It is catchy and has two simple and measurable tests. First, retire from work—in other words, stop the activity completely—and second, do so by forty-five or earlier. Pass or fail, there's no wriggling out of.

The problem is that "retire" implies stopping something (in this case, work) and marks the end of an activity in your life, whether you like it or not. This goal ignores the question of what kind of life you expect at retirement. Stopping work completely at a certain date now seems unnecessary and unappealing. The concept of an age target has appeal, but not in this form.

More than everyone I know
As a relative test that can be met by ditching wealthier friends, this is a temporary ego massage unlikely to inspire for long.

Focus on other endeavours, and leave money to sort itself out
By taking this line, you abdicate responsibility for building wealth. For some, it is a genuine choice, but for many, it is an admission of defeat and an attempt to make virtue of necessity.

Live it up—spend and enjoy it all now, and let the future look after itself
While this may be a chosen path, it hardly amounts to an objective, because it is too easy to be of any value. For these cash-flow hedonists, the only way to sustain spending is to carry on working for it.

Have it all—live it up now, and retire early with a collection of goodies and a pot of money
Although for most players, this goal is clearly impossible, many players blindly follow it, hoping for the best until they reach the cliff edge.

Work until state retirement age and beyond that if necessary
This is the state-sponsored default option chosen by millions. Its problem is that as the developed world's population ages, costs become unsustainable, and pension payouts fall short. In signing up to this, you deny yourself the chance to improve on it. It is, in effect, no objective and encourages drift and a lack of personal attention as well as a false sense of security that another, such as the state, will look after you.

No strategy whatsoever
Somewhere in this person's system is a desire for money and an understanding of its value, but no tangible objective exists. This bucket is full of people with halfhearted aspirations and wishy-washy dreams that drift in and out of view with the current.

It is common to adopt one or more of these approaches at the same time and move from one to another to suit circumstances and the mood of the moment. The problem is that they don't all combine well, and you can end up with the financial equivalent of a Brown Windsor soup. For those of you who never worked in the British catering industry in the 1970s or 1980s, this is a soup made of leftovers and usually served on Friday. It's invariably brown and most often recycled into gravy for the Sunday roast.

The entire premise of the wealth game is that you finish it. To enter without this aim, for the fun of playing or any other reason, is to mistake its purpose. At the finish line, you tick the box marked "enough," cast off all the associated pressures and shackles, and move on to something else. It doesn't matter what; by all means, carry on making money, but do so in the knowledge that you don't need to and that, beyond a certain point, what you do in life is more important than what you have. Winning the game opens the door to a place you have imagined but never set foot in and heralds a new beginning, a chance to start afresh at a higher level.

On August 22, 1968, Bernard Moitessier left Plymouth in his thirty-nine-foot steel ketch *Joshua* as part of the first Sunday Times Round the World Race for single-handed yachts. There was no need to officially enter, and the challenge was to leave any English port between June 1 and October 31 and return to it after rounding the three capes of Good Hope, Leeuwin, and the Horn. He deplored the idea of a race and had planned to circle the world before its conception but was attracted by the prizes, a golden globe for the first to finish and five thousand pounds for the fastest voyage. Seven months into the race, he announced his retirement in a communiqué to the newspaper, giving the reason "because I am happy at sea and perhaps to save my soul."

Instead of stopping, Moitessier carried on sailing around the world for another three months, effectively circling it one and a half times. Sir Robin Knox-Johnston, as the only legitimate finisher, won the prizes and became the first person to circumnavigate alone without stopping. It is impossible to say whether Moitessier would have won had he continued to the finish line, but his legendary status as one of the greatest ocean voyagers was only enhanced by his actions.

In the wealth game, whether you choose to cross the finish line, carry on past it, or redraw it to a different place altogether is up to you. Whichever way you choose, you need to know where the line is. The place not to be is doggedly flogging on without knowing that you have actually crossed it. I know plenty of people who have won the game without realizing or accepting it. At best, they miss the satisfaction of knowing that their efforts are now optional, and at worst, they just waste their time. Who wants to look up one day and realize that he or she could have stopped work years ago but didn't?

INTRODUCING O

The Swedish use the term *Lagom* to mean "just enough," "not too much or too little," "enough to go round," "fair share," or "just right." It is used in answer to all manner of questions: How are you? What's the weather like? What's your financial situation? It indicates balance, not perfection and reflects the country's cultural and social ideals of equality and fairness.

There is no English equivalent, and anything close, such as "sufficient," "average," or "adequate," tends to invoke negative connotations of scarcity, abstinence, and failure, which don't apply to the Swedish word.

Definition and meaning
O is the objective in the wealth game. It is designed to meet the requirements for an effective goal and be achievable without magic, extraordinary skills, or disproportionate luck. I don't suggest for a minute that everyone can reach it, but it is within the grasp of many more people than currently recognize it and who are busy cooking up Brown Windsor soup.

Like *Lagom*, O also balances needs and resources, but it is solely interested in the maths and makes no comment on appropriateness, equality, or fairness. Those issues are for you to decide. You win the wealth game if the numbers stack up.

Here is the meaning of O: I can live the life I want without needing to work for money again.

Why not say it out loud a few times, as if you are savouring the aroma and flavour of a fine wine? Perhaps emphasize certain words as you examine its sound and feel from different angles. What images and sensations arise? Notice these and enjoy the moment.

Now go ahead and ask this question: How on earth does this fulfill the criteria of being measurable or believable? Somehow, you need to work out what kind of life you want, how much it's going to cost, and how long you're going to live. And where's the money coming from to pay for it? Isn't this just legalistic trickery wrapped up in smooth semantics?

At first glance, it reminds me of a correspondence writing course I signed up for some years ago. The introductory warm-up exercise was something like "write about your interests or family." The next task was so impossibly challenging that I gave up and didn't pursue the course. It was a brilliant business concept—a virtual head office with minimal overheads and self-employed tutors paid by the number of assignments they reviewed. Courses were paid for in full up front (no refunds), and there was a 90% dropout rate after the first exercise.

You've bought or borrowed this book and barely into the first part find that the grandly titled objective appears impossible to fathom, let alone realize. It is circular, with the unknowable driving the unknown. So perhaps like "world peace," "ending poverty," or "equality for all," it's laudable but, in all practical senses, useless. If true, this makes things far too easy and leaves you where you started. Fortunately, it is not true.

Let's say that this was called *The Health Game: An Ordinary Person's Wellness Companion* with an objective "to live as long as your genetic coding allows." The title looks equally fanciful, and the objective, suitably unfathomable, but would this stop you trying your utmost to live longer? Not necessarily. The health game is vast and all encompassing, with individuals, businesses, and governments feverishly pursuing every conceivable avenue to prolong and improve life, a kind of Darwinian struggle to evolve.

Health is universally accepted as important to the well-being of individuals and society. From a young age, we are taught or learn that safety and health are our own personal responsibilities and that prevention is better than cure. In developed countries, it is promoted to greater or lesser degrees by the family, is on many school curricula, and is written about ad nauseam. We have access to our own personal health counsellors in the form of general practitioners and, for those who are in real need or who can pay, to specialists. While there is no health school for ordinary citizens, the educational resources, materials, and range of support is immense.

Scientists unpick genetic coding, environmental factors, and human activity, such as our diet, lifestyle, metabolism, and response to stress, in order to better understand the pathways to longevity. The pharmaceutical industry cures us, and governments regulate to keep profit-hungry food and drink companies in some kind of line, because bad health makes people miserable and is costly. As citizens, we feed hungrily on new knowledge, diets, supplements, exercise regimes, alternative medicine, and spiritual guidance. Success breeds success; we feel better, look better, and then work harder at it. Of course, none of us knows whether all this good activity will offer us a longer life. At an individual level, it's unprovable, but we're content with improving our chances and reaping the immediate rewards of fitness and good health, so we carry on anyway.

Whether we live to sixty or 120 is not the point, and it doesn't matter that we don't yet understand our genetic code or its implications. We just *know* that being fit and healthy is enjoyable and leads to good things, so we do what is in our power and control to achieve it. We may fail abysmally, but we do have a go.

Clearly, some people have no practical interest in longevity; sales of cigarettes, alcohol, sugar and its substitutes, saturated fat, salt, and processed meat and the corresponding lung, liver, and heart diseases and obesity and diabetes are testament to this. But the point is that in most cases, at least in developed countries, we have a choice. We can play the health game if we want.

So having an unfathomable objective doesn't in itself stop us from playing the health game. We simply redefine our objectives into ones that are easier to measure and achieve but still point us in the right direction.

In the wealth game, the components of O *can* be understood and measured. You just need to know how.

"Live the life I want."

Roll the clock forward to O, and ask what your mission statement or personal motto is, which values you embrace, and what you still want to achieve in life, personally, materially, spiritually, socially, and so on. This is a big step up from practicing new signatures, describing your perfect partner, or plotting a career, but why not ask these questions? Isn't it what people do as teenagers and forget to do later?

As an exercise in visualization, let your imagination run free, and explore current and past ways of living, including those forgotten or never considered. Design the existence you want on the basis that you don't need to work to fund it and are free from financial constraint. Only when the picture is complete or drawn as far as possible should you layer onto it the rough financial effects as far as you can estimate them. Whatever landing you reach now will be temporary, as nothing is permanent, and your outlook will change as you move through the game. You should consider this carefully.

This is a long way from the conventional image of retirement, with connotations of giving something up at the end of the line, being forced to live within your means, questions about your new identity, and a worrying void ahead.

It doesn't matter if your early efforts are clumsy or naïve. The more you practice over time, the sharper the results will be in light of changing conditions and maturity. My answers have evolved dramatically over the years, never more so than in the run-up to O. And at no point has there ever been a shortage of content and ideas for a life beyond.

As I drew closer to my O, different subjects began to come into view, some from the past and others completely new. A space had begun to open up with the knowledge that, soon, I wouldn't need to work for money, and it was quickly being filled with new ideas. It was hard to rationalize them all, and for some time, I didn't try. I just opened the receptors and let them in from all sides. There was a giving up and letting go of things through a kind of small back gate, but this was nothing to compare with the flood of new things that had overcome all resistance and were literally pouring in and springing up all over. It was a wonderful return to boundless imagination and creative thought, bigger and better than ever before, colourful, noisy, and jostling for space. Certain areas of my brain began to open up,

THE THEORY OF O

sections that had long been closed due to lack of need, and yet more storage space was created. The lights came on, and fresh air breezed in.

During this time, a curious thing happened.

After leaving student life and joining the working world, as soon as I was out of debt and on solid footing, I began to measure all of my decisions and actions—except for those relating to my love life and, later on, health—against certain questions: Does it make financial sense? How will it affect my goal of financial independence? There was room for other considerations, but not much. As time went on, the test expanded to include financial independence for the family rather than myself, but the financial test remained foremost, and it drove decisions powerfully.

As I drew nearer to financial independence and to shedding the need to work for money, this financial test began to recede into the background. It didn't disappear, but it did hand over the steering wheel and move to a backseat. Of course, the financial effects of actions still needed to be understood as part of good stewardship, and a certain amount of cash planning remained unavoidable, but concerns over sufficiency simply weren't there anymore.

The heady influx of new ideas and thoughts took time to settle, but before long and without much conscious effort, views began to form, and fresh priorities emerged. Driver and navigator roles were split, and into the vacant seats jumped new coalitions of equal partners. This sounds like a recipe for either getting lost or having a nasty road accident, but fortunately, the car slowed down, and no one seemed to mind quite as much where it was going. In fact, it began to stop rather often, as the occupants got out to stretch their legs, admire the scenery, and chat with the locals.

As time moved on, other vehicles became fewer and fewer until there were none. The roads themselves were swallowed back into the land, and the car began to hover over the ground, propelled by the collective will of the occupants.

Determining the life you want becomes a joy in itself. Living it is better still, and there is a fair chance that while your horizons grow and experiences magnify, your needs and wants will crystallize like shards of ice and gradually melt.

"Without needing to work for money again."

The first section of O asks you consider your wants and needs. The second addresses the means. To realize this part, you need to hold sufficient money and assets to meet your financial requirements without working. This means all costs of any kind for the rest of your life and no work—not full time, part time, or as a one-off contribution. Think about this for a minute.

Remember also that O is the final goal in the game, and you can reach it only once. If one day you think you have the means but later find that you don't because you run out of money, it proves that you never reached O and were mistaken. This raises a conundrum: How do I know for sure that I have crossed the finish line?

The answer is in two parts: one is mechanical, which I deal with later, and the other is intuitive and holistic, which, like *Lagom*, is subtler and all encompassing. I call it the "way-of-the-wealth game." You will explore and discover this yourself in the same way that a Buddhist develops mindfulness or a martial artist develops a heightened sense of awareness. It is a way of being and living in which your thoughts and actions lead you inexorably towards O, and, once there, you have no doubt whatsoever that you have arrived. What starts as hesitant, awkward, and stiff becomes natural and effortless as your body and mind attune and develop through open-minded investigation and practice.

This is the most important element of the game, the art and the alchemy—the rest consists of skills and techniques that can be learned.

Your needs and financial resources occupy a personal ecosystem and are dynamic and constantly changing. If something falls too far out of line, it will upset the balance. Why not create a healthy environment that accommodates ebbs and flows and restores itself to equilibrium? They are, after all, *your* needs and *your* financial resources, and the challenge set down by O contains the solution. If your needs are too complex, simplify them! If they are too costly, reduce them! If they are too uncertain, wait until they are certain, and, in the meantime, overprovide for them! Respect natural cycles and phases rather than ignore them! Take charge and direct proceedings! This is not rocket science but cause and effect.

Traditional financial prudence instructs you to "cut your coat according to your cloth," so buy only what you have sufficient money to pay for. What a dismal image, a painful cure to a nasty problem. Follow this path of mealy abstinence and make do. Oh, and by the way, you'd better carry on working for money, or else it'll get worse. Why not do away with the need for a cure at all by cutting off the problem at its root? Move somewhere warm, and you'll soon forget what a coat is, let alone need one. Use your cloth for something more useful. Design a life in which the only thing being cut down to size is craving and attachment.

It is easy to mistake the approach as asceticism, but you should guard against so simplistic a view. Asceticism is abstinence and austerity, a kind of poverty, a denial of what one wants, a retreat from temptation behind manufactured barriers, and, as such, it is a blunt instrument. Instead of a balanced middle way, it creates a troublesome state of constant tension, guilt, and dissatisfaction tempered with self-righteousness. Think of the sexually repressed monk or the binge eater.

Humans focus attention on the objects of their desire and displeasure, hungering for the desirable and yearning to avoid the unpleasant and undesirable, but we tend to ignore the underlying causes of these sentiments. The brouhaha of the superficial obscures a path leading to greater reward.

Pare back craving and clinging, abstain from being led by the nose or whatever other body part has lashed you to consumption, and achieve a kind of freedom of will. By travelling light, you can go farther, see more, sense more, feel more, experience more, and understand more. Everything is more intense, deeper, and richer—the space, sounds, colours, feelings, smells, and tastes—and you have greater capacity to savour and experience it, because, instead of craving it and hoarding it, you let it come when it comes and pass naturally away. You never fill up. Displeasures come and go too, but without sticking or hurting. As a neutral receptor, your need to control and influence fades, and any thoughts of asceticism vanish.

Your opponent is suddenly very manageable.

Let's consider the work element of the goal. Whereas retirement implies an end to work, O does not; it simply means an end to the *need* to work for money. This is important, because work of some kind is necessary for a healthy and fulfilling life. You may wash clothes or tend bees in a monastery, grow vegetables, study, learn a new skill, look after people, or build a business. In fact, "work" is a misnomer and is better termed "activity with purpose"; personal benefit arises from physical and mental exertion, as well as the engagement and the connectedness necessary to pursue it. Inactivity and purposelessness, physical and mental inertia, estrangement, and disengagement over a sustained period benefit no one.

Reaching O allows you to work for a nonfinancial purpose, which changes the terms of the bargain between employer and employee, client and service provider, capital and labour. If you choose to work for no money, by definition, you expect a different return, either for yourself or someone else. You wouldn't do it otherwise. If money is still part of the equation, you view it more dispassionately.

Adding an age target
An implicit assumption behind O is that you reach it with time and energy ahead of you, so an age target helps focus the mind.

I don't exactly remember when I set mid forties as a target. It would have been sometime into my late twenties or early thirties, once I was established in work and getting a sense of what it was all about. At this stage, however, it was no more than a rough working assumption, an aspiration without any real foundation, and too far away to matter.

When I married at thirty-five, Jessie, my wife, was three months pregnant. Within a year, number two was on the way, and the family was nearly complete, so I had enough data to calculate our collective future needs and complete the equation. Forty-five quickly emerged as the target age to stop paid work and change tack. Ten years was a round number and, although ambitious, seemed just about achievable. Fifty was a common target for many in the professions and public sector, so why not aim to beat it by a few years? Fifty-five would have been another very respectable target and sits well with personal pension accounts becoming available, but twenty years seemed a long way off and bang in the middle of the stampede of baby boomers and early Generation Xers doing the same thing, so it didn't seem like much of a prize. State retirement was out in the long grass and left too little time to do everything that was stacking up in my mind.

In short, my age target needed to be properly worthwhile, a real prize, realizable with a fair wind while allowing a margin for slippage. It didn't matter if it was reached at forty-six or forty-seven. In no time, the date was about as set in stone as it could be. It became accepted in the family that this *would* happen, and lifestyle decisions were based on it.

It is for you to decide whether to set a date, and if so, when. The concept seemed alien to most of my friends—too mechanical, brutally efficient, almost German, perhaps on account of my part-Bavarian grandmother. In fact, I can't remember anyone confessing to setting a target date so far ahead of the event. This immediately made it more appealing to me and added grist to the mill.

Eleven years after marrying, I resigned and stopped paid work to write, travel, and spend more time with my family.

PHASES OF PLAY

There are three broad phases in the wealth game.

Beginner phase—this begins at the moment you proactively adopt wealth as a personal life goal. Until then, you may be on the field of play but aren't consciously participating. You may be young and ambitious, a latecomer who, for some reason, hasn't previously set out to achieve it, or a returner who adopted the idea but dropped it along the way and is now lining up to start again.

Here, your focus is on gathering materials and skills and making a start on the pot of money. The job is clear. There is no asset pot—or at least nothing big enough to service your needs for very long—and you may even be in the red with a negative-balance sheet. Unless you build an asset base, all bets are off, and any future-needs planning is futile. All effort is on producing surplus cash and directing it to growth platforms, with minimal regard for current needs and no place for expensive luxuries.

Central phase—the transition to this phase arises when you have built at least two significant bases for future wealth generation, such as equity in residential property and a pension, and generate sufficient surplus cash to make further investment choices. You can bypass the beginner phase and enter here if you already have an asset base and cash flow and have made wealth a priority outcome.

This is a consolidation period, when players build on their asset base and begin to sketch out future needs in more detail. The central phase is the most dangerous section of the game. It envelops players, smothers them with comfort- and energy-sapping demands, encourages needs expansion, and subtly erodes their will to escape captivity. The only certain way out is through single-minded determination to avoid the perils of neediness and waste and reach O without delay. You can easily let yourself succumb and put O aside "just temporarily," with an intent to pick it up again, only to find that years pass, and you are caught. Suddenly there is a mountain to climb, and you are not fit to tackle it.

Many players never progress beyond this phase. They struggle on, forced to work for money in order to meet everyday needs, and O is either forgotten completely or becomes a mirage, an unattainable trick of the light truly available only to others. The end is often a messy combination of extended graft, forced sacrifice, and hardship tempered by state bailout.

Final phase, or end game—the end game arises when O appears clearly on the horizon and is reachable within five to ten years. How do you know that O is reachable within five to ten years? First, you have a sizeable asset base and a clear pathway to growing it further. Second, all categories of your future needs are known, and the constituents of each are identified and quantified. Third, you perform the analysis at the end of this book, and the results confirm that O will be reached in five to ten years. At this point, you will know that you are in the final phase.

If you bash on, blindly building the asset pot with no regard for its sufficiency, you will miss the signpost for the final phase, but if you regularly take stock of your net assets and needs, you will see the signpost and can make the turn at the earliest opportunity. Once O is clearly in sight, you will naturally begin to accelerate towards it. The knowledge of being in the final phase and the sight of O engenders confidence and excitement, reinforces resolve, injects energy, and pushes doubt, restlessness, lethargy, and other obstacles out of the way.

For the first time, O—until now a guiding light helping shape and direct actions—becomes real. You can almost reach out and touch it.

III

WHAT TO MEASURE

The wealth game balances two numbers, *net worth* and *needs*, each made up of many other numbers.

NET WORTH

This is a measurement of your wealth at a point in time. You have a net worth right now, and the sooner you know it, the better. Whether positive or negative, large or small, solid or uncertain, it is your starting point. Every player should know his or her approximate net worth and be no more than an hour away from calculating a reasonably accurate figure.

The definition of your net worth is the total value of all your cash and assets, less any debt or other obligations for which you are liable. Other commonly used terms are *net assets* or *balance sheet*. They all mean the same.

Assets can split into two categories: real and financial. Real assets are property and other physical assets, and financial assets refer to money in its various forms, securities, and receivables. Debts are obligations to repay loans in all their forms: term loans, mortgages, overdrafts, IOUs, credit, hire purchase, finance leases, and so on. Other liabilities refer to any other sums due.

Why is net worth so important?

Net worth is the little porridge pot, the well or font of wealth that delivers the cash we so desperately need to live. When you have no wealth, the only route to survival within your gift is to work for money. State benefits, bequests, or charity are at the discretion of others and, therefore, are outside your control. There will come a point in your life when you are physically or mentally unable to work any longer, and, more often than not, there will come a stage sometime before this when you don't want to work for money anymore. Your net worth now steps in, allowing you to feed, house, and clothe yourself and your dependents; to remain self-sufficient; and to be free of financial poverty.

A new approach to assets

You might think that real and financial assets are self-evident, and on one level, they are. A starting definition of an *asset* is something that has positive, realizable monetary value. In other words, it can be exchanged or sold for a positive cash sum after selling costs. Such items should be fairly easy to spot.

But in the wealth game, what matters is whether your asset is trending up or down in value. All assets, including cash, don't stay the same value for long. Some inexorably appreciate over time, others waste away to nothing, and some bounce around without any clear sense of direction. Many are consumed and disappear immediately. An asset may have a positive value one day and a negative one the next. It may even become a liability if the costs of keeping and maintaining it outweigh the benefits.

From the outset, it's important to realize that everything tangible we call an "asset" falls into one of three baskets. You should learn and understand the names and characteristics of each, as they all directly affect your wealth, either for good or bad. I have never seen them labelled in this way, but more than thirty years of personal practice bears them out. Every time you see an asset from now on, ask yourself, "Is it this type or that type?"

Appreciator

This is an asset whose value can be expected to increase over time, despite short-term fluctuations. The time frame we are concerned with is how long we plan to hold the asset. Will its value increase over the period you plan to hold it for? If the answer is yes, it is an appreciator. You need to understand its value and the drivers for it in order to have a reasonable basis for believing this. Some of this is intuitive or common sense, but more important are acquired knowledge and experience.

There are two types of appreciators: one that, as well as appreciating in value, produces an income or is capable of doing so is called a productive appreciator, and one that does not is called an unproductive appreciator. Examples of a productive appreciator might be residential property that can be rented out or company shares that pay a dividend. Unproductive appreciators include precious commodities, such as metals, jewels, art, or antiques.

You might ask whether a business is an appreciator. The answer depends on whether it is likely to prosper. If it is run badly and losing money or its products or services are falling out of favour with customers, it is unlikely to appreciate.

Appreciators are the bases for building wealth. Your job as a player in the wealth game is to find, acquire, and, if you are able, build them.

Depreciator

These wasting assets have a value that inexorably declines, possibly to nothing or to a negative value. Their value literally wastes away, perhaps because they wear out or become obsolete.

Again, the concept of productivity applies, as even a wasting asset may generate income during its life. A car, boat, caravan, bicycle, television, or computer may be rented out to others for money and become a productive depreciator. If used as a private asset, it is an unproductive depreciator. Cash is a productive depreciator, because although inflation erodes its value over time, it can earn interest if deposited with a bank or other borrower.

Even though you include depreciators in your personal balance sheet, every penny you spend on them erodes your net worth over time.

Consumable

A consumable is literally that—an asset that doesn't survive long enough to merit inclusion in your balance sheet. It is destined for near-term consumption and has no realistic resale value in the meantime. For example, if I spend two pounds on ice cream and then eat it, for a moment after purchase, I hold an asset possibly equal in value to the money I have spent. Once eaten, I'm down two pounds and up a few ounces in weight. A poor deal were it not for the pleasure hit. All food and drink are consumables, as is fuel in the car. I also include all personal effects, like clothes, shoes, books, CDs, DVDs, toys, leisure and hobby items, and so on.

Do not include consumables in your net worth calculation. They have no meaningful value and don't produce income.

Let's consider the car as a prime example of a depreciator, a rapidly wasting asset that may become a liability. No income is generated, so its financial value is the open-market resale price. This reduces each year, as the car depreciates until it has only scrap value. At the same time, the license, insurance, and MOT fees rise each year in line with inflation, and maintenance costs grow exponentially as the vehicle gradually wears out. In simple terms, at the point when the annual running costs exceed the resale value, the vehicle has a negative net worth and becomes a liability in your personal balance sheet.

It is no more than a solution to your land transport needs. It may outlive you or not, but, either way, it has a temporary life-span. If you buy it outright, you are making a payment in advance against these needs, and if you rent it, you are paying as you go. Either way, it is money you won't get back.

The first proper car I bought was a red Alfa Romeo. It sat gleaming in a small mews off Lancaster Gate in West London. Up until then, my cars had been bangers—bought cheap, often shared with friends, and driven hard until they died or were towed away and left in the pound. The Alfa brought a smile to my face every time I saw it, and accelerating through fourth gear at about seventy miles per hour, she pinned us back in our seats and made us laugh for joy. In the second year, insurance rates doubled, and the garage at the mews took her back for half the original cost. After interest and a few meagre repayments, the purchase loan hadn't changed much. I repaid the shortfall out of savings.

Does anyone view a car as a financial investment? I hope not, unless he or she is a collector of rare marques with a large garage. For the rest of us, cars are there to satisfy our needs. In the case of the Alfa, my only need was the desire to drive fast and look good. I lived in London, so I had no practical need for a car. A blast to the south coast and beloved Isle of Wight was bonus territory. Before that, I'd happily caught the train. Beyond pure hedonism, our needs include transport to work, getting to the shops, doing the school run, and escaping from it all without encountering the general public. We tick our preferences against a long list: acceleration from zero to sixty, top speed, brake horsepower, torque, miles per gallon/litre, emissions, safety record, boot space, number of seats, optional extras, service costs, tax bracket, and so on. Depreciation may be on some people's lists but is unlikely to top many.

But who considers a car to be an asset? I suspect rather a lot of people, judging by the number of new and expensive cars being sold or leased each year, recession or not. As well as the sheer pleasure factor, cars represent an outward sign of success, status, and style. People might live in dismal homes or have hopelessly indebted statuses, but many see cars as pure life enhancers, potent drugs worth almost any price if they can muster the means to pay for them.

Aside from food and drink, clothes are a popular consumable. Their basic utility is in covering our nakedness and shielding us from the elements. Beyond that, clothes are used to enhance our physical appearance, to signify membership of one group or another, and to make a personal statement. You should consider this carefully and understand it. Imagine a world in which everyone wears a versatile and adjustable garment of the same style and broad type of natural fabric, depending on what's readily available—a thick, heavy one for cold climates and a thin, lighter one to wear in the heat. Dyes could be used to add any colour or shade desired. Production requirements would be standardized, with no need for designers, and without brands, retail would simply be a case of purchase and delivery.

Life would be simpler for everyone, and much time would be saved— no creating wardrobes or planning outfits. Just buy a standard garment, wear it until it falls apart, and buy another one.

In our global consumer society, the range and volume of depreciators and consumables dwarfs appreciators. They are everywhere and overwhelm us. Your only escape is to cut off or heavily restrict Internet and media sources and stay away from shops, which is hard to do while you are engaged with the world of working for money. All you can realistically do is to develop a constant and deep awareness. In the cold light of day, when the packaging and the embossed shopping bags have been thrown away, the credit cards have been paid off, and the sun has gone in, our assets are more often than not exposed as valueless clutter, like sediment at the bottom of an empty wine bottle.

I now want to deal with another important matter. This simple three-way categorization of assets is based purely on their financial characteristics, but how do we account (if we can at all) for the nonfinancial benefits they can provide? The pleasure, pride, excitement, thrills, and so on.

The answer is quite simple. In the wealth game, only the financial consequences of a decision matter. Nothing else. It is a trap to place the financial and nonfinancial effects of a decision on the same footing. By doing so, you encounter the double risk of first not being dispassionate in your financial assessment (it's very easy to tweak the assumptions), and second, when comparing the two, placing equal or greater weight on nonfinancial benefits that are large, colourful, and immediate. Objective financial analysis is overshadowed, and muddled thinking follows. And this applies not just to important life-changing decisions but also to small, everyday ones that you make without discussion or even conscious thought.

It is vital to develop a mind-set that measures every decision against its impact on your net worth, now and in the future. Once you've done that, pause and reflect. In the financial industry, this is called "cooling off." Then, weigh the nonfinancial benefits of your proposed decision, and decide whether they are an adequate reward for any negative impact the decision has on your net worth. They may be, or they may not be, but that's for you to decide. This may be new territory. You enter a zone where, despite being able to afford something with ease, you choose not to buy it because there is a bigger game afoot.

There is clearly much more to be learned about assets, but if you get no further than grasping the contents of this chapter, you will benefit. Consider the game Snakes and Ladders. Depreciators and consumables are like snakes, which send you backward, and appreciators are the ladders that propel you ahead.

The debt-and-liabilities side of the net worth calculation is instinctively easier to comprehend, as it tends to be solid and unavoidable. All I would say at this stage is that debt is one of the most powerful sources of wealth creation and destruction in existence, and as such, it deserves to be studied, understood, and respected. I devote a section to it later.

NEEDS

Needs make up the liability side of the equation. They erode your net worth, so every pound reduction in your needs adds to your net worth. Think about this for a minute.

A need is something that you must have in order to function and live. You can't survive without it. A want, on the other hand, is something you'd like but isn't absolutely necessary. Economists often assume that our wants are limitless. In reality, what you want is a personal choice.

Your task in the game is to identify your needs and decide on a range of wants that satisfy you as well as allow you to reach O as quickly as possible. Only include those that cost money, and ignore all others, even if they take up time in which you could be earning. Too expensive a package will hold you back for years and may halt your progress. This is a challenge that I explore in detail later.

Throughout this book, references to *needs* mean the wants and needs chosen by you.

Design your own package

Here, you become the architect of your needs instead of letting others define them.

Lifestyle is sold to us by those who wish to profit. Businesses want our money; media want our attention; government wants our vote and our cash, through taxes; and religious institutions want our patronage. We are the prize at the centre of a gigantic bun-fight between contenders rooted in self-interest and a powerful will to survive. Our collective behaviours determine whether they live or die, and they fight hard to influence them.

These peddlers and purveyors combine to service our lifestyle and needs. Between them, they cover the subject; in fact, they create and define the subject before giving us their solutions. Like a vast autoenrolling outsourcing machine, they take over this department of our lives and run it for us: what to wear, eat, drink, read, watch, listen to, learn, drive, believe, think, and care about; where to live, work, holiday, invest our money; how to be healthy and safe; and who to respect, disrespect, value, emulate, like, dislike, love, hate, reward, and pity.

From the industry corner, here are some examples of the guidance directing us to never knowingly underspend:

"Because you're worth it"—You deserve it and owe it to yourself. It's your right to buy this treat. Don't compromise. After all, you are precious and valuable, rare and unique. You've worked hard. It's just a little something to reward yourself. What harm could there be in that? In fact, what reasonable and loving person in their right mind would deny you that small pleasure?

"Because your husband or wife is worth it"—For all his or her unstinting efforts, the hardships he or she puts up with, and the sacrifices he or she makes for the good of the relationship and family, it's the least you can do. Build that pedestal high, and polish it.

"Because your children are worth it"—After all, they are the most beautiful, wonderful offspring on the planet, are young for such a short time, and deserve your generosity before facing the hard world out there. The best parties, party bags, Christmas and birthday presents, foreign holidays, clothes, games, and gadgets are surely not too much to ask.

"Retail therapy"—Yes, it is actually good for you, physically and mentally, to go out or online and buy things. It's stimulating and fun and takes your mind off difficulties and worries.

"Live the dream"—No matter that the last one never quite lived up to the brochure; this time it'll be different, and your dreams will become reality with this simple purchase.

"Life's too short; live for today" or *"YOLO: you only live once"*—Spend it while you can, because you may not be around tomorrow, and if you are, tough luck, because the money will have run out.

"You can't take it with you when you go"—On that basis, why bother about anything?

"Cash rich, time poor"—You'd better spend your money to equalize matters.

"The latest version"—It's better than before. It's smarter and more functional and will please you more. Who wants to be seen with an old version?

"Petrol head"—Wear this badge of honour proudly, drive fast and large, and look down on all beneath or behind.

"It's sale time"—Buy three for the price of two, even though you only want one. Spend to save, and grab a bargain.

"Only the best/you get what you pay for"—Under this snob's charter, it really is better quality, even if you wouldn't know it on a blind test.

"Brands are best"—Pay a lot of money for our product, and then advertise it for us by wearing the label on the outside. It's really cool and just proves your good taste and affluence.

"Dress to impress"—As a "manic impressive," you will garner more lovers, better jobs, and greater status, and people really will like you more.

"Learn to be a collector"—Become a "connoisseur," an expert in your field, and an authority on the subject, and perfect the art of buying.

"Out with the old; in with the new"—Spring-clean your life, make a new beginning, and start all over again with some new purchases, this time getting it right.

"Don't let the side down"—Avoid the humiliation and embarrassment of being the shabbiest on the street, being the tattiest at the school gate, or having dull holidays at home, so-called "staycations." Think of your family, neighbours, and friends. And worst of all, don't let yourself down with poor standards. Where's your self-respect? Take a leaf out of Hyacinth Bucket's book.

"You can afford it"—Of all people, you shouldn't be holding back!

"Do your bit to help the economy"—Everyone knows that recessions are caused, or at least prolonged, by demand drying up. Spend, spend, and spend some more to do your bit to lift us all out of this mess.

"Fair trade"—Help poor people by buying this product.

Who are these pushers, and how can we opt out of autoenrollment in their messages?

As to who they are, look around and in the mirror. What are you selling? Can you think of anyone who isn't selling something? This is no "us and them" situation. It's a human condition; we're hardwired to act at least partly out of self-interest. Whatever you think about the messages and methods of other sellers, blaming them for your own or society's problems is misguided and pointless. It's like blaming rain for making you wet. The answer to this fact of life is in your hands—stay out of it or take an umbrella.

Opting out of being led to spend in the wealth game is surprisingly easy, as long as you can disconnect. Choose what to listen to and when, and to those who do manage to reach you, just listen politely and say no thank you. Design your own lifestyle and needs from scratch instead of using default options. The information, transparency, and connectedness delivered by the Internet make it a buyers' market. You design, specify, research, select, and purchase on your own terms.

A tendency towards willful and independent thought and a certain two-fingers-up attitude to what others think is essential. Instead of "because I'm worth it," try "because I'm worth more." And as for "live for today, not tomorrow," how about "live today and provide for tomorrow"? The joy of slogans is that they are so versatile.

To complete the wealth game fast, concentrate on your needs above all else. Yes, you must generate wealth, but decouple it from your needs. Treat the two as separate exercises and distinct entities. Build one large, but design and manage the other small. Why should what you have influence what you need in the slightest? It is a cardinal mistake to allow net worth to contaminate needs. By doing this, you will lose sight of the ground.

Untrained needs multiply like an interconnected root system, spreading and sucking more water and nutrients from the soil. Rarely do they stand alone. One luxury, treat, or upgrade leads to another across every department until anything simple and basic looks out of place, whether it is fit for purpose or not. Foods, clothes, furnishings, car, house, gadgets, gardens, personal fitness and beauty, leisure, hobbies, and holidays all demand to be made over once the money supply is switched on. Children catch on fast and join the queue. Rampant materialism not only directly erodes your wealth but it also saps your energy and, as we'll see later, in many cases promotes unnecessary suffering. It is an obstacle to your reaching O—probably the biggest of all. As you earn money and build wealth, do not succumb to this trap, however much your own cravings and the pressures from others push you towards it.

Big life or small life

A big life suggests that everything is large: house, car, family, social network, and spending style. At one level, this is true. At another, it is false.

There is an inverse relationship between the scale of your lifestyle infrastructure and your ability to pursue activities and interests outside of it. The potentially immense time and cost spent providing for, managing, and tending to a large house, family, pets, cars, and other appendages directly reduces the time and money you have to do other things, perhaps with the same family. A big infrastructure, pleasurable to a point, can inhibit and stifle, constantly forcing you to look inward. Rather than a big life, you have a high-maintenance, small one.

If you adhere to the notion that what you do is more important than what you have, this is relevant.

On the other hand, a small lifestyle infrastructure enables a large and outward-facing existence—a big life. Instead of devoting your time and energy to feeding a large, hungry beast, you can lock up and leave, travel, learn, pursue your interests and passions, and spend valuable time with those you love. You can travel light.

The choice is entirely yours. It is easier if you start and stay small, but if you find yourself servicing a big lifestyle and yearning for a more outward-facing life, make the change!

In early blue-collar outsourcing contracts—for example, cleaning and buildings or grounds maintenance—the performance measures were input types. For example, x number of tasks, y number of people for each task, z number of visits to site, and so on. Suppliers soon worked this out and convinced their customers that such prescriptive arrangements denied them any real opportunity to improve the service, create efficiencies, and drive the costs down. Tenders began to focus on performance and specific outcomes. New style contracts rewarded or penalized workers depending on whether the buildings were kept clean and safe, grounds were usable and neat, or infrastructure and machinery were functional. Contractors were free to manage themselves and their tasks in any way they liked. The smart ones completely reengineered the way services were delivered, made better profits, and pleased their customers.

The big-lifestyle infrastructure never suited us, although I was slow learner. Having ticked the box and enjoyed the pleasure and pain for a few years, we sought simplicity and a connected base from which enterprise and endeavour could flourish separately from the homestead. We realized how narrow, yet demanding, our life had become. There was simply too much else to do other than carry on supporting this edifice. Taking a knife to the structure was a pleasure.

We listed our priorities and needs and constructed a new life that was fit for purpose. We found a school that felt right and a functional, undemanding home in Portsmouth, a city brimming with amenities and spirit, right next to the sea and my beloved Isle of Wight. Yes, there was more upheaval and hard work, but I had never seen Jessie happier; a bright horizon beckoned. The reengineering took six years in total, by which time I was through O and had stopped paid employment. It was completely worthwhile, but six years is a long time. Dismantling a big-lifestyle infrastructure is quite a job, and ours wasn't even that big by many people's standards.

You will have read of hugely successful investors and entrepreneurs who stay rooted, perhaps living in their childhood home; driving a twenty-year-old car; and dressing, socializing, and living like an ordinary person. Warren Buffett is one. Challenge and test your needs independently of what you earn or have accumulated. Keep the pursuit of wealth in its box as a limited objective, rather than the main event. Shift all emphasis to self-management of needs, and turn the telescope around the other way. Instead of being magnified to match your wealth, your needs are tiny. Once this fact is firmly lodged in the system, throw away the telescope altogether.

HOW DOES CASH FIT IN?

The Problem
Many people mistake cash flow for wealth and confuse the two. They think that having cash makes them wealthy, and they behave accordingly.

The problem is that when they spend their cash, it is swapped for something else. If they buy an appreciator, wealth is preserved and should grow, but if they opt for a depreciator, value will waste away over time, and for a consumable, value is lost immediately. You might think it self-evident that spending choices affect wealth, but this simple truism is widely overlooked or forgotten, as you can see from consumer debt, which continues to balloon.

Plenty of ordinary people have high net cash flow for a phase of their lives. They can live well, consuming and pleasing themselves without a financial care in the world. This cash may be a new experience, novel and exciting, and perhaps follows years of doing without. They may treat being asset light as a virtue and enjoy freedom from responsibility. This is no way to prosper in the wealth game. Pleasure, such as it may be, is sustained only by the cash fuelling it, and at some point, for the ordinary person, this cash flow will stop; the job or career will end. Without the porridge pot of wealth, the only course is to downscale and live simply on whatever money can be eked out from earnings or state benefits. This may be exactly what the player always wanted and foresaw, but on the other hand, it may not. The point is they won't have any choice in the matter.

At the same time, some people have wealth but struggle to manage, because they are short of cash. This situation is often mistakenly used to justify the superiority of cash relative to wealth.

Imagine a large country house owned by the latest impoverished member of a long family line or the beneficiary of a will or perhaps the sole survivor of a hard-working marriage. The house, beautiful and substantial though it is, needs a major overhaul on the roof, brickwork, window frames, joists, ancient electrics, and a heating system that requires several trees or a private oil well to fire up. The kitchen garden has gone to seed, and the remaining grounds are returning to nature, while the perimeter fencing slowly disintegrates. The art and antique collection is largely sold, and visitor and event days are just about keeping the place going. In short, it's a pretty sorry state of affairs.

The estate, however, is situated in prime English countryside, untroubled by neighbours, roads, or any blights, and it offers a tantalizing dream home for many an aspirational family. It's worth well over a million pounds and is mortgage free. The owner is "wealthy" but aging at twice the normal rate.

The solution is straightforward—sell the house, buy or rent something smaller, and live off the proceeds. Only when all this wealth is gone will this person be in the same financial position as the newly impoverished cash-flow hedonist. And depending on how old this person is and how well he or she manages money and spending, this situation may not arise during his or her lifetime.

The Way Forward

You should be clear as to the nature of cash flow. It is like the element of water, fluid and moving. It is the fuel for wealth creation, since without it, you cannot buy or develop assets. At the first sight of it, you should put as much of it to work as you can.

Second, it is a by-product of wealth, because assets, whether productive appreciators or productive depreciators, generate income, and all assets deliver cash on sale.

Cash flow is not wealth itself but a measure of solvency, and it is not the same as cash, the asset that can be exchanged for something else. It is measured over a period of time, rather than at a moment in time, like net worth. A person's net cash flow is £x over a week, £y over a month, and £z over a year. Measured weekly or monthly, it may dip into negative territory, as the timing of income receipts and payments vary, but over a period of time, it should be positive. A negative cash flow is unsustainable and, if uncorrected, leads to insolvency.

It follows that to succeed in the game, you need to keep a close grip on cash flow and take care not to trade wealth for short-term lifestyle.

IV

WHAT'S THE PRIZE?

It has been said that "to travel hopefully is better than to arrive." I disagree. Future hopes and dreams undoubtedly comfort in the warm, fuzzy way of fantasy escapism and may inspire and motivate, but they provide precious little preparation or assistance. "Hopefully" implies uncertainty and doubt, and journeying with it suggests that we lay ourselves open to chance in a kind of blind bet that everything will turn out all right.

The suggestion that this state is better than the target destination implies an extremely stupid or naïve traveller who has failed to think through the purpose of his or her journey. Is it possible that the destination was never considered or defined or, if it was, not properly evaluated? Or perhaps the prize was misrepresented, and if so, by whom?

A preferable aim is to travel surefooted, knowing that the target is worth all your effort and sacrifice to reach it, and with an unshakable belief that you will get there.

How can you achieve this? To replace hope with conviction demands an understanding of the underlying principles and rules (in this case, the rules of finance and human nature) and certain knowledge that you can play the game. The commonest failure arises from an inability to grasp basic financial concepts and/or a fatalistic view that one is different, through circumstances or design, and has somehow been singled out to fall short. For example, thoughts like these: "I am pathologically disposed or forced by circumstances to obesity, ill health, addiction, dependency, ignorance, laziness, greed, overspending, poverty, and so on," or "I have no chance compared with others."

I have yet to meet someone in the developed world whose poverty has not been caused either by their own actions or inactions or war. Challenge this statement, and by all means reject it! Perhaps you know someone who was robbed of all he or she had. Observe the financially poor around you, and ask why they are in this position. Follow the chain of causation, consider each outcome, the cause behind it, then the cause behind that, and so on, until the whole picture is laid out before you. Now ask what part the person played. No doubt, the circumstances into which they were born, their parenting, and their education will have influenced their behaviour, but such factors, whether helpful or unhelpful, apply to everyone. Short of being physically detained in a place where free choice and action is prevented so that someone can't take steps to improve his or her situation or mentally abused to the point that he or she can't think straight, how can that person not have played the lead role?

To be certain that the prize is worth the effort, examine it, visualize it, and meditate on it. Interrogate and challenge every hope, dream, and preconception, and take nothing at face value or solely based on someone else's word. Seek out others who are financially independent, both old and young, and observe them, listen to their stories, and observe their suffering. Adopt wise and compassionate role models, and learn from them. You may need to travel to find such people, but they do exist and can be found. Your open-mindedness and energy, research, investigation, applied reason, and meditations will combine to reveal the true nature of the prize.

Now you can decide if it is worth the effort. If the answer is yes, and you set out to win it, the trip itself becomes immensely enjoyable and continually satisfying. Of course, it will be tough in parts, but players understand that achieving any worthwhile goal requires effort and dedication through adversity. Certain hours, days, weeks, or months will be painful, but they are painful for a purpose, a grand design, and this knowledge sustains. The remainder is either painless or enjoyable. As you develop mastery of your needs, together with associated resourcefulness and creativity, the journey begins to deliver quality and richness at every level. Wonderful though it is to travel, arrival at O still beats it hands down.

In the wealth game, the prize is set at the outset, and no number of winners will dilute it. Every player is allocated one prize of equal value. It is not transferable between players, and there are no rollovers, so any prize not won or claimed is cancelled. Prize details and related information, including implications of being a winner, are fully disclosed and available to any player who wishes to review them at any stage of the game.

It's time to tear off the wrapping paper and open the box.

YOU WIN

Every child's fantasy is to conjure up a genie who grants three wishes. Let's say that this particular genie, being wise and knowing the human condition, offers three baskets of wishes and allows the child to pick one from each. A wish must relate directly to the child or someone close to him or her, rather than anonymous beneficiaries, so it can't include things like "end poverty" or "world peace," nor can it be a wish for more wishes.

The first basket contains tangibles—anything material that can be touched. The picker might opt for unlimited sweets, chocolate, ice cream, gold, diamonds, supercars, jets, boats, a farm, a castle, an island, and so on.

The second basket contains personal qualities, so it might include such rewards as a perfect physique, beauty, superhuman strength, eternal youth, immortality, a cloak of invisibility, the ability to fly or time travel, x-ray vision, or the power to read others' minds.

The final basket contains outcomes. Examples are good health, loving relationships, happy and successful children, fame, power, and status.

In the wealth game, the prize is more of a hamper, bulging with items that are all available to winners. Like the genie's offering, these fall into the same three groups: tangibles, personal qualities, and outcomes. The inventory sounds a bit like a box of fortune cookies, although less abstract.

The tangible prize
You win a money pot that yields cash year-round sufficient to meet your needs as long as you live. This organic marvel requires minimal attention and is self-sustaining if treated with care and respect.

As a virtual pot, it is fully portable and divisible and can be protected from theft or damage. It is your own, private domain, a resource to be utilized.

The personal quality prize
You win a selection of exceptional, life-enhancing personal attributes, each with a free upgrade, should you desire it. Those marked with an asterisk are major qualities with greater-than-average upgrade potential.

The ability to control all your nonsubsistence needs.* You have learned restraint and self-discipline. Upgrade allows complete mastery of all sense-related pleasures and displeasures. With this, you can appreciate and enjoy the sight of natural and human beauty and man's creations, sounds, smells, tastes, and touches, but without craving them or needing to utilize, possess, or cling to them. Every sense pleasure received is a delight to enjoy without the suffering caused by wanting. Nothing is off-limits or out of reach. Similarly, ugliness and man's destruction, natural decay, death and disaster, loss, unpleasant noises, foul smells and tastes, pain, hunger, thirst, tiredness, excessive cold or heat, and all other forms of displeasure can be witnessed without the suffering that arises from aversion and a craving for the unpleasantness to cease. These things exist and are there, but the upgrade allows you to duck the personally inflicted suffering that generally comes with them. And far from cold dispassion, this detachment from self allows understanding and compassion to flourish.

Patience. Through incremental saving, utilizing compounding, and living within the financial laws, you have developed patience and seen its rewards. This will only grow over time.

Mental endurance.* The marathon that is the wealth game leaves you highly toned and possessing considerable stamina. This mind training, however, has been a by-product rather than the main event. The free time and space afforded by O allows you the option to switch focus and develop mindfulness and concentration as a priority and to enjoy the insights and equanimity that these deliver.

Detachment.* You have learned to be dispassionate, recognizing that everything is impermanent and subject to change. The higher-level award offers a deeper understanding of this and promotes objectivity and perspective. You become aware that cravings, aversions, and clinging cause suffering.

Resourcefulness and creativity. These have been precious commodities during the game and now flow naturally, allowing you to add colour and vitality to all activities. No thing or action, however mundane or thankless it might appear, is beyond your power to rekindle as interesting and rewarding. Like a child not yet worn down by obligations and restrictions, your imagination is firing and free. Your skills of rejecting convention, refusing to accept rules and norms, and setting your own course independently of others have enabled this, while self-imposed restraint and sacrifice have demanded it. Subject to the laws of nature and physics, these skills can be developed without boundaries and limits.

Energy. Your training has created a well of energy that, although depleted, is deep and refills naturally. The game has forced you through a kind of physical and mental boot camp. The call to action is now deeply ingrained and won't leave you. This feeds effort and endeavour. Your energy will not be sapped by the now-unnecessary mental and physical efforts of providing financially; it can be spent carefully and economically to maximum effect elsewhere.

Finance skills. An ability to grow wealth and use money to make more is now second nature. Technical knowledge has combined with experience and learning from past mistakes to create a powerful platform for continued wealth creation. You can choose whether to continue to engage and take this further or to adopt a passive approach. Finance is fun, as is making money, and just because your needs are now satisfied, it doesn't mean that it can't be pursued as an intellectual and practical hobby. A surplus of money after reaching O is not a problem, as there is always a worthwhile home for it.

Commercial nous. This is now ingrained. Its effect is to simplify and reduce, to direct you to sound decisions quickly and efficiently, without fuss or waste. In the distilled, potent world beyond O, your commercial skill sits comfortably. Further practice and application sharpens it.

Self-sufficiency.* Not only do you understand this, but you have also lived it. You are now fully aware that from birth, we have no innate rights or entitlements, that all we want must be acquired or developed, and that very little in this world is given up for nothing. You have also observed that inequality isn't solved by people being dependent.

This gift transcends financial and material needs and applies to every sphere of life. It is the foundation and means of all personal achievement. Gandhi spent his entire life experimenting with and honing self-reliance in his quest for personal and social improvement. To be self-sufficient and turn from a net consumer to a net producer, from a burden and a drain to a contributor, from a liability to an asset, must surely rank as one of life's great opportunities and challenges.

Confidence. This flows from your success in reaching O and every other achievement along the way. It dispels doubt, promotes modest self-assuredness, and has universal application.

Humility. Reaching O by your own efforts has taught you how difficult a challenge it is for the ordinary person. Further time spent in the field will only serve to broaden this sentiment.

Compassion.* Arising from humility, your own suffering, and the practice of detachment and objective insight, you now have a more than adequate grounding from which to exercise this, if desired. It feeds numerous virtues and promotes actions and results that lead directly into contentment.

The outcome prize
You win one guaranteed outcome: the freedom to stop paid work. If you choose to take up this option, you win a great deal of additional spare time. Based on forty-eight five-day weeks, this amounts to 240 free days every year. In addition, the remainder, which was supposedly free before you stopped work, also expands. Your newfound space is also free from thoughts and worries about the job, the commute, the people, and the money.

If you choose to continue work, whether paid or not, you can set the terms—for example, only doing something you feel is worthwhile and enjoyable, with people you like. No longer will financial necessity force you to compromise. You can simply walk out at any point.

In at least two rather significant areas, however, wealth can't guarantee outcome. The first is nature, which operates on its own laws. Money cannot control climate and weather patterns, the health of the planet, its oceans, landmasses, and atmosphere, nor can it govern time or alter the impermanence of all things. The second is human behaviour, which is equally unconstrained. At a group level, money has failed to end poverty, inequality, institutionalized corruption, larceny, rape, hatred, and wars or promote tolerance and sustained harmony, even on a small scale.

At a purely individual level, money cannot guarantee good health, long life, beauty, physical appeal, intelligence, humour, skills, fertility, friends, loving relationships, fulfillment, happiness, or an end to suffering.

And this list only scratches the surface. The more you investigate and peel back the layers, the more you see that the power of money and wealth to deliver certain outcomes is a fraction of the power lying elsewhere, in such places as nature and human behaviour. And then you begin to question even the limited claims of the wealth camp. In the world of trade and commercial transactions—which is home territory for money and where cause and effect is most direct—outcomes can be upset by nature or human activity. Even the best-laid plans can be ruined like an expensive wedding or garden party spoiled by torrential rain or a deal delayed because someone is on holiday or unavailable.

If the outcome sought is more layered than simply "this item for that price" and extends to "this item to serve this purpose for that price," while you may get the item you ordered, it may fail to deliver the outcome you wanted because of some intervening event. Imagine an expensive wedding or garden party in perfect sunshine in which the bride changes her mind at the altar or the host and hostess have a dreadful fight, which tarnishes the whole event.

Money can buy a large house and grounds in a location and climate to suit you, perimeter fencing, CCTV, security guards, staff, a collection of luxury cars, a supermodel wife or husband, surrogate or adopted children, a top-notch education, an instant social life, gadgets and toys galore, luxury holidays, and endless hobbies and other diversions to fill acres of spare time—but it still can't guarantee the outcomes listed previously. Anyone failing to grasp this or, in fact, anyone interested in the subject of wealth should watch Lauren Greenfield's multi-award-winning 2012 documentary *The Queen of Versailles*, which follows the story of David and Jackie Siegel's quest to build the largest and most expensive single-family home in the United States. The rot had set in well before their time-share resorts business began to struggle, but the eventual speed of disintegration still surprises.

While wealth can't guarantee most outcomes, it can legitimately claim a contribution to them, and herein lies the difficulty. Because it can be so helpful, money is too easily seen as essential to the result when it isn't.

The notion that wealth overpromises and underdelivers is well illustrated by the frustration and distress suffered by those with money and influence who try but fail to control the events around them.

It is in the nature of successful people to be aspirational and ambitious. Where success brings wealth, social status, and influence, an illusion of personal omnipotence can arise quickly. As we've seen, the list of what money buys, although finite, is long and impressive; the list of what it can influence is virtually endless. It is easy for items on the second list to seep onto the first, either through arrogance and "master of the universe" attitude or a cocktail of blind optimism and desire. Suddenly, money is more powerful than ever before. The holder has inflated its buying power to fantasy levels.

The problem is that fantasy is just that—a type of imaginative fiction or make-believe, an appealing illusion. There is nothing certain or reliable about it. Does this knowledge check people's behaviour? Apparently not. Like gamblers bent on playing the odds to get rich fast with minimum effort or parents compensating for their neglect or failings by spoiling their children with gifts and costly experiences, they convince themselves that spending their money in this way is the right thing to do.

In many cases, however, trying to buy outcomes with readily available cash is the default option compared with the alternatives, and it lures players into another trap, one of mindlessness or laziness. Either they don't explore other possibly more effective routes, or they reject them as too slow or demanding. Players can spend money needlessly and fail to achieve their goals.

Naturally, at certain times, they may strike lucky and win a chosen outcome. But is it as valuable? Is buying a husband or wife as rich a prize as meeting, falling in love, and committing to each other? Do opportunist friends measure up to true friends? Will a child gently wafted through elite schooling, eased into a grand university, and steered to the top of the job pile via the money, connections, and relentless pushing of parents feel as worthy as one who has forged his or her way through grit and determination?

None of this suggests that you shouldn't use your money and status to try to influence outcomes that can't be guaranteed, but you will avoid wasting it as well as unnecessary suffering by fully considering other, cheaper options first, and, if you still want to spend, recognizing the limits to your power and staying detached. If you have done your utmost and the result still isn't what you wanted, you having nothing to reproach yourself for. Let go, and move on.

SPENDING SUGGESTIONS

The three prize groups are available in full when you reach O; how you use them will determine whether you win other even more valuable outcomes.

On inspection, none of the prizes is an end in itself. Money is a medium for buying things. Personal attributes determine our thoughts, words, and actions, and the freedom to stop paid work is a doorway to lots of new spare time. What will you buy? How will your thoughts, words, and actions evolve? Can you use your spare time well?

O is only a staging post, not an end in itself, and here's the proof: your rewards for reaching it, valuable though they appear, are useless until they are put to work. For this, new goals are needed, which, as always, are entirely up to you.

If this sounds like a return to the start of a game, it's because it effectively is. Not the wealth game but whichever other game you now want to play. Since all of these games are part of your life on earth, one might call the entire box the life game. Other games in the box include the mating game, the parenting game, the health game, the skills game, the achievement game, the philanthropy game, and so on. There is no end to the others that you might dream up.

All games can be played concurrently or sequentially. They can be started and stopped at any time and resumed at a later date. Each has definite and measurable targets, and once these are met, the relevant game is over, unless you choose to continue it.

Finishing one or more games helps your progress in the life game but isn't a guarantee of overall fulfillment. A player can have a lifelong mate, wonderful children, and reach O in the best of health but still be unhappy or riven with suffering, while another who has completed no games at all may be content and free from suffering.

Not long before he died in 1924, Franz Kafka wrote, "The reason posterity's appraisal of a man is often more correct than of his contemporaries is that he is dead. Only after death does a man's true nature emerge." In the same way, assessment of your overall performance in the life game is essentially an end-of-life exercise, since only when you are dead can it be fully considered. During its course, you can review the past but only guess the future.

O is a natural point for reflection. Where you stand regarding other games or objectives is irrelevant. Completion of the wealth game allows a major rethink and reallocation of resources into other areas. Each of the prizes you have just banked is individually significant, but if you combine them, you can raise your sights towards superhuman achievements.

More than ever, it is time to rebel, to reject and cast off lingering rules and conventions. Why not grow your hair long or shave it off, replace your wardrobe with tunics or kaftans, stay up all night, become a vegan, jettison fools, stop consuming news, say hello to everyone you meet on the street, upgrade everything, or downgrade everything? The list is endless. If people think you are in some kind of midlife crisis, let them. The point is to upset and challenge your personal order, to shake things up, releasing energy and creativity, and to begin a period of renewal, leading to a new direction and fresh purpose.

What exactly will emerge from this is anyone's guess, but something is sure to, and chances are it will be worthwhile. Perhaps it will be a long-forgotten theme, a small, barely formed idea or instinct you once had that has lain dormant but can now be dusted off and given life. Such was the case for Joseph Knecht, the Magister Ludi in Herman Hesse's 1946 Nobel Prize winning novel, *The Glass Bead Game*. Step by step, this player reached the natural summit of a gilded career, building on each task completed and test passed only to effortlessly abandon the comforts and privileges of office and leave his mystified colleagues behind, journeying on towards a destination glimpsed in fragments many years before.

A WEALTH WARNING

The prizes in the wealth game are immense, but in the course of playing and winning, dangers arise that, if not avoided or overcome, will impede your efforts and diminish your happiness. These are worth bearing in mind.

Fears and worries

Boston College's Centre on Wealth and Philanthropy has been investigating wealth and the wealthy since the 1970s. Its four-year study, "The Joys and Dilemmas of Wealth," published in 2011—the focus of which is more on the dilemmas than the joys—offers fascinating insights. Partially funded by the Gates Foundation, which wanted to understand how and when philanthropy overtakes accumulation as a personal driver for the wealthy, and the John Templeton Foundation, whose interest is in the spiritual aspect, the centre canvassed 165 American households on what it meant to be wealthy. Of these, 120 had at least $25 million in assets, and the average net worth of the respondents was $78 million. The goal of the surveyors was to include only those at or just reaching complete financial security.

Children were their number-one concern, mentioned by nearly every parent who responded. Would wealth or the knowledge that it's coming around the corner make their offspring spoiled brats, cause them to lose their drive and ambition, give them a corrupted view of the world, prevent them from developing empathy and compassion, sabotage their love lives, or make them fall out with each other? Quite possibly all of the above, according to the researchers, who gloomily reported that they had yet to see a strategy for mitigating these risks that worked. Warren Buffet said, "I gave my children enough to do something but not enough to do nothing."

The next worry was not having enough. Incredible though it sounds, this is also a general concern that echoes numerous other studies. Dissatisfaction with even sizeable fortunes is almost standard, and in the Boston College report, most respondents didn't consider themselves financially secure. For that, they said they'd require, on average, one-quarter more wealth than they currently possessed.

Third was a fear of losing it. "Sometimes I think that the only people in this country who worry more about money than the poor are the very wealthy," says Robert A. Kenny, a trained psychologist and coauthor of the report. Worries about losing their wealth plagued the respondents. Would their investments fail? Were they getting sound impartial advice?

Self-worth concerns followed, although these seemed to be the preserve of those who inherited rather earned their money. "The lucky sperm club," as Warren Buffett labelled them, aren't all arrogant and carefree, and many doubt their ability to live up to expectations or the highs achieved by their forebears. They don't enjoy the confidence-building satisfaction of having succeeded in their own right, and they often drift.

Loneliness is also a common problem. According to the report, many of the superwealthy felt isolated and unable to connect with people. This is particularly problematic for those with "sudden-wealth syndrome" and those who arrived at the point of not needing to work again at a young age. Existing friendships are tested, and money encourages new—but possibly shallow—acquaintances to appear. Generosity loses some of its meaning when it becomes commonplace or recipients grow to expect it as a matter of right.

Finally, in relationships, "Are they after me or my money?" is the classic worry, rather like the supermodel being courted for her mind. It may well be that the interest is genuine, but doesn't any of that fabulous store of wealth or that beautiful bone structure have some bearing on the matter?

It is easy to become mistrustful of genuine affection, and the cold, hard job of sifting contenders for love often becomes a family affair, like it or not; parents who insist on protracted due diligence of potential partners, prenuptial agreements, and trust arrangements dampen the romance. The report concluded that many relationships fail due to money-related issues.

Materialism

Materialism involves placing a high value on money, possessions, appearances, and status. Players can become addicted to the accumulation aspects of the game and lose sight of O. In his book *The Selfish Capitalist*, Oliver James tracks some of the many academic studies that support the notion that unmaterialistic people are less likely to suffer emotional distress than those who are materialistic. Of these, the work by Erich Fromm, a German psychologist and member of the Frankfurt School, stands out as pioneer thinking, and Fromm's prescient book, *The Sane Society*, written in 1955, remains as relevant as ever. More recent empirical research confirms his original findings and delves more deeply into the causes. The evidence is overwhelming, and no player should ignore it.

Fromm argues that through capitalism and, in particular, its focus on abstract concepts—like profit and loss and the quantification of activity and output—rather than concrete and direct observation, man has become alienated or estranged from himself and his surroundings. He quotes the famous line by Gertrude Stein, "A rose is a rose is a rose," which is her protest against this "abstractification." "For most people, a rose is just *not* a rose, but a flower in a certain price range, to be bought on certain special occasions; even the most beautiful flower, provided it is a wild one, costing nothing, is not experienced in its beauty, compared to that of the rose, because it has no exchange value."

Marx describes the same problem: "Money...transforms the real human and natural powers into merely abstract ideas, and hence imperfections, and on the other hand, it transforms the real imperfections and imaginings, the powers that only exist in the imagination of the individual into real powers…It transforms loyalty into vice, vices into virtue, the slave into the master, the master into the slave, ignorance into reason, and reason into ignorance."*

* Karl Marx, "Nationalokonomie und Philosophie," *Die Fruhschriften* (Stuttgart: Alfred Kroner Verlag, 1953), 300–301.

Fromm describes the alienating function of consumption as follows:

Beyond the method of acquisition, how do we use things once we have acquired them? With regard to many things, there is not even the pretence of use. We acquire them to *have* them. We are satisfied with useless possessions. The expensive dining set or crystal vase that we never use for fear they might break, the mansion with many unused rooms, the unnecessary cars and servants, like the ugly bric-a-brac of the lower-middle-class family, are so many examples of pleasure in possession instead of use…the act of consumption should be a concrete human act, in which our senses, bodily needs, our aesthetic taste—that is to say, in which *we* as concrete, sensing, feeling, judging human beings—are involved; the act of consumption should be a meaningful, human, productive experience. In our culture, there is little of that. Consuming is essentially the satisfaction of artificially stimulated fantasies, a fantasy performance alienated from our concrete real selves.

According to Fromm, alienation also corrupts our relationships and leisure activities, the latter being 'consumed' as time fillers and distractions, rather than experienced and enjoyed.

A great deal of what goes under the name of love is a seeking for success, for approval. One needs someone to tell one not only at four o'clock in the afternoon but also at eight and at ten and at twelve: "You're fine, you're alright, you're doing well"...This creates someone who is a passive, empty, anxious, isolated person for whom life has no meaning and who is profoundly alienated and bored. If one asks these people whether they are bored they answer, "Not at all, we're completely happy. We go on trips, we drink, we eat, we buy more and more for ourselves. You aren't bored doing that!"...In fact, the anxious, bored, alienated person compensates for their anxiety by a compulsive consumption...Boredom comes from the fact that man has become purely an instrument, that he cultivates no initiative, that he feels not responsible, that he feels like a little cog in a machine that someone could replace with another at any time...he tries to compensate for it through consumption.

Labour-saving devices don't help: "He does indeed save time with his machines, but after he has saved time, then he does not know what to do with it. Then he is embarrassed and tries to kill this saved time in a respectable way. To a large extent, our entertainment industry, our parties and leisure activities are nothing but an attempt to do away with the boredom of waiting in a respectable manner.

The bluntness of these observations shouldn't be mistaken for pessimism. No one can reasonably doubt that such problems exist and on a large scale. So far, governments, religious institutions, social pressure groups, and movements have failed to cure the disease en mass, but society's woes should not be automatically imputed to the individual, as they are far from inevitable. Whether taken as a cure or a vaccination, once you are aware that a problem exists, you can reevaluate and reconnect as you choose, make your own rules, and, to a large extent, avoid alienation. Studying the collective behaviour of community and society and analysing the policy implications for governments is of no more practical help to you than waiting for the state or society to solve your problems. It is futile and misguided. Focus entirely on your own self-improvement and the path to O.

It is quite possible to be financially wealthy and not materialistic or rigidly attached to your money and assets. You can act as a custodian or trustee of funds and assets for the benefit of others. You disengage from the superficial benefits of your wealth. You still need to steward the pot and decide how to distribute it, which takes time, but your personal needs or desires are removed from the equation.

Complexity

One of the most common complaints I hear from those with money is how complicated their lives are. The time spent buying, protecting, maintaining, administering, and ultimately selling houses, cars, boats, and other collections often gets in the way of enjoying them. It can be a full-time job, yet these assets constantly cry out to be used, making us feel guilty and frustrated if we don't.

In his 1884 essay "England's Ideal," Edward Carpenter, the Victorian socialist philosopher and radical involved in founding the Fabian Society and the early Labour Party, included a chapter called "The simplification of life."

> If you do not want to be a vampire and a parasite upon others, the great question of practical life that everyone has to face, is how to carry it on with as little labour and effort as may be. No one wants to labour needlessly, and if you have to earn everything you spend, economy becomes a very personal question—not necessarily in the pinching sense, but merely as adaptation of means to the end. When I came some years ago to live with cottagers (earning say fifty to sixty pounds a year) and share their life, I was surprised to find how little both in labour and expense their food cost them, who were doing far less work than I was, or indeed the generality

of the people amongst whom I had been living. This led me to see that the somewhat luxurious mode of living I had been accustomed to was a mere waste, as far as adaptation to any useful end was concerned; and afterward, I decided that it had been a positive hindrance, for when I became habituated to a more simple life and diet, I found that a marked improvement took place in my powers both of mind and body.

Chinese writer and scholar Lin Yutang, who wrote that he first found himself and came alive in the Widener Library while studying a doctoral degree at Harvard, picked up the theme in his 1937 book, *The Importance of Living.* "I do not think that any civilization can be called complete until it has progressed from sophistication to unsophistication, and made a conscious return to simplicity of thinking and living."

Dr. E. F. Schumacher, author of *Small Is Beautiful—A Study of Economics as if People Mattered*, published in 1973, also railed against complexity, the misuse of resources, and exploitation. In the chapter "Technology with a Human Face," he discussed "self-help technology or democratic or people's technology—technology to which everybody can gain admittance and which is not reserved to those already rich and powerful...It is my experience that it is rather more difficult to recapture directness and simplicity than to advance in the direction of ever more sophistication and complexity. Any third-rate engineer or researcher can increase complexity; but it takes a certain flair of real insight to make things simple again."

In his chapter "Buddhist Economics," he takes issue with overconsumption, echoing the themes of Erich Fromm. The modern economist "is used to measuring the 'standard of living' by the amount of annual consumption, assuming all the time that a man who consumes more is 'better off' than a man who consumes less. A Buddhist economist would consider this approach excessively irrational: since consumption is simply a means to human well-being, the aim should be to obtain the maximum of well-being with the minimum of consumption."

A corrupter?
Studies carried out by Berkeley psychologists Paul Piff and Dacher Keltner and published in 2012 indicate that as people climb the social ladder, their level of compassion towards others declines. Social standing was measured by wealth, occupational prestige, and education.

One experiment observed a busy four-way road intersection and found that luxury car drivers were more likely to cut off other motorists than wait for their turn. This applied to both male and female drivers at any time of day, however busy the conditions. In a related study, they found that luxury car drivers were also more likely to speed past a pedestrian trying to use a crossing, even after making eye contact.

In order to test whether selfishness leads to wealth or vice versa, the academics ran another study. A group of subjects was asked to spend time comparing themselves to people richer than themselves, another group to poorer people. Both groups were then shown a jar of sweets and told that they could take home as much of it as they wanted and that any left over would be given to children in a different laboratory. Individuals who had spent time imagining they were better off than others took significantly more sweets than the others, leaving less behind for the children.

One series of studies directly tested compassion. A first found that less affluent individuals are more likely to demonstrate compassion regularly to others. They are more likely to agree with statements like "I often notice people who need help" and "it's important to take care of people who are vulnerable." A second experiment monitored heart rates of viewers watching two videos, one showing a person explaining how to build a patio and another featuring children with cancer. Participants with lower levels of income and education were more likely to report feeling compassion while watching the young cancer patients, and this was supported by a drop in heart rates consistent with paying greater attention to the feelings of others.

Seven study areas in the work revealed that "upper-class" individuals behave more unethically than those in lower classes. They are more likely to

- break the law while driving,
- exhibit unethical decision-making tendencies,
- take valued goods from others,
- lie in a negotiation,
- cheat to increase their chances of winning a prize, and
- endorse unethical behaviour at work.

Mediator and moderator data demonstrated that these behaviours are accounted for, in part, by upper classes having a more favourable attitude towards greed. Piff and Dacher also suspect that wealth and abundance give a sense of freedom and independence from others, leading to disconnectedness and insensitivity.

Their work continues a rich seam of study pointing in the same direction. Real-life evidence adds to the mix, whether it be a UK MP's expense scandal, news editors hacking private telephones, Ponzi investment schemes, bankers manipulating interbank interest rates, match fixing, FIFA or Olympic bribes, lawyers falsifying mortgage applications, hedge fund managers trading on inside information or dodging train fares, oil majors and industrialists cutting corners on health and safety and environmental protection, and so on. All of these behaviours begin with the individual.

If you embrace them fully, the scale and quality of prizes and upgrades offered in the wealth game fill available space with a kind of wholesome richness that dissipates fears and worries, cuts through and simplifies life, releases you from material attachments and cravings, and dilutes tendencies towards antisocial behaviour.

PART TWO
GETTING STARTED

V

WHERE ARE YOU ON THE GRID?

YOUR NET WORTH

It's now time to see where you are in the game. The first step is to calculate your net worth.

You can do this on a single piece of paper, and I suggest you start this way. Keep it simple, and note any estimates used or outstanding questions to one side. Step one is identify all your assets, list them, and place a value against each asset. This should be a realistic and conservative market value after any expenses and tax on sale. Step two is to list all of your debts of any kind and currently outstanding liabilities (ignore future ones not yet incurred) and place a value against each one. Next, deduct the value of your debt and liabilities from your assets to reveal net assets—or net liabilities, as the case may be.

By completing this task, you are behaving like a commercial enterprise that has a strong interest in understanding its financial position. There are many books and online resources available to help you answer questions about the details of preparing a personal balance sheet, and it is worth investigating these.

The face of your balance sheet shouldn't change much whether you have negative or positive net worth or have a lot of money or a little. I would recommend that once you are familiar with the process, you type it into a spreadsheet. This allows easy updates and printing for your records. As your skill develops, you can add detailed supporting schedules for each asset and liability class or group that feed directly into the summary output page. You can also add formulas to help highlight particular themes, such as asset allocation or loan-to-value ratios, and make the spreadsheet addressable (i.e., dynamic so that you can play with illustrative numbers).

Try also grouping your assets into appreciators, depreciators, and consumables.

A typical balance sheet will be a variation on the examples for each phase of the game, set out below:

Table 5.1

Example balance sheet

		beginner £	central £	final £
assets				
productive appreciators	private pension pot		25,000	250,000
	rental property			150,000
	other shares		15,000	75,000
appreciators	home		280,000	450,000
	antiques			5,000
depreciators	cash/bonds	3,000	10,000	15,000
	car		10,000	10,000
	boat			10,000
	caravan			10,000
	tv/hi-fi	2,000	5,000	5,000
	computers	2,000	5,000	5,000
consumables	clothes	1,000	2,000	3,000
	furniture	1,000	5,000	8,000
	miscellaneous	1,000	3,000	4,000
total assets		10,000	360,000	1,000,000
liabilities	mortgage		200,000	
	term loan	1,500	6,000	
	student debt	50,000		
	overdrafts	2,000	1,000	
	credit cards	1,500	1,000	
	hire purchase		2,000	
total liabilities		55,000	210,000	–
net assets/liabilities		-45,000	150,000	1,000,000

The beginner-phase example takes a recent graduate who hasn't built up any meaningful assets and carries student and other debts. The central-phase player has begun to build an asset base with home, pension pot, and shares and has a positive net worth of £150,000 after mortgage and other loans. The final-phase player has paid off all debts and has a range of assets.

Notice the proportion of productive appreciators to total assets for the second two examples. The central-phase player has 11% (40/360), and the other has 48% (475/1000).

What are your net assets, and how do your assets split between categories?

I calculate my net worth once a year, on December 31. It takes me about thirty minutes, assuming that I have realistic, updated valuations on my properties. Values of my other assets are maintained in supporting spreadsheets or online, and I update these at least quarterly.

What are the benefits of measuring net worth?
Your personal balance sheet is the pinnacle of all financial planning. No matter how much cash flow or other analysis you do, it is a mistake to ignore it. Aside from the fact that it is the other side of the needs coin in the wealth game and that without a grasp of it, you're unlikely to reach O, there are a number of spin-off benefits.

Efficiency—All your assets and liabilities are listed and valued on one page. You can dispense with laboured searching through files and documents and reinventing the wheel every time you want to see the picture. It is easy to update and for others to understand, and it's very useful if you're not around.

Confident planning—Whether the picture is pretty or horrible, there's something refreshing and liberating about knowing where you stand. By operating in the dark, you *will* suffer, either by worrying when you don't need to or living it up when you shouldn't be or by simply getting stuck like a deer in the headlights and making no decisions. Your personal balance sheet allows you to plan spending and saving patterns for the year based on fact, not fiction.

Capital structure—It shines a light on the scale and types of debt you carry relative to overall assets, helping you make decisions about the right levels.

Asset analysis—You can segment assets with particular characteristics, such as appreciators and depreciators, or liquid versus illiquid. For example, cash, shares, and bonds versus property and personal possessions, or short versus long term. Subtotals can be easily calculated, and weightings can be shown and analysed.

Asset allocation—A balance sheet delivers an accurate picture of your asset allocation between all categories, both major, such as property, shares, and cash, and secondary, such as chattels. From this, it is easy to consider adjustments depending on the state of the markets, your needs, and your appetite for risk.

Performance management—The simple scrutiny that a balance sheet promotes leads, in no time, to a more critical assessment of the performance of each asset class and the assets within. This leads to a sharpened focus, a reluctance to tolerate underperformers, and a reorienting around quality.

Target to beat—No one enjoys going backward, and the fact that you can't hide from your net worth provides an incentive to improve on it for the next calculation point.

The overall effect of giving attention to your personal balance sheet is that you shift from "here and now" cash management to proper asset management. You begin to steward and nurture your hard-earned and precious assets.

YOUR NEEDS

Your net worth is a fixed number today, and to be comparable, your needs total must also be a fixed number today. The difficulty is that your needs are uncertain and continue to the end of your life, so how can you quantify them?

Fortunately, in the beginner phase of the game, it isn't necessary to try. As you move through the central phase, you should develop a working model for them and refine this as you approach O. Of course, there's no reason that you shouldn't have a go now, even if you are just starting out. Treat it as a blue-sky exercise, a chance to start shaping the kind of life you want and to design a needs framework to suit you.

The easiest way to explain how to quantify future needs and express them in a single balance sheet number at today's value is to consider the categories in turn. Some can be calculated using a common approach; others have their own treatment. Certain cost categories, like food and energy, will run until you die; others, like school or child care fees, are for a few years only; some arise early in life; others arise later; and some expenses tail off, while others increase. At this stage, the objective is to keep the calculation as simple as possible.

In my own planning and the analysis below, I assume life ends at ninety, but it's up to you to set your own target. The major needs categories and approaches for capitalizing them are easy to apply to your life:

1. Accommodation
This includes your home(s) (i.e., places you live in or use rather than hold for investment or rental). A home is an absolute need; the scale or quantity is your choice.

Approach—First, ask yourself whether your definition of O includes a home that is owned or rented.

For an owned home, include today's market price of the type of home you expect to die in. I call this the *final home value*. Whether it is a £2 million or £200,000 home, include the relevant figure. The reason for setting the price at death rather than at some other point is that it allows you to assume that any excess value in property above this number is not a need but a source. The value of any home you currently own is irrelevant for this step. Once reaching O, however, you must recognize that if your home at that time is worth more than your then *final home value*, it will be called upon either through sale or equity release to deliver the surplus in cash at some point before death. The decision as to how and when you release any excess value will be for you to decide based on your circumstances and needs at the time.

Let's say that in calculating your needs today, you set a final home value at £500,000 but currently own a house mortgage free with a value of £850,000. For the calculation, your accommodation need is recorded as £500,000. If today is the day you reach O, you are effectively agreeing to release £350,000 in today's money at some time before death. If, on the other hand, you have no intention of moving house at any time before death, record your need as £850,000, which effectively becomes your final home value. The only point at which the question of final home value matters for real is when you reach O. Until then, it is an aspiration.

For a rented home, multiply rental costs in today's value by the number of years you expect to pay that rent. If you are fifty and expect to pay rent at £15,000 per annum for thirty years and then to downsize to a smaller place at £10,000 per annum for ten years, the total is £550,000 (£450,000 + 100,000).

2. Subsistence living expenses

This includes food, utilities, and transport, plus any day-to-day expenses you consider to be essential, other than those in other categories. If you need help calculating it, consult one of the many budgeting guides available.

Approach—The simplest method is to multiply today's annual total by number of years until age ninety, so subsistence living expenses of £35,000 per annum add up to £1.4 million over forty years. Alternatively, you can divide your remaining years into low-, medium-, and high-spending periods to match your expected needs—for example, ten years of high spending at £50,000 per annum; ten years of medium spend at £35,000; and twenty years at a lower rate of £25,000, totalling £1.35 million.

3. Children

The day-to-day costs of feeding and clothing children should be included in the previous category. This section is for specific nursery and early-care charges, school and university fees, and financial support after leaving school. These involve personal choices that can have a big impact on outcomes.

Approach—Calculate total remaining costs for each child in today's money. How much, if any, do you expect to contribute to these categories? Nursery and early-care charges are hard to avoid, but from primary onward, the choice is between private or state-funded schooling. Similarly, the burden of university fees and living costs can either be added to your list of needs or shifted to the child to fund through student loans, part-time work, and later, full-time salaried employment.

The total cost of needs under this heading may be anything between £0 and £400,000* or more per child, depending on your decisions.

*Assumes private schooling at £8,000 per annum from age four to eight (£40,000), 24,000 per annum from age nine to thirteen (£120,000), £33,000 per annum from age thirteen to eighteen (£165,000) university tuition fees at £9,000 for three years (£27,000) and a £10,000 per annum living allowance for five years after leaving school (£50,000). This totals £402,000.

4. Holidays
This section refers to an allowance for all future holidays.

Approach—Multiply chosen annual cost of holidays by the number of years until age ninety. Your holiday needs will change over time, as family numbers ebb and flow, your appetites evolve, and physical capabilities grow and decline. You can try to predict and cost these variations, but I prefer to start with the largest possible number and assume that you'll be able to spend it one way or another, whatever the circumstance. This way, any leftover is an upside. Include the cost of weekends away and short breaks as well as longer time out.

Over forty years, an annual budget of £10,000 amounts to £400,000.

5. Cars
This section refers to the purchase cost of all cars you expect to buy in your lifetime.

Approach—One way is to multiply the cost of your chosen car by the number of upgrades you expect to make. For example, if you are running a forty-year forecast and expect to change your car every five years starting in five years' time, that's eight cars. If the cost of your chosen car today is £25,000, your needs are £200,000. Alternatively, list all the cars you think you'll buy over the forecast period, including run arounds, luxuries, people carriers, vans, and off roaders, and add the total cost in today's money.

6. *Maintenance or settlement obligations*
This includes any known future obligations, such as payments to ex-partners for children, unless accounted for already.

Approach—Add up the total cost of future payments in today's money. An obligation to pay £400 per month for ten years amounts to £48,000.

7. *Other luxury spending*
This is where you can be as expansive or frugal as you wish. Though it's often hard to be specific, this category includes presents, pampering, and other nonessential items.

Approach—Include a monthly and annual budget for these things. An allowance of £500 per calendar month or £6,000 per annum over forty years is £240,000.

8. *End-of-life care*
This includes an allowance for nursing and other care ahead of your death.

Approach—Add a provisional total sum. Let's say you are budgeting for yourself and a partner and want to allow £40,000 each. Include £80,000 in needs. Given the shifting nature of available care provision and its costs, this is a hard one to be clear on until you are well into the game, and even from the point of reaching O, it is certain to change again. The trick is to recognize your needs and include a reasonable estimate for it, based on circumstances today.

9. *Fixed legacies*
These are any specific cash amounts or appreciators that you want to pass on to beneficiaries on or before your death. By definition, like your final home value, these are ring fenced and, therefore, not available to service your needs between O and death.

Approach—Include today's value of any such legacies. A legacy of £50,000 to each of your four children is a need of £200,000.

10. Miscellaneous needs

This section refers any other needs not included in any of the previous categories. These can be entirely manufactured from a wish list of future luxuries. For example, life after O may seem pointless without a boat or a camper van or paid staff, so provision for these costs should be included. Similarly, you may feel the need to pay for private health insurance after a certain age, in which case the capitalized costs of this should also be included.

Approach—Add the item's cost or capitalize as for other needs.

What about debt and related interest repayments? For many, the cash outflows for these are the dominant outgoing. In the wealth game, borrowings are treated as a source of funds to meet your needs rather than as needs themselves. These stand alone. Needs arise from your own physical requirements and wants, so they are quite distinct from the means you can muster to pay for them. Your job here is to cost your future needs, irrespective of how you fund them. Debt and its related costs are counted in the net assets side of the equation.

Adding the totals of these categories plus any others that you think apply gives today's value of your total future needs.

Depending on your age and choices, this may be a very large number. For example, an ambitious thirty-year-old with a new family and home and forecasting sixty years to live will generate a much larger number than a steady fifty-five-year-old whose children have left home and who is nearly mortgage free. And if today's number is big, future values will be enormous if compounded over fifteen years or more. One of the entertaining aspects of periodically running the numbers is watching your needs figure change as your tastes and outlooks mature or as your asset position firms up.

As you get older, your needs will become clearer, and your time periods will become shorter. What begins as a fairly rough-and-ready indicator with big risk around future assumptions gradually becomes a very reliable calculation. Clarity around the home you choose to live in, either rented or owned, and the number of children you parent helps greatly.

Here's a very simple example for a forty-year-old:

Final home value—£300,000
Subsistence income—£25,000 per annum × 50 years = £1,250,000
Children—2 × £75,000 = £150,000
Holidays—£5,000 per annum × 50 years = £250,000
Cars—10 over the remainder of life at £10,000 each = £100,000
Other luxuries—£10,000 per annum × 50 years = £500,000
Care—£40,000 per annum × 5 years = £200,000

Total needs = £2,750,000

This shows just how large the numbers can become for even a relatively modest lifestyle. Through your decisions and actions, you have the power to expand or shrink your needs total by hundreds of thousands—if not millions—of pounds and set your rate of progress towards O. It is as powerful a force as your lifetime earnings, yet more under your control.

THE NAN GAP

Once you have calculated your net worth and your needs, you can compare the two. The result is your net-assets-to-needs (nan) gap, either a shortfall or a surplus. At this stage, it is no more than an indicative guide, a glorified back-of-the-envelope calculation. The joy is that you can use rough-and-ready estimated figures to produce a quick ballpark result that will almost certainly be helpful and enlightening.

Later in the book, I explain how to refine and use it so that you can better assess whether you have reached O.

In the meantime, there are four important principles to note:

1. Numbers are capitalized and expressed in today's money value.

    The NAN gap compares your net assets today with your total future needs, also expressed in today's money value. It is a snapshot position of assets and liabilities at a point in time and quite different from traditional profit-and-loss and cash flow forecasting.

    Future asset returns and cost inflation as well as exact timing of future income and needs are all put to one side for now.

2. Net asset values are calculated after tax and selling costs have been deducted.

    Tax is a real cost to your wealth and therefore needs to be factored in, whether it has been paid yet or not. All assets included in your net worth are valued after selling costs and capital gains or other taxes payable have been deducted.

    Let's assume that you own an investment property worth £150,000 that, if you were to sell today, would incur a capital gains tax liability after reliefs and allowances of £10,000 and transaction expenses of £5,000. You should record its value as £135,000 (£150,000 – 10,000 – 5,000). The logic behind this approach is that your needs, together with the resources you set aside or generate to meet them, should be directly comparable. A need of £100 cannot be fulfilled by an asset worth £100 if the net proceeds of its sale after tax are only £80.

    Add up the gross value of all your owned assets, and calculate a net of tax and sale expenses total, using current rates, reliefs, and allowances applicable to each. It is reasonable to factor in some tax planning, such as phased sales to utilize annual exemptions, rather than assume complete liquidation at once.

3. The NAN gap includes you and your dependants.

O is a personal target, so the test is oriented to you as an individual, but if you provide financially for a partner, spouse, children, parents, or anyone else, you must include their costs.

4. It's a relative test.

The entire premise of O is matching resources to needs. Absolute totals, however large or small, are meaningless in isolation.

YOUR PROSPECTS

"We spend thousands on your education" was a common half joke in our family when I was slacking or somehow not delivering. Over time, I began to feel like an investment opportunity. My parents poured in money and emotional support, and I, the time and effort—the exams, qualifications, and training.

When all this was done, I started thinking about the potential payback on our collective investment. I was worth everything I could earn in the future, and that made me more valuable than someone who had a lower earning potential, even if he or she started out with more than me. And if I could steward my earnings better than others, I would have a further advantage.

Here is a short test known in the vernacular as a "quick and dirty," which will reveal roughly where you are on the starting grid. It's highly indicative and certainly not worth getting hung up on, but it has the merit of being quick and easy to complete, because the answers are all estimates, some highly subjective. Scoring too is a matter of personal interpretation, so it's open to cheating, but that would be rather pointless. Of more relevance are the questions themselves and your thoughts around them.

Questions are scored from –10 to +10 points. It's up to you how you score each answer.

1. What is my current net worth, including any certain wealth coming to me in the near future (e.g., trust fund or inheritance)?
If you don't already have a rough net worth estimate from your personal balance sheet, do it now.

If the answer is negative (i.e., you have net liabilities instead of net assets), mark a negative score. Your early efforts in the game will be spent eliminating this deficit before you can move into positive territory. Typical ways to do this are to pay off debts and liabilities, separately grow an asset pot that exceeds them, or do an element of both.

Neutral worth (i.e., zero net assets) scores 0 and means that you can start building positive value immediately.

A positive net worth places you ahead of the pack and provides a pot to steward and nurture. Score depending on how large it is relative to your likely future needs.

2. How much surplus net cash am I generating per year?
As discussed, cash flow is the fuel for wealth creation. Negative cash flow erodes wealth and is unsustainable indefinitely. It scores a negative number in this test.

Break-even cash flow, scoring 0, represents no more than solvency and limits your ability to grow net worth. Without it, all you can do to make a difference is wait for assets to appreciate over time or shuffle them between classes. While the surplus cash flow tap is switched off, you are exposed to falls in asset prices and escalating needs without an opportunity to replenish.

Surplus cash flow can be directed to feed and nurture your net worth and scores positively.

3. What is my earning potential in the next five to ten years, given my skills and qualifications?
Potential future earnings have value today. Two businesses with the same risks will be valued differently depending on their profit potential. One that has the potential to generate substantial profits will be valued more than one whose profit opportunity is small. Individuals are no different, and employers or investors will back and reward those with promise, even if they have limited or no experience.

Like choosing a rich nation or prosperous region, allying your potential to an industry or activity with money requires research and accurate knowledge, but it pays. You may have exceptional potential in flower arranging, but if no one values that activity financially, you'll score low on this test. Certain industries are inherently poor, and workers in them are destined for low pay. These might be public sector services reliant on taxpayer money or industries in decline, where new technologies, products, and solutions are replacing people. Alternatively, certain activities will pay poorly irrespective of industry—think low or unskilled ones that anyone can perform.

It doesn't matter whether or not you have a job now, and, if you do, what type it is. Think about your capabilities and their commercial value, but be realistic. The younger you are, the more time you have to achieve. A sixty-year-old player who is still trying to work out what he or she is good at should temper his or her optimism.

Scores for this question are universally positive unless you are one of the exceptional people like Frank Spencer in *Some Mothers Do 'Ave 'Em*, who appeared to have negative prospects.

4. How secure is this earnings potential?
Your potential might be enormous, but some risk weighting is necessary to keep it meaningful. In other words, how likely are you to achieve it? The answer partly lies in your chosen industry but mainly in your own temperament.

Is your chosen field the hire-and-fire, boom-and-bust type or the hero-to-zero type? Mark it down. Planning to beat the system is an unreliable strategy.

Are you a long-distance runner, an endurance specialist with stamina and mental resources, or a sprinter living off fast reactions and explosive power? Perhaps you are somewhere in between, a middle-distance expert with a quick finish. Either way, are you a winning platform? Would you back yourself? Delve into your own makeup, and risk adjust your potential score. It is quite consistent to have a low potential score in the previous question but a high probability one here and vice versa (a high potential but low probability). Scoring high on both tests places you strongly in the game.

5. What are my likely financial needs as well as those of any dependants over the next five to ten years?
If you haven't already had a go at estimating your needs, do it now. Do you currently have dependents, or are any expected to arrive over the period? Ignore any hopes or fears that lie outside this time frame.

You can answer this by listing and quantifying needs (or simply estimating as small, medium, or large) and scoring accordingly. All answers should be negative, because needs erode wealth potential. An ascetic scores near zero, a glutton near –10.

6. What sort of life would I like for myself and dependants longer term?
The final question is another negative scorer.

It purely aspirational and covers lifestyle and key financial aspects, like home, hobbies, holidays, and schooling for any children as well as your attitude to spending. Reach further than your known or reasonably foreseeable needs in the previous question, and imagine the style of life that you want. Where on the spectrum are you? Are you a hermit, monastic, a self-sufficient homesteader thriving on spiritual nutrition and nature, or a larger-than-life player or family, immersed in a free-spending material bubble?

Before you start, here are five example types that I have already scored:

Grace is twenty-three and single, has just finished her studies, and is beginning work; Mike is thirty-five with two children and well established in low-paid but steady work; and Gemma is forty-five and a high flier with four children. Chris is fifty-five in reasonably paid work whose children who have left home and are self-supporting. Laura is thirty, works part time, and has two teenage children. Each of these people is the sole breadwinner in his or her home. In some shape or form, all are in the game.

Table 5.2

Prospects

	Grace	Mike	Gemma	Chris	Laura
net worth	-2	2	5	6	2
annual cash surplus	0	2	2	3	1
earnings potential	6	3	9	1	3
security of earnings	4	5	6	6	3
needs over 5-10 years	-2	-5	-8	-3	-5
longer term needs	-4	-4	-8	-5	-4
total	2	3	6	8	0

Chris scores highest due to his accumulated wealth, ongoing surplus cash flow, and modest needs. Gemma follows with a combination of wealth and income potential, despite a costly lifestyle. Mike, whose costs and needs are offset by solid income potential and reliable cash flow, is next. Grace proves that starting with debt and no surplus cash flow isn't terminal as long as there is potential and near-term needs can be kept low whilst part timer Laura lags the field with a neutral score, held back by her family needs and weak earnings potential.

Despite the different circumstances and needs of each, none of the players starts behind the line, illustrating that the combination of scores matters more than any one score. Questions with the greatest scope for negative scores (i.e., 1, 5, and 6) have a huge impact on overall starting position, but helpfully, these are the ones over which you have most control.

Someone with a high score is theoretically closer to O than someone with a lower one. A positive overall score indicates a favourable starting position; a negative one indicates that major change is needed in order to play the game with any real chance of winning.

How do you score?

VI

COLLECTING CHIPS

THE GAME CURRENCY

To begin or stay in the game, you need to be solvent. Whether or not you already hold assets, the more cash you generate, the greater the wealth you can build. It's time to explore cash flow in more detail.

Cash flow can be measured in different ways, depending on what you are interested in finding out. At one level, you may be checking that you can pay your way over a period of time, that you are solvent. At another, you may want to know what free cash is available to spend on something, such as holidays or wealth generation. Alternatively, you might want to analyse the sources of your cash to distinguish the money earned from work versus that generated from assets or other sources. Whatever the objective, it is best to start with a basic definition and work out numbers based on that. The one I propose is a catchall that saves listing all the possible categories and entries:

Personal net cash flow is the difference between the money you have incoming after tax and your outgoing cash measured over a period of time.

Incomings include all cash or money that comes into your possession in the chosen period, even if it is advanced for work yet to be done or as a loan to you. Tax is deducted at current rates after applicable reliefs and allowances.

Outgoings are all payments out of any kind, except for tax that has already been deducted from the incomings side. Outgoings include loan interest and repayments.

The result is a surplus, a deficit, or a zero balance.

If you want to calculate the cash available to fund a particular purpose, add back any outgoings in the period that are allocated to that purpose—to reveal the cash available to fund holidays in the period, add back the cost of all the holidays. Alternatively, you can exclude the relevant payments from your outgoings subtotal. Either way, it will deliver the same result, and it works for considering any particular area of spending.

In the wealth game, a key driver is the cash available to grow your wealth. Throughout the book, when I refer to surplus cash flow, this is what I mean. In calculating this figure, you must ignore all payments into:

1. Saving—For example, into a pension, a tax-free scheme, a bank or building society account, bonds or other products.
2. Investing—Payments made for the purchase or maintenance of appreciators. If you are currently renting a home but want to check your ability to buy instead, you should also separate your rental costs to avoid counting your accommodation costs twice. Depreciators and consumables are left as part of general outgoings, because they erode wealth.
3. Finance costs of appreciators—Interest paid on mortgage or other loan costs secured or relating directly to an appreciator.

Add these back to your overall net cash flow total, or exclude them from outgoings in arriving at that total, and you'll have net cash flow after tax and before investment in net worth—your surplus net cash flow number. This is the game currency.

KEEPING TRACK

Unlike net worth, which can lie inert and hidden until resurrected through your balance-sheet calculation, cash flow has a dynamic life of its own and is unavoidable. It is constantly ebbing and flowing, enabling you to pay your way or not, depending on whether you have enough. However wealthy you are, your cash needs must be satisfied, and money must be in the right place at the right time. The decision here is not whether you measure or monitor it but *how*, and an early question is this: "Are you interested in historic cash flows or future ones?"

Measuring cash flow over a past period involves fact-finding to trace all the incomings and outgoings that actually happened during that time. This can be laborious or even impossible, depending on the state of your record keeping. If done properly, the result is an accurate picture of how much money has come in and how much has been paid out—a story of your financial activity.

Forecasting cash flow over a future period is a completely different exercise. You are no longer bound by history, and although elements of spending are nondiscretionary, such as rent or mortgage interest, utility bills, and insurance, much will be partly or wholly up to you to decide. The past is only a guide.

The first exercise is like doing a postmortem, while the second is a health assessment, an eating and exercise plan for someone still living. Medical or financial health history is useful, but only up to a point. What matters is how the patient is going to behave and fare from now on. You should devote your energy to planning and forecasting future cash flows. In doing this, refer to past spending to support your assumptions. Once you are living the plan, check at intervals to see how accurate your guesswork is, and refine it where necessary.

Having chosen your review period, the next task is to decide on the level of detail and approach. Your own style and circumstances will determine this, as well as how much time you wish to commit. If you are living on the edge of your means and feel the need to police your spending rigorously, you may opt for prescriptive, hands-on planning with constant forensic review. If not, a more relaxed and less time-consuming method can suffice.

I have seen a number of approaches.

Cash in hand

There is no listing or measuring of any ins or outs—this involves simply looking at what's in your wallet or bank to decide whether you can afford something or not.

This primitive approach can work if you have all the cash you need, but in all other cases, it leads to money controlling you and your life. It is a blunt instrument that can leave you short of funds and is to be avoided.

Micromanagement

This is usually a weekly or monthly record of all incomings and outgoings by category, reconciled to bank balances—a comprehensive and detailed audit of your or your family's ongoing and projected financial activity. This can be diced and sliced to show categories of income and expense, percentage contributions, and ratios. As time passes, you can compare actual performance against your forecasts, and it builds into the kind of record a finance director keeps.

Avoid this kind of exercise if at all possible. It is very time consuming and takes a lot of pleasure out of the process of living, like being electronically tagged and monitored or having to report daily to a parole officer. Unless you are a pathological recidivist, there is likely to be a better, more effective way.

Further dangers exist with overanalysis and excessive detail. This can take on a life of its own, becoming overbearing and dominant so that users become something of a slave to its requirements and lose the will for independent thought. Second, the often-spurious accuracy creates a false sense of security and overreliance, an "it must be right because the spreadsheet says so" mind-set. Finally, you risk getting lost and not seeing the wood for the trees—in other words, you may be unable to get a general understanding of the situation because you are too worried about the details. Simple but powerful actions or strategies may be overlooked as you burrow through the minutiae and complexities.

Annual, half-yearly, quarterly, or monthly look forward
In this case, you might prepare a summary output page for the chosen period with sources at the top, uses at the bottom, and a calculated difference between the two. It picks up known or projected cash inflows and outflows based on the past but allowing for changes, including inflation. Supporting pages in the spreadsheet can include more detail and feed into the output page. This will reveal total receipts and payments in the period by category and contain sufficient data to allow further analysis if you wish.

All players should know, without needing to look it up, approximately how much it costs them to live for a year, both at a minimum (if times are hard) and living with a few luxuries.

Equally, your total annual and average monthly income from all sources after taxes and before any bonuses should be a number that instantly comes to mind. This is basic commercial sense. Yes, it does take a bit of effort to set up the spreadsheets and calculations and update them every so often, but the benefits far outweigh this small time cost.

If your income comfortably exceeds your outflows, you may choose to drop the income section and just keep a schedule of expenses over the year to keep tabs on the overall shape and scale of your spending. The performance of your assets is picked up elsewhere, and there is no merit in calculating something if you don't need to.

Manage by feel
Often an evolution of the last method, you can, over time (and assuming no major changes in circumstances), develop a sense of the numbers on an annual basis without needing to do the calculation at all. If a major financial change takes place, such as new job, the start of school fees, a new mortgage, or retirement, you can return to an annual look forward for a year or two until you have the numbers in mind again.

This is a marvellous point to reach, as it is highly efficient and economic. You can shift your attention completely to the far more important exercise of asset management and building net worth, which will further enhance your cash-generation capability. It is like sailing without a wind indicator or telltales, which are essential for novice sailors or for absolute precision in a race but not for a capable helmsman sailing for pleasure, guided by the feel of the wind on his or her face.

Event-specific management
However accurate your feel is, there will still be occasions when you need to shift money into the right place, perhaps to pay for a major purchase or event. Funds may be on timed deposit or tied up in assets that need to be sold. A certain amount of advance planning can't be avoided.

In choosing which one or combination of these to use (or any other variation), ask yourself what you are trying to achieve from the effort, and limit your objectives to the simplest and most useful. There are other, more direct ways of identifying and policing overspending. If you think it's happening, then it probably is, and rather than trying to deal with the problem by recording it in a detailed spreadsheet, it is far more effective to just stop doing it.

HOW MUCH CAN YOU GENERATE?

Here's a simple exercise to test the amount of game currency you might earn from employment over a forty-year working life between the ages of twenty and sixty.

The two variables are the level of your after-tax earnings and the percentage of these you are able to save. The following table shows pot sizes in pounds for a range of these:

Table 6.1

Pot sizes over forty years at different annual earnings after tax and savings percentages

average annual earnings after tax	savings %				
	100%	50%	40%	30%	20%
£25,000	1.0	0.5	0.4	0.3	0.2
£50,000	2.0	1.0	0.8	0.6	0.4
£75,000	3.0	1.5	1.2	0.9	0.6
£100,000	4.0	2.0	1.6	1.2	0.8

Note that pot sizes are £m.

At age sixty, a thirty year needs total can easily reach £1.7m. The table shows that even if you have earned £75,000 after tax every year for forty years and saved half of it, you will only have put aside £1.5m!

The missing ingredient is assets, so appreciators and productive depreciators that generate income and cash proceeds—only with these can the equation balance.

Run the numbers for yourself from wherever you are now to your date for reaching O. What is a realistic total?

VII

GROUND RULES AND A PLAN

Many people have a natural tendency to overengineer and complicate matters; to waste effort and time on the unimportant; to clutter minds, days, and lives with fruitless activity; and to chase, accumulate, and expand rather than discern, inquire, and focus. When this approach meets the unavoidable complexity of finance, the result is confusion and unsound actions.

It's no wonder that we seek solace in step-by-step guides and simple formulae for achieving goals, that we love systems and sound bites, and that we latch on to rules and regimes. They tantalize us with hope, and our optimism knows no bounds. The problem is that rules, regulations, principles, and procedures can rapidly take over as major subjects in themselves, restricting free thought and creativity, stultifying us, and sucking in precious time so that we lose sight of the game.

No rule should be accepted unless it is either unavoidable or materially helpful to your cause. Reject and ignore all others, and keep what you accept to a minimum. By doing this, you will escape all manner of distractions and dead ends.

Ask yourself this: What is the origin of a rule? Is it a natural law of nature, science, or mathematics, or is it man-made? If the latter, is it your own self-imposed rule, or one that others seek to bind you with?

In driving, the laws of physics and biology govern speed, cornering, stopping, loss of control, and impact, as well as fuel economy and driver concentration. For the sake of personal survival and cost management, these unavoidables are best understood and accepted. Man-made speed limits, licences, insurance requirements, and drink-driving and other road laws that carry fines or criminal sanctions if breached are physically avoidable but best accepted, because the sanctions can be costly versus any benefit accruing. All others are optional, and a driver can select from a wide range. You can choose to respect and be polite to other road users (whatever their behaviour), drive as fast or slow as possible at all times, never drive on motorways or in the snow or after dark, minimize fuel consumption, have a break every three hours, keep spare fuel in the boot, and so on. The list is endless.

In finance, there are certain natural laws that it pays to understand, as they can work powerfully in your favour or against you, and they can't be ignored. Fortunately, beyond these and outside of tax rules and general criminal law, we are largely left alone to do what we want. You should, therefore, aim to develop the smallest possible kit of the most useful multipurpose rules. If you carry around a vanload of them, it is hard to remember what you have or to find the ones you want. Travel light on the rule front!

A FOUNDATION

Before considering laws specific to finance, such as the time value of money, risk and return, and compounding and debt, there are three universal concepts to understand.

1. Impermanence and change

Our natural instinct is to crave security and stability, to be able to anchor ourselves to something solid, reliable, and constant, but since all things are impermanent and subject to change, this is an impossible and therefore futile task. It is better to accept that nothing stays the same for long or exists forever. Temper your craving, and recognize that clinging is misguided. This promotes detachment, objectivity, and balance, and it reduces suffering. By adopting this rule, you will learn to focus all effort and energy on matters that you can control and to ignore those that you can't. Strangely, this liberation creates a sense of more overall control.

The principle that nothing is permanent is well established and hard to challenge, but it is often overlooked or forgotten. In Buddhism, it is known as anicca. What can you think of that is permanent and will last forever? Our universe is not, nor is human, animal, nor plant life or anything man-made. Furthermore, what can you think of that is not dependent (in part or whole) on something else, that is not related to anything and exists in complete isolation? Whether you challenge the notion with scientists or philosophers, mathematicians or historians, or anthropologists or theologians, you will find no certain exception within current human knowledge and science.

Once you accept that everything is (a) transient and in a perpetual state of flux, and (b) dependent to a degree on something else, you lift one of the veils that otherwise masks your ability to see things clearly. Think about this for a minute.

How does this apply to wealth?

Earning ability
We move from being useless and dependent as infants to being useful and able to contribute; then we go back to being useless again when we're infirm or dead. During that pitifully short time, nothing stays the same for long. The lesson from this is to make hay while you can. By squandering any of the few good seasons that you have, your barn will be emptier than it could be.

Not only are our working lives short, but during them, earnings don't stay the same or follow a consistent path. They will go up or down or stop altogether when you are between jobs. In good years, you might receive a profit share or bonus or cash some share options; in bad ones, you may be fired or forced to take a pay cut. Furthermore, your earnings are dependent on many factors, and you can't control all of them. It is good to recognise this.

A further consideration is that while earnings prospects and profiles vary between industries and firms, if you choose to earn money by working for someone else or as a self-employed practitioner, you will have a finite period of maximum earning capacity linked to physical and mental abilities and the state of your industry. And there are no exceptions; footballers, actors, supermodels, designers, engineers, bankers, production workers, nurses, electricians, carpenters, and plumbers all have shelf lives. I have seen many people behave as if the good times will last forever. They basked in money, but they became slack and complacent, and instead of being psychologically or financially prepared, they were shocked and upset when the inevitable happened, and they lost their earning power. By failing to recognise earnings highs as the short windows they are, these people overlooked the opportunity to squirrel away funds for the inevitable tougher times.

If you own a business or have accumulated a property portfolio or library of valuable rights, the dynamic is slightly different, as you can employ managers to run the thing. If all goes well, your business will continue to thrive as long as you need it, but its profits and dividends will still fluctuate and cannot be guaranteed.

Why not refine your estimate of lifetime employment earnings from before? Factor in your views on future economic cycles and the effects they will have on the health of your industry and your earnings; consider the total number of maximum earnings years that might be available to you. When will you reach the top of your game, and how long might you stay there? Perhaps ten to fifteen years at most? In sports, this might span an age range of twenty to thirty-five; in the professions, industry, or media, thirty to fifty-five; and in the arts, any age. When will you run out of steam and go part time? Now revisit your lifetime earnings and savings totals.

Needs
Since the age of twenty, I have not known a period of more than two years without a significant change in my needs, and I don't expect this pattern to alter for some time. My own personal needs have steadily reduced and continue to trend down, but those of children and the wider family have grown. Layered onto this have been the big structural changes of moving house and buying and selling significant appreciators as well as changes in borrowing costs, each of which has generated a new pattern of cash needs. Continuous flux has been the order of the day.

Try overlaying a rough needs profile onto your earnings chart. The absolute numbers matter less than the interaction between the two. Over which periods are you likely to be most cash rich or poor, and how might these match wider market cycles?

Decay, depreciation, and death
As humans, we age and die, and most of us get sick in between. Physical things, whether living or not, also have finite life-spans. Buildings crumble, ships sink or get broken up, trees die and fall over, cars rust or wear out, computers malfunction and become uneconomic to repair, clothes rot, paintings fade or craze, and pots break. Even diamonds and gold or nuclear waste will not last for eternity. And if things are not wearing out, they're running out, like natural resources or space for homes in certain urban areas.

Assets, whether appreciators, depreciators, or consumables, are in the same boat here. Show me a company that can survive indefinitely, however great its current generation of management or products, or a farm that will always remain economic. Appreciators, by their nature, grow in value over time, but only through continued demand and the efforts of man to maintain, nurture, and manage them. Without our appetite, attention, or interest, all will ultimately depreciate and become valueless.

A friend of mine runs a successful business restoring gardens. He is busy year-round clearing rotten structures and dead plant life and replacing them with new ones. Small town parcels and large country spaces, owners young and old—the process of change escapes none. Just think of the industries that maintain and restore physical assets, buildings, boats, planes, cars, and machinery, prolonging their lives to the utmost.

Does this universal characteristic mean we should eschew assets, ignore liabilities, and abandon the quest for net worth? Not at all. To me, it argues for a little more discernment between things and a lot more detachment, a change in our relationship with assets and liabilities, and sense pleasures and discomforts. Understanding the difference between appreciators, depreciators, and consumables is a good start, but we can go further. What is the life-span of an item? What, if anything, will I need to do or spend to keep it fit for its purpose? How will I feel about it when it is a few years old and surrounded by shinier, newer, better-specified versions?

In the United Kingdom, people change their cars on average every four to five years, their mobile phones every two to three years, and PCs or tablets every four years. We introduce our own changes to an ever-changing world. Do these really benefit us, or do they just distract and occupy our attention? Is it wise to anchor your financial security or happiness to any asset or circumstance?

You should consider this carefully, as it will change your perception of material things and sensual experiences. When you dwell only on decay, depreciation, and death, you risk becoming maudlin. To ignore or deny these things risks wasting time chasing illusions and denting your personal wealth prospects, as well as bringing about a good deal of unnecessary suffering.

2. Opportunity cost

In microeconomic theory, the opportunity cost of a choice is the value of the best alternative foregone, where a choice needs to be made between several mutually exclusive alternatives, and you have limited resources.

Opportunity cost is a foundational plank in economics that expresses relationships between scarcity and choice and applies to anything that provides utility, such as money, time, or pleasure. In personal finance, it lies at the heart of commercial nous and rational behaviour and forms the basis of a sound financial strategy. In simple terms, can you spend your money more effectively in the quest to reach O?

Imagine that you buy a Mercedes SUV for £50,000, which depreciates at 15% of the purchase price each year. What is the best available alternative? Let's assume that you can buy a Ford Focus for £5,000 and generate a post-tax return of 8% on cash and that both cars cost the same to run and maintain and depreciate at the same speed.

The financial opportunity cost of your decision in year one is the extra cost of owning the car (i.e., its depreciation versus that of the Ford, plus the benefit you have lost by ignoring the best alternative):

Extra cost of Mercedes = (15% × £50,000) – (15% × £5,000) = (0.15 × 50,000) – (0.15 × 5,000)
= £7,500 – 750 = £6,750

Foregone return = 8% × £45,000 = 0.08 × 45,000 = £3,600

Opportunity cost = £6,750 + £3,600 = £10,350

This doesn't account for any additional utility or pleasure you have received. Is this worth an extra £10,350 for a year? That is the question you should answer before you make the purchase.

You can also measure the opportunity cost over the life of your car. At annual depreciation of £7,500 for the Mercedes and £750 for the Ford, both cars will be worthless in 6.67 years. Your opportunity cost becomes the difference between the initial price of each car plus the foregone interest on cash.

$$\text{extra cost of Mercedes} = £50,000 - 5,000 = £45,000$$

$$\text{foregone return} = £45,000 \times (1.08^{6.67}) - 45,000 = £30,188$$

$$\text{opportunity cost} = £45,000 + 30,188 = £75,188$$

Over 6.67 years, your pleasure has cost you £75,188 versus the best alternative, equivalent to £11,273 per annum. This effective annual loss exceeds the year-one loss because of returns compounding on the cash saved. Imagine what you could do with £75,188 compounding over another five or ten years!

Another example is university fees. If annual tuition fees are £9,000, and living expenses are a further £6,000, you might think that the opportunity cost is £15,000 for each year you study. This is not the case, as the best alternative is that you use the time to work for money. Assume that while you are at university, you could alternatively earn £20,000 per annum after tax. These foregone earnings are a further cost to you, making an opportunity cost of £35,000 per annum before factoring in possible investment returns on any savings.

The question to ask before signing up to a three-year course is whether a cost of £105,000+ is likely to be outweighed by extra future earnings or other benefits from having a degree.

3. Virtuous and vicious circles
A virtuous circle is a recurring cycle of behaviours or events, the result of each one being to promote more and to increase the beneficial effect of the next—one good thing leads to another.

A vicious circle or spiral is a sequence of reciprocal cause and effect in which two or more elements intensify and aggravate each other, leading inexorably to a worsening of the situation—a domino effect of damage.

These are extensions of cause and effect, and personal finance provides a rich source for both. Examples crop up throughout this book.

The car purchase scenario earlier also contains the seeds of both. Imagine that you borrowed half of the £50,000 purchase price for the Mercedes and that interest rates go up. Both your purchase and choice of funding contribute to a worsened situation that may in turn lead to further negative events, such as missing payments on other loans, suffering stress at work, losing productivity and pay, discord at home, traumatized children, and so on. The best alternative delivers a profit of £75,188 in comparison. This could be the difference necessary to fund a much bigger home in a richer neighbourhood, which in turn will deliver a gain, an improved living environment, better schools, a happier family, and so on.

If you study hard at school, you'll achieve better exam scores and be able to access higher education, which in turn raises your skills and value in the marketplace, leading to higher pay and the ability to help others achieve. If you fail at school, your chances of high pay will be reduced, and you will have less to spend on yourself and others, who in turn will be deprived of your help.

The economics of agglomeration are used to explain the benefits that firms obtain by locating near each other. These clusters of economic activity provide enhanced networking opportunities and a chance to save costs. An old proverb is "Money begets money"—the more you make, the easier it becomes to make still more. A more recent saying is "The first million is the hardest."

In personal finance, there is no doubt that money earns money. Cash is a productive depreciator, and money in the form of appreciators grows whether the appreciators are productive or not. The effects of compounding are profound, as you'll see later.

Whether there are additional financial upsides from having a cluster of assets and managing them holistically against ongoing needs has not, as far as I am aware, been the subject of studies, but it seems highly probable and has been borne out by my own experience. Economies of scale can arise, and savings, both cost and time are spread over a larger base of wealth. More wealth justifies and provides resources for more research and analysis, leading to better decisions. Greater wealth presence inexorably leads to more networking, not least because wealthy people are sought out by others. These effects can foster a positive and productive environment for wealth creation.

There is overwhelming evidence to support the phrases "Success breeds success" and "Cycles of poverty." Your task in the wealth game is to spot possible virtuous circles and take steps to promote them, while avoiding any of the vicious variety. You are in one or more circle of some kind right now...but which?

MAKING A PLAN

Let's say that I have a burning desire to drive from London to Nice, a trip of about 865 miles, and to arrive next Monday afternoon. I have the car and the skills to handle it, the money for fuel, understand the relevant natural laws of physics and biology, and have read up on the European rules of the road, border control, and customs requirements. I also have the exact address and a map of my destination in Nice.

An element is missing, however, and whether I am the forward-thinking, organized type, or a laid-back dude, it can't be avoided. I need to make some decisions about the journey. One simply can't be ducked: Do I cross the English Channel by Eurotunnel or car ferry? Choosing the latter immediately raises the question of which port of departure and ferry line, since there are several. There are a few more questions I might want to consider:

What day and time do I leave London?
Should I book the channel crossing or just turn up?
If I book, for what time?
If I take the ferry, do I want a cabin?
Once in France, shall I do the trip in one go, or arrange an overnight stopover?
Should I do some sightseeing, detour to see friends, or buy wine on the way?
What route will I take?
Am I happy to pay toll fees on motorways?
Should I take some euros with me or rely on credit cards?
Are there any likely traffic congestion hot spots to avoid?
Do I want to drive at night when the roads are quiet?
Will I buy food and drink along the way or take it with me?
What music should I take with me to listen to?

My decisions on these and other questions relating to the journey amount to a plan. Even if the answer is "I can't decide any of these things. I'll just get in the car and see what happens," it's still a strategy called winging it.

How about tinkering with the objective? Perhaps remove the "Monday afternoon" part and just arrive when I arrive. That makes life much easier and raises fewer questions, but some still remain. What happens if I drop Nice as a destination altogether? Now we're getting somewhere. The sky's the limit here—no decisions or strategy of any kind is needed. I can just drive and see where I end up.

So in order to achieve a set objective, however simple the task, you must make choices and trade-offs to achieve it. These choices and trade-offs constitute your strategy. To fix O as your goal and set off without a strategy is a sure way to somewhere, but it's unlikely to be O. This seems patently self-evident, yet a surprising number of people jump on the bandwagon, enjoy the company and party spirit for a while, and then find themselves out of road, in a dust bowl in the middle of nowhere.

Another important point is that your finance skills, starting position, chips, understanding of the rules, and chosen strategy link to your objective like the connections in a circuit. If one of the components doesn't fit with the others or malfunctions, the whole system fails. Imagine the circuit without any one of these.

So what is a good strategy to achieve O?

A good personal financial strategy should be short and clear, help you every day, and endure so that you don't have to change it.

As this book isn't concerned with the source of your earned income, the question is this: "How do you use surplus cash flow to generate net worth and manage your net-assets-to-needs gap to achieve O?"

Here is the strategy I recommend to achieve the first part of this: maximize surplus cash and apply it to a mix of appreciators that you understand; use leverage (where appropriate) and compounding to boost returns while maintaining adequate liquidity throughout.

The second part of the question is about managing needs, and the generic strategy is simple: design the needs package that most helps you reach O, and stick to it.

PART THREE

BECOMING A PLAYER—EARLY SKILLS

VIII

QUIET REBELLION

In short-course sailboat racing, if you aren't leading the race, it pays to be on the tail of the leading boat and track its every move until a chance to pass arises. Joining one of the chasing packs is generally a recipe for finishing there; there's lots of noise and crowding with "dirty" wind, and everyone is watching each other. The solitary world of ocean racing is different; there, you profit from taking your own carefully planned path from the start and largely ignoring the competition.

In both cases, someone occasionally takes a flyer and heads off in a completely different direction, hoping to catch a favourable tidal stream or wind pattern, and then either wins by a spectacular margin or limps back long after the prizes have been awarded.

Taking a flyer in the wealth game suits those who have nothing to lose or who don't mind losing what they have—in other words, they have a very robust attitude to risk. "All or nothing, but anything's better than the boring mediocrity of being in the middle" is the mind-set, where terms such as *employee, manager, commuter, pay raise, promotion, mortgage, pension,* and *savings* become bywords for *losers.* These adventurers may be desperate, misguided fantasists, or both, but a small number are genuinely exceptional individuals who emerge through elements of brilliance, tenacity, and shades of good fortune to cook up enterprises that make them and others rich beyond the dreams of the ordinary people they once were.

I applaud them. They are the sporting elite, the rock stars, the Nobel Prize winners, and the political giants of business and wealth, and their achievements are inspirational and uplifting. What a rich resource of role models we have to study and emulate. If you aren't one of them, you should still strike out on your own; there is no safety in numbers, and any comfort or security you might feel in a group of followers is misguided. Just look around. If there is a rich resource of elite to study, how much richer a resource is the remainder? You will end up becalmed in a middle ground, neither here nor there.

The trick is to adopt the attitudes, energy, and chutzpah of the stars, but instead of heading into the unknown and risking everything, apply them to a guaranteed strategy that you know will work, like the one set out here. For this, you need a certain private temperament: subversive, confident, independent minded, determined, and focused. Why private? Because for now, unlike the elite, you are still in the pack, and until you can break free financially, you must pay lip service to its rules and customs or be trampled on. Learn to be an outsider in the system. Find a cause unrelated to your own self-interest. Your will is toughened by this.

A PARTICULAR TEMPERAMENT

As a youngster, I found it far easier and more interesting to observe the folly of others than my own shortcomings. The scorn and arrogance of youth, idealism, and early successes have given way to compassionate observation. First, spot the dreadful mistakes and judgement errors of others, and second, step carefully around them in your own life—voyeuristic perhaps, but infinitely preferable to blundering forward without studying the terrain or reading any of the signposts along the way. However carefully you plan and prepare, there will always be more than enough to occupy you.

And what others do still shocks me. Squirrels and beavers gather food and build homes for the winter season. Apparently, humans in much of the developed world haven't yet worked that out. When winter comes in the form of economic downturn, banking collapses, and the drying up of cheap money, we cry for help rather than delving into our larders and store cupboards that, of course, are bare. If ever there were a case for taking a different path, this is it.

In 1854, the American transcendentalist and friend of Ralph Waldo Emerson, Henry David Thoreau, published *Walden* after spending two years living on his own in the woods near Walden Pond, Concord, Massachusetts. The first chapter is titled "Economy" and opens with this message: "I do not propose to write an ode to dejection, but to brag as lustily as chanticleer in the morning, standing on his roost, if only to waken my neighbours up."

He explains the purpose of the adventure as follows:

I went to the woods because I wished to live life deliberately, to front only the essential facts of life, and see if I could not learn what it had to teach, and not, when I came to die, discover that I had not lived. I did not wish to live what was not life, living is so dear: nor did I wish to practice resignation, unless it was quite necessary. I wanted to live deep and suck out all the marrow of life, to live so sturdily and Spartan-like as to put to rout all that was not life, to cut a broad swath and shave close, to drive life into a corner, and reduce it to its lowest terms, and if it proved to be mean, why then to get the whole and genuine meanness of it, and publish its meanness to the world; or if it were sublime, to know it by experience, and be able to give a true account of it in my next excursion.

In the wealth game, only by making choices different from the general population's can you hope to achieve a better than average outcome. You are more loner than leader and never a follower.

GUERRILLA TACTICS

If you still wonder how being contrarian can help you in the wealth game, here are some examples of the personal philosophies that I adopted as part of my "be different" strategy. They're here to illustrate. Adopt any of them if you wish, but remember that it's your own personal strategy that matters.

Work—treat it (to yourself) as a game

The first lesson of work is to understand your position in the enterprise. What does the firm exist to do, how exactly does it do it, who does what, and where do you fit in? Stand in the shoes of the owners and managers separately, and ask, "Why have we employed this person, and what do we expect from him/her?" Think as they think; understand what motivates them. Learn to anticipate their actions.

Second, work out where the value lies and how it is apportioned. A law firm or architect practice sells human services. The staff *are* the firm and should demand the lion's share of profits, allowing for brand value that also contributes. A manufacturing plant is a mix of premises, plant, machinery, and people (i.e., capital and labour). Value tilts towards the capital. For a theme park with rides attractions and landscaped gardens, the physical structure is the business offering, and the staff on site play a supporting role.

This approach is commercial. Many people get no further than asking these questions: Is this a job I enjoy? Do I like the people, is the pay acceptable to me? Can I travel to it? Is it the best option I have? These questions are fine, but they are narrow and wholly self-oriented. By understanding your environment and the motivations of those you work for or report to, you will perform more effectively.

Specific tactics include the following:

Targeted over delivery—Select tasks and times where extra effort will have maximum effect, particularly when others are asleep or cruising. Slow down and preserve energy when undertaking menial tasks. In varying pace and activity, you avoid becoming a predictable journeyman, and your actions will be more explosive.

Hunt efficiency—Don't waste time, and avoid the impractical. Let others handle long or pointless meetings, protocols, and activities that won't in some way add to your worth.

Pick your battles—Let opponents win if their victory does not harm you. It will help preserve harmony, and when you do choose to fight or resist, your actions will stand out. Only take action where there is real benefit to your cause, recognizing your standing in the firm; bright and questioning is good, but a difficult junior will be "short-dated stock," as they say in the city.

Know your opponent—It is said in martial arts that you control the light when you can see into your opponent's mind as he attacks. If you show him that you will control his methods with strength, he will be controlled by that strength and change his mind. In this way, you can head your opponent off in advance.

Close down victory—On any issue that matters, such as a sales pitch, promotion bid, bonus discussion, or client fee negotiation, as soon as victory is in sight, close it down without hesitating or slowing down for a minute, and stop speaking as soon as you have won.

Selected openness—Freely disclose information that does not harm you, your clients, or your firm but that is of value or interest to the recipient. This fosters a trusting environment and elicits much information in return. Holding your cards constantly to your chest breeds tightness and cramps. Only genuine secrets should be guarded.

Be yourself—Avoid any kind of constructed surface persona. It is like carrying a heavy weight. Humans are quick to spot authenticity and are attracted to it.

Stay grounded—By all means, let others coo at your status, but remember that it won't last, and you are just another person trying to get on in life. Never be deceived into thinking that you really are important or that your identity is defined by what you do. I know incredibly talented and successful big cheeses who were either fired or retired and fell apart mentally because their identities disappeared. De-emphasize the self, and focus more on the world around you.

Know your value—Understand the commercial value of what you are doing, and get paid what it's worth—or more if you can—but don't delude yourself that a job is worth more than it is, however skilled, important, or dangerous it is.

Keep perspective—Cut through the fluff, and recognize why you are acting. There's a big world and a wonderful life to be enjoyed outside of working for money.

Beware of "experts"
We are brought up to respect age and authority. It is unsettling to discover that wisdom doesn't automatically follow age and that authority doesn't equal competence or integrity. And just because something is written in a newspaper, that doesn't mean it is true or can be relied on.

In fact, you should respectfully assume that all utterances of so-called experts are wrong until they or you have proved otherwise. If it's impractical to prove their validity, treat them lightly. Remember that this is a quiet rebellion, but if you need to speak plainly and directly, do so, as you are not in a popularity contest.

A problem in personal finance is the perceived gulf between ordinary people and experts that disarms players into thinking that they are not up to the task. Often there is no gulf at all. With basic tuning in and training of the kind discussed in this book, you will be far better placed to improve your own situation than most others.

Accreditations, qualifications, industry regulators, and ombudsmen are no more than a state-sponsored attempt to promote minimum standards and safeguards across the widest possible population. They may satisfy the electorate at large or box tickers in Whitehall, but you should ignore them and demand more at every turn.

Think and act poor until you reach O (because until you're there, you are)
Early in the 2009 film version of *A Christmas Carol*, an animated Jim Carrey is seen counting coins in a dark room, his face lit grotesquely by a single candle whose light bounces off grim wood-panelled walls. In the hearth, a solitary piece of coal glows.

Inspiration for the character was reportedly drawn from the renowned miser John Elwes, known as "Elwes the Miser," who also features in *Our Mutual Friend*. Born into a family of niggards, his wealthy mother starved herself to death, and the young Elwes became rich at the age of four upon the death of his father. The boy's uncle, Sir Harvey Elwes, who took pride in spending no more than £120 per year, mentored him, and the two spent many an evening together bemoaning the profligacy of others while sharing a single glass of wine. On his death, Sir Harvey left £250,000 to his nephew, who continued the tradition of meanness, although he was described by his biographer as "chiefly an enemy to himself." Despite many poor investments and loans that were never repaid, John managed to finance the construction of sizeable parts of Georgian London, including Portman Square and Portman Place, as well as parts of Oxford Street, Piccadilly, Baker Street, and Marylebone, and on his death, he left £500,000 (over £18 million today) to his two sons, born out of wedlock, and a nephew.

As one who reached O when he was four and devoted his adult life to asceticism, there was nothing ordinary about Elwes. As a role model, however, he and his like have something to offer—at least up to a point.

Personal parsimony, or an extreme unwillingness to spend money or use resources on oneself, is a powerful ally against spending on poverty-promoting depreciators and consumables. You can recognize the folly of frittering and the value of investing without living in rank squalor, ignoring personal hygiene, or obsessing over your wealth pot, and you *can* practice compassion and generosity towards others. Once you reach O, you can bid farewell and thanks to this friend and raise several glasses in memory over the coming years as you gently enjoy winding down your net worth. At its heart is the plain fact that whatever your net worth, you are not financially rich by any standard until you have reached O, and you fool yourself if you think otherwise.

Look at the "rich" around you. Are they what they seem?

For the rebel player, this is the big one to crack. This is the hardest subject personally and socially because of the enormous pressures from our own cravings, loved ones, friends, society, the marketplace, government, and the global forces of capitalism. Not a day passes without feeling the pressure or need to spend beyond subsistence.

By thinking and behaving poor, however, even when the cash is rolling in, you develop and exercise creativity and resourcefulness, two deeply satisfying attributes. There's nothing clever about spending money, but spending money cleverly is a skill to be honed that will serve you throughout life. Let others act rich while you quietly get on with growing your wealth.

Time and again, I hear stories and experience the joys of the alternative holiday or activity, the makeshift wedding, the impromptu party, or the simple social gathering at home—all generally more fun and rewarding but also cheaper by a factor than showy corporate style, faux cool, or traditional alternatives. All you need is courage and enterprise. Courage is the big one, because only by abandoning your fears of others' judgement, the unknown, the unscheduled, the discomforts and the inconveniences—large or small—will you take the plunge. Break with convention, embrace originality, and get used to eccentricity in the quest for more fun and a quicker journey to O. What's the worst that can happen?

Thinking and behaving poor also keeps you rooted and in touch. You will see money and wealth as they are, as opposed to something grander and more important. Do you want to enter a twilight zone disconnected from ordinary people, where values are hideously distorted and success is measured solely in terms of money, possessions, and a certain lifestyle—where spending thousands on a pair of shoes or a handbag or tens of thousands on a trip is not only fine but essential, and where insulating yourself from any discomfort or want becomes mandatory?

Challenge tradition, convention, and received wisdom
These enemies are like experts, but they are worse, because they are completely unaccountable. No one takes responsibility for them; they just exist, manufactured by nameless inventors and adopted over time by communities—feared, respected, loved, or hated, but always clung to in some way or hidden behind by those who encounter them.

While man-made conventions are intrinsically empty of substance, many of them need to be respected if the entire social system isn't to disintegrate into chaos. Take names and other forms of labelling as an example—entirely constructed and essentially meaningless, but necessary for order and effective communication. Money is another artificial product, a convention with which goods and services are traded, and whether you'd prefer a primitive barter system instead is not the point; it exists and can't easily be ignored. Endless and varied social customs span cultures and peoples, constructed and lacking any substance in reality, but to trample on them is to invite offence, hurt, and confusion. The dilemma is that clinging to conventions and traditions burdens and limits us, yet defying them completely leaves us isolated and in conflict.

Somehow, the quiet rebel needs to let go, to detach from the illusory importance of customs and conventions without needlessly upsetting the apple cart. By standing back and coolly observing the landscape ahead, a player can more easily discern those actions most conducive to reaching O and those likely to impede progress. In certain circumstances, you will need to get tough, to rediscover your warrior spirit, and to rail hard against something, but such action should always be calculated against its effects on your journey to O.

Responses like "It's always been done this way" or "This is the absolute truth" should invite scepticism from any right-thinking human. Of course, you haven't got time to challenge or take issue with every such platitude; to do so in today's society would keep you permanently occupied with no time for anything else. As long as you remain an ordinary person in the world of wealth, it is best to challenge convention quietly but effectively, through actions rather than words. Let others form their own views about your behaviour without you telegraphing it for them. And most importantly, rebel not for its own sake or because it is fun to do so; do it to liberate yourself, follow your own instincts and judgements, and lighten the path to O.

IX

MAXIMIZING SURPLUS CASH

Surplus cash is the essential nutrient for building and sustaining wealth. Without it, you're stuck. To reach O before normal retirement age, you must therefore take all possible steps to maximize it, but how many people set out to do this?

It's worth revisiting our earlier definition:

surplus cash = after-tax earnings from labour + after-tax earnings from assets – spending of any kind except that relating to investment in net worth.

Earning from your own labour requires skill, commercial nous, hard work, opportunity, and a degree of luck, particularly around timing. It helps for at least some of your career to be the right person in the right firm in the right industry in the right economic cycle, and no one can be sure to align all these stars.

To earn cash from your assets, you need to have productive assets and the disposition and energy to make them pay. This source of money is a powerful stimulant that can grow exponentially and ultimately dwarf and replace your earnings from labour.

First, it's time to face spending. This is the most controllable element of the equation, yet probably the most overlooked. It's as simple as this: spend less to generate more surplus cash, and spend more to reduce surplus cash.

How much you spend and on what is a central and recurring theme of the wealth game. Not only does it help determine your surplus cash flow, which in turn drives your net worth, but it also shapes your needs. Get it right, and you enjoy the double benefit of more cash and net worth as well as less need. Your net-worth-to-needs gap can be hugely positive, allowing you to reach O quickly. Get it wrong, and you face the double whammy of less cash and net worth trying to service greater need. Your net-worth-to-needs gap can be deep into negative territory and O no more than a fantasy.

My remedy for containing spending is to think simple. After all, the problem is a simple one—too much spending. The more complicated and involved the solution, the less likely you are to remember it, let alone stick to it. Take killing a person as an example. The way to avoid this antisocial behaviour is not to do it—no ifs, and, or buts, whatever the circumstances.

A SMALL IDEA

Siu Lim Tao is the first form of the ancient martial art Wing Chun and can be loosely translated as "way of the little idea" or "little idea form." It is composed of three sections of movements that can be learned easily but that are foundational to the entire system. Mastering them doesn't mean that you will be good at Wing Chun, but to be good, you need to master them.

In Buddhism, four observations called noble truths underpin the practical cure for human suffering. Deceptively simple and quick to recite, two and a half thousand years of analysis, development, and discussion begins and ends with them.

A third example of small idea and large effect is that of *satyagraha*. In 1906, where no word existed in Gujarati to accurately describe his principle, Gandhi set up a competition in the newspaper *Indian Opinion*. What emerged were two Gujarati words that Gandhi tailored through their Sanskrit equivalents, *satya* (truth embodying love) and *agrahara* (firmness), into a new one meaning "holding to what's right," a kind of obstinate virtue. Although he had been living this principle since childhood and was inspired by a Gujarati poem extolling good action against evil, the New Testament's Sermon on the Mount, the Bhagavad Gita, and Tolstoy's antireligion polemic, *The Kingdom of God Is within You*, this was the first time he was able to simply articulate it and communicate the idea widely. The principle of practicing nonviolent action in a good cause galvanized a divided nation and led to India winning back its independence.

For Gandhi, *satyagraha* was only one of several small ideas that inspired his behaviour. By the time he joined a ship from Bombay to London when he was nineteen, he had already sworn a vow of vegetarianism. From then on, his "experiments with truth," as described in the autobiography of the same name, continued daily and involved various forms of self-sufficiency, asceticism including *brahmacharya* (celibacy) at the age of thirty-seven, and self-improvement that continued throughout his life. His fierce intellectual independence and lack of fear or need for acceptance allowed him to select the ideas that he found most acceptable, whatever their sources, and to reject at will beliefs and dogma that didn't resonate, whatever their apparent authority and standing. In doing so, he carved a path of his own choosing.

The Swedish term *Lagom* is another such small idea.

If you take up any simple but profound idea of this sort, you will find that, over time, it changes the way you think and behave. Naturally you will test the notion, and if it doesn't stack up, drop it, but if it is genuine and you are open-minded, it will stick. In order to live the idea, all manner of rules, protocols, and practices naturally arise to facilitate it. Some may have already been constructed by others and are there to be learned and obeyed, like helpful road signs; others spring up organically when circumstances require them. As you adopt and internalize these and discover your own personal methods, they build into an entire pattern of conscious and subconscious behaviour, impossible to fully articulate or comprehend at the outset, but impregnable and capable of very significant force.

Conversely, if an idea is not taken up, its associated rules, protocols, and practices seem empty and meaningless. You may follow it, but without zeal and passion. It will be easy to drop. This is a common problem for people trying to economize. They approach the task by creating or following someone else's microprescriptions for saving cash at every opportunity and end up becoming dispirited.

Think about this. Your small idea may be a goal or a cause or just a musing, it may be personal or connected to something external, or it may be specific or general. Which will you adopt?

Although I didn't realize it at the time, I lived according to the principal of a small idea related to personal finance from the moment I started earning more than my subsistence needs. It didn't matter that I had no name for it or that I didn't speak of it; it just existed, and I followed it. Only later, after reaching O, did I learn that there is a recent body of academic theory supporting the effectiveness of the technique that gave rise to this particular idea. It's called mental contrasting, and studies indicate that by pursuing it, people are more likely to fulfill their goals.

Begin by imagining, as clearly and vividly as possible, the benefits you can experience by reaching O and claiming the prize, such as freedom, space, tranquillity, and time. Next, reflect on the obstacles that could impede this goal, again as starkly as you can—for example, boredom, restlessness, fatigue, limited opportunities in your town, the wrong skills, distractions at home, and so on. Take time out to dwell on this for a moment or two. The first part is good old-fashioned visualization, peddled as a "get rich" or "success" technique for as long as I can remember. Adding the second element is the clever part, as it does away with the fantasy that wonderful results come effortlessly or that they are somehow deserved, not earned. It reminds us that we have to make success happen through our own careful planning, sound actions, and determination.

The studies show that those who practice mental contrasting around an objective they are confident they can achieve—as opposed to one that they doubt is possible—will have the following characteristics:

- They are better prepared to overcome obstacles, because they will already be primed to act in the face of any given obstacle. Mental contrasting increases the association between future possibilities and challenging realities. Even words that represent challenges will automatically invoke words that represent inspiring possibilities.
- They are more motivated to overcome these obstacles by appreciating that challenging realities represent obstacles to future possibilities.
- They embrace all the information needed to proceed with any given action. In contrast, those who enjoy only positive fantasies tend to neglect vital information; in particular, they feel motivated to overlook complications and other insights they perceive as undesirable impediments to their progress. In a form of selective exposure bias, they shift their attention to the benefits of the pursuit and deliberately disregard alternatives or foreseeable difficulties. Rash or ill-considered actions result, increasing the likelihood of failure or setbacks.

In my late teens and early twenties, life was one great voyage of discovery. Everything was new. I simply spent all I had to generate the maximum amount of fun. In my third year at university, the bank ran out of patience, set my overdraft limit in stone (no further breach allowed), and sent two men to our student house to collect my cheque guarantee card. In those days, no sensible trader would accept a cheque from a student without a guarantee card, and in my town, they were used to our attempts. The confiscation was a relief in a way. It forced me to make do with the little I had and what my friends loaned me, and I became increasingly resourceful in my pursuit of sustenance and pleasure. At the same time, the bank letters began to dry up, and I started opening my monthly statements for the first time in a long while.

There was no point in planning or setting objectives. I had nothing to plan with, no job or income beyond my student grant, and no idea what I wanted. Life was the here and now, keeping warm and fed, sleeping, and having fun while clinging to university study so as not to get thrown out. My good friend Joe, a larger-than-life budding guitarist, sage, and purveyor of many things, departed at the end of the first year, leaving the place less colourful. We continued in the spirit, and for a long moment, we were oblivious to the outside world of work and responsibility. As the time approached for job applications, however, the switched-on people tuned in, and the rest of us thrashed around, peddling our impending qualifications or setting out to garner more. In one of those seminal Technicolor days forever etched in my memory, I spent a blissful few lunchtime hours in a pub with one of my great college friends, discussing the lives that lay before us, dreaming and hoping with the innocence and ignorance of true idealists. It was the only such conversation I remember.

I don't remember trying to visualize financial independence in my early twenties, but I always assumed it would happen at some point. This confidence was not inspired by a view of where my nascent career was heading, which remained a mystery, but rather through an awareness that I could manage my needs as necessary. It became clear to me that wasting what little surplus cash I did have was a major obstacle to achieving financial self-sufficiency. I must have considered other obstacles, like losing interest in work, being in the wrong firm, failing to progress, or getting distracted by something or someone, and found ways to overcome these. But the standout small idea relating to spending was and still is this: don't waste money.

From this rather general idea came this specific maxim: Spending on consumables and depreciators is an obstacle to reaching O.

At every point, at every turn, and in every given situation, this notion guided my behaviour. As long as O still mattered to me and it never stopped mattering, positive behaviours sprang up to overcome this obstacle. Whether I found what I wanted at a lower cost or for nothing, chose an alternative, or dropped the desire completely, there was always a route around the problem. I didn't need specific rules for this or that spending—it all fell into the same basket. Spending hard-earned money on consumables and depreciators was such a blindingly obvious obstacle that no further consideration of the subject was needed. There was no agonizing about the rights or wrongs of a purchase; it was clear-cut. Unsurprisingly, this simple approach became second nature and made life easier. It became so normal that I never felt as though I was denying myself anything of importance. To deny myself the chance to reach O quickly—now *that* would have felt like an intolerable sacrifice.

Others around me certainly had difficulty with my approach at times, but I remained quietly resolute, certain that it was the right thing to do.

Where are you on this? Reflect on yourself and what matters to you. Be realistic.

From your small idea springs a range of others that, together, will form a personal style of spending behaviour that is genuine to you and, as such, fits easily. An opportunity for creativity arises. Ask yourself, "What spending style do I want and why, and what are my underlying values?"

Clearly the objective is to develop a package that leads to lower spending and greater free cash flow, but even within this remit, the options and nuances are considerable. There is far more here than simply being a spender or a saver. Your style and values can be clever, discerning, eco minded, compassionate, highbrow, lowbrow—in fact, they can be anything you want, as long as they're fit for your purpose. The point here is that it is considered and designed. You set it from the outset.

Styles change, but the more elements you can nail down, the better. Ideally, the overall blend is not only versatile but also classic and timeless. The following are some of the many available suggestions to help get the process underway. They are not all directly related to spending but affect it:

- *Simplicity*—This might be stark minimalism or extreme selectiveness.
- *Purity*—A return to nature and the natural way. Roll back technology, resist labour- and time-saving gadgets, shortcuts, processed and mass-market factory products, and return to basics. Wholesome and simple.
- *Utility*—Everything should be functional, fit for a purpose only, and not overdesigned or overly specified or unnecessary. This one sits well with simplicity, and both apply widely to potentially high-spending areas, such as home, food, clothes, possessions, relationships, work, leisure, and travel.
- *Economy*—Use only what is necessary and avoid waste.
- *Efficiency*—Don't overengineer or overcomplicate. Find the most effective and straightforward line between you and your goal, and quietly follow it. Distill actions to create the maximum effect from the least expenditure of time, energy, and money. Don't zigzag around and make a lot of noise.
- *More for less*—A simple motto that reaches far. Allied to efficiency and economy, it means more benefit for less cost. The output may be material things or intangibles; the input may be time, effort,

raw materials, or money. Just think about the power and potential of this. Is there anywhere it can't be applied?

- *Creativity and resourcefulness*—Let necessity be the mother of your invention, only manufacture the necessity as well. Why deny yourself this proven and valuable spur? The simple solution is to behave as if you are poor, whether you are or not, and apply lateral thinking, innovation, agility, and brazen opportunism to meet every need. Only when you have exhausted all options do you fork out cash for it, assuming you haven't lost your appetite by now. Once developed, these qualities deliver colour, brightness, and levity to all corners and push many established needs to one side.

- *Good things come to those who wait*—Whoever first said this was spot-on. It has served me well, and I was not surprised to find, yet again, that recent scientific studies bear it out. Humans, it appears, have an unusual ability to defer gratification: "I'll resist this instant gratification for months or even years if it means a better return in the future." Apparently, it stems from the fact that we prefer larger rewards to smaller ones, and the more vividly we imagine the future gain, the more likely we are to wait for it.

Walter Mischel's recent book, *The Marshmallow Test: Understanding Self-Control and How to Master It*, revisits his seminal 1960s experiments. What happened to the hundreds of six-year-olds who were invited to take a marshmallow from a pile or to wait fifteen minutes and take two? The Columbia professor discovered that the 25% of children who deferred their pleasure have performed better academically and socially than the instant-gratification majority. They have also been more successful in their careers and relationships and less prone to obesity, overdrinking, or drug problems. The brain science is fascinating and surprisingly accessible, chiming with common sense and reason. Mischel's work shows that people with good self-discipline and emotional control tend to have more success, leading to greater confidence and a sense of being able to overcome whatever obstacles and negative outcomes are thrown at them. You should look at it.

Internalizing one or more of these or other such notions as part of your personal ethos and style provides the intermediate structures necessary to bridge the space between where you are right now and O, some way into the future. The whole exercise is entirely positive, and it works in practice.

And it all stems from a small idea.

FITNESS TRAINING

The best small idea in the world is of no use if you aren't fit to implement it. You may also have the necessary technical skills and know-how, but these too are meaningless without the physical or mental strength to utilize them fully.

You must train and develop strength, not for a particular objective or outcome as an athlete does but just for strength itself, as a platform to help you overcome whatever obstacles or challenges you encounter. It is more like training your core muscles as a prelude to any other physical endeavour.

What is meant by "strength"? On the physical side, I mean toughness and durability. You need to be able to endure physical discomfort, tiredness, and a certain level of pain without being overcome with suffering or giving up. This is easy to practice and goes far beyond the gym. As well as your regular exercise routine, try a week or two of sleeping on the floor, turning the heat off in winter, eating once a day, eating vegetables raw, going to bed and getting up an hour or two before your usual time, and starting the day with stretch exercises or meditation. Or perhaps replace alcohol with water and healthy juices, or stop watching television for a while. Train yourself to tolerate greater and greater levels of discomfort, whether it is cold, heat, hunger, pain, noise, fatigue, boredom, and so on.

By doing this, you reduce your physical neediness, wean yourself off cravings, and become more self-disciplined.

Conduct your own assessment, and design a fitness course to suit your needs. Focus where you are weakest or neediest. Remember that training and self-improvement are to be lifelong, so don't take on too much at the start. Build it up gradually. A classic mistake is to focus only on giving things up, which becomes a tedious exercise in abstinence. Concentrate on what you will do, rather than what you won't, and where you do choose to give up something, replace it with a more wholesome product or activity—meeting friends rather than Facebook time, dried fruit and nuts instead of sweets, reading a book instead of watching a screen, visiting a new town or hiking somewhere versus staying in, creating for yourself rather than consuming others' creations, quiet contemplation instead of constant diversion...The list is endless.

Much neediness, particularly the need to spend and consume, is driven by fear—of discomfort, of being without, and of falling behind. Fear is pervasive and contaminates all areas of life; it is a major obstacle to action. By training yourself physically, you can face down fear and overcome it. Ask yourself, "What is the worst thing that can happen to me by doing this?" Consider your answer carefully, and then set it against other risks you routinely take without a second thought, like travelling by car or eating unhealthy food. With simple practice, you can quickly discover directly that a frightening vision is overdone. It is not as painful as it might have appeared, and after a few sessions, you will laugh at the notion that you were ever scared of it or put off by the thought.

The idea of getting on a plane and flying to a foreign country without booking any transfers or accommodation in advance has fuelled an entire industry that offers packages and itineraries to remove the fear of the unknown. Do it once or twice yourself, and you'll wince at the overdesign and mollycoddling quite apart from what you miss out on as a result. Learning to swim can inspire great fear in children. A day after they swim their first length of the pool, they're old hands. Giving up sugar in my tea was uncomfortable for a few days, but I can't imagine returning to it now. It was relatively easier many years later to cut out milk as well. A far wider appreciation of tea resulted. More to the point, what is the worst that can happen if you turn up at the school gate in a ten-year-old car and scruffy clothes? Can you live with that?

Such training and fitness breeds confidence and detachment. It's not so much bravery as a lack of fear. This is a great asset in the game, and I'll return to it later.

Research by Australian scientists Megan Oaten and Ken Cheng of Macquarie University put volunteers on a two-month programme of physical exercise requiring willpower. At the end of the period, those who had kept to the programme demonstrated better self-control than another group who had not tried it. The subjects also started to smoke less, drink less alcohol, eat healthier food, monitor their spending, and improve study habits, suggesting a positive link from physical exercise to other areas of life.

This accords with research into self-control that describes it as being like a muscle that gets fatigued with heavy use. It must be rested occasionally, and once you recognize this, you can develop healthy strategies for giving it time off, rather than running it down to empty and falling into the first temptation. Fortunately, just as muscles are strengthened by regular use, so is willpower. In order to preserve your willpower, researchers advise that you apply it to goals one at a time, so creating a New Year's list of resolutions is the worst possible approach, since depletion in one sphere will reduce it in others. Studies also show that once a good habit is established, you don't need to draw on your willpower to maintain it. Healthy habits become routine.

Mental strength and self-discipline allow you to override and ultimately eliminate tendencies that obstruct your path to O, like being unable to resist temptation or say no, impressionable, easily led, flaky, halfhearted, or weak.

I have observed that people's lifestyle decisions are generally correlated to their degree of neediness—to fit in, to be appreciated, valued, loved, admired, respected, remembered, comfortable, pampered, entertained, thrilled, pleasured, served, safe, and secure. The more needy people are, the more they demand in compensation, whether it be material trappings, stimulants and substances, distractions, or escapism. Ironically, all this does is compound the underlying problem of neediness by inflicting the difficulties associated with wealth, materialism, and overconsumption observed by Fromm. At the extreme, instead of becoming part of the cure, lifestyle turns against them like a kind of Frankenstein monster.

Neediness is a burden in all areas of life—to the subject, to those around them, and to society at large. In the wealth game, it is a major obstacle to progress. It is a weakness that arises from being overattentive to self. In communist countries or others with strong caste systems, social hierarchies, or religious commitment, personal ego is often forcibly suppressed. In the developed and increasingly secular West, these overarching forces don't exist. It is your job as a free individual to address your own weaknesses and neediness. Fitness training becomes essential.

PRACTICAL MATTERS

Since this book is a companion, not a spoon-fed step-by-step solution (if there even were such a thing), a small idea, the neural network that flows from it, and the necessary fitness should be all you need. No plan to manage spending will work if it isn't your own design. It'll evaporate like facts and figures crammed for an exam.

Before leaving the spending subject, however, here are some further thoughts.

The Changing Shape of Needs

Mapping your priorities and the needs and spending that arise from them is entertaining. The pattern and themes arising from your earlier work should be investigated further and in more detail, with the counterbalance of realism. What can you actually afford to have and do, now and over the next few years?

List the things that matter to you most right now and those that register as being significant in the future. Order them by importance, but leave out financial security as a goal; when the picture is complete, shade or cross out anything that looks superfluous.

This exercise should become routine every few years, as your attitudes and outlook change. At age twenty-seven, my list was quite different from those that followed.

Now

1. Career—All-important driver of my earnings, in my own hands, and can't be built overnight, so a top priority. Also, determined to obtain a tangible return for all the years of hard study and exams.
2. Home—Get on the ownership ladder in the best area I can afford.
3. Women—Meet and entertain lots.
4. Clothes—Look sharp, high quality, and bespoke.
5. Car—Buy a fast one.
6. Travel—As much and as far as possible, given constraints of career and cash.

Future

1. Wife—Important and likely but could happen in a flash, so focus on that later or when it happens.
2. Children—Desirable but uncertain. If they come, the best education I can afford.
3. Home—Trade up to something big.

4. Car—Fast and luxurious
5. Sailing boat—Capable of offshore cruising
6. Hobbies—Numerous

This loose shopping list added purpose and direction to my work endeavours, as all entries were costly. Hitting the road and dropping out altogether was not an option.

Given the law of impermanence, it was bound to change, and it did. What was vital and essential at twenty-seven became trivial and unimportant over time, and new ambitions arose. My early list is now a slightly embarrassing historic footnote, and twenty-five years on, now and future aspirations have merged into one list, on which the only nonessential areas of meaningful spending are the children's education and travel. Qualitative objectives have replaced material ones.

This profile is not unusual. Just as adopting good behaviours leaves your willpower free to tackle other challenges, once you have established the foundations of your life, you can spend less without a reduction in quality, allowing your available cash to go further. It is a further incentive for getting on with the groundwork without delay.

Raising the bar
Since spending money on consumables and depreciators is an obstacle to your reaching O, a high bar helps, but how high?

The two most obvious questions are to ask these: "Do I need it?" and "Can I afford it?" As we've seen, *need* is a subjective term and open to wide interpretation. Another approach is to mentally redesignate consumables and depreciators into essentials and nonessentials, or subsistence items and luxuries, but does this help?

Somehow, you must decide what is essential to you and what isn't, what you absolutely must have, and what you can do without. In order to do this, you need to choose your own position on a continuum between subsistence, the bare minimum for physical survival, and lifestyle, the bare minimum to sustain your current or aspirational life. Depending on the size of your lifestyle, there can be some distance between the two. The closer your mark is to subsistence, the more items fall into the nonessential, or luxury, bucket. At the lifestyle end of the line, all related spending is essential.

A purist would regard any starting position other than subsistence itself as a lie. "Your basic need is what it costs to feed, clothe, and house you," the purist would say. "Anything else is nonessential and therefore a luxury!" A determined spender can designate all manner of needs as essential, rather like someone fiddling expenses. A pragmatist might opt for a subsistence-plus position that measures essential spending as subsistence together with an amount necessary for good health, learning, and enterprise.

An advanced player might leapfrog this intellectual retrofit and design his or her life to fit the definition. Instead of sifting through cost components, trying to decide which are essential or not, the advanced player would design or pare back his or her lifestyle to a level that he or she feels is appropriate and treat the associated spending as essential, so everything else is treated as luxury.

Whatever approach you adopt, the exercise is worth undertaking. It is an extension of mental contrasting and obstacle analysis in that it prompts you to develop another behaviour technique to overcome the obstacle of wasting money. The tighter and leaner your definition of essential spending, the easier it is to resist or defer that luxury and avoid the obstacle altogether. Conversely, in treating all costs of a high-maintenance life as essential, you are effectively disregarding the drag effect it has on your journey to O. This is fine if you have sufficient income and wealth to power your way to the finish line in an acceptable time period, but if you don't, you have taken action that will hamper you. You have been stopped by the obstacle.

It follows that anything you treat as essential is by definition no longer a luxury, so by widening your definition of what's essential, fewer luxuries are available to you than to someone with a narrower definition. For these people, your essential is their luxury. And luxuries are wonderful things to be looked forward to and savoured. Smoked salmon and champagne once a month are delightful; having them once a day every day make them routine. There is a parallel here, with the inverse relationship in the big life–small life discussion. The smaller your essential needs, the larger your universe of luxuries.

And it gets worse. One of the features of essential spending, whether small or large, is that it is just that—essential, the bare minimum for your survival. Without it, things go wrong and you suffer. So the greater your essential needs, the more you have to lose and the greater the risk of having to do without some of them from time to time. The pressure to fund essentials can become such a worry that the whole thing stops being enjoyable.

Out of harm's way

Hardiness, self-discipline, and raising the bar are not infallible. A skillful player also steers away from trouble. There are two components to over-spending—you and your money. If you're under control, you won't spend. If the money isn't there, you can't spend. You should develop strategies and policies for addressing both.

Why not redefine shopping as a chore instead of a leisure activity and do it only if you must? By all means, reserve some as a luxury, but enjoy it sparingly. Instead of wandering round the shops or perusing Amazon or eBay in your leisure time, do something else. As a matter of course, avoid situations where your willpower is likely to be overtested, and stay away from people who pressure you to overspend. Like giving up sugar and milk in your tea, your taste buds will be liberated, and you will discover greater pleasures.

The second part is easily addressed with a savings plan that automatically removes money each week or month before you have a chance to spend it, like pay-as-you-earn taxes. It can be a direct debit or a physical withdrawal to either a structured product, like a pension, or to any account or safe place of your choosing. A mortgage is an excellent forced-saving tool, because you treat it as an essential. A mandatory saving strategy works partly because it is a positive action. Instead of trying not to spend your money, you are putting it somewhere worthwhile and helping yourself reach O.

An uneven ride
In 2002, my lower back finally gave way as I bent over and pulled up my jeans in a tent at a music festival. Disc L5/S1 prolapsed, fluid and gel seeped out, and the whole mess squeezed against my spinal cord. Over the next week, all feeling in my right leg and foot ceased, and I lost all ability to rise up on my tiptoes. On seeing the MRI scan and examining me, the surgeon recommended an operation the next morning. I could see the pound signs in his eyes as he checked his schedule and reached for the surgical gloves. This expert was a little too keen, and I couldn't help but feel that my otherwise healthy body should be given a chance to heal naturally.

I returned home to my bed and the floor. Food was served on a plate next to the cat bowl, and we found a physiotherapist who wouldn't touch me but each week instructed me on a gentle exercise programme to stimulate recovery. It was her counsel and reassurance that kept me on track despite the snaillike pace of progress. Worst of all were the days when all progress seemed suddenly undone by a careless move that set off excruciating muscle spasms and pain. The co-dydramol dose that I'd been reducing as fast as possible was stepped back up, and my spirits sank. My faithful physiotherapist explained that these episodes were no more than minor setbacks along a steady journey to recovery, that the body's healing process doesn't run in a straight line, and that they should be expected but not feared.

She was right, and eight weeks after crawling away from my tent, I was up and hobbling back to work, where a good friend introduced me to an Indian osteopath operating from a semidetached house in north London and whose devoted clients came from as far as Canada. His eyes were frighteningly magnified by Coke-bottle glasses, but as if to compensate, his hands worked a kind of magic over three sessions, at which point he said, "You're cured," and the spell was broken. A year passed before I returned to anywhere near my previous condition, and I still do regular core exercises today to ward off these times.

In maximizing surplus cash flow to feed your net worth pot, *every* step counts, however, large or small, and setbacks happen. Change is ever present, and cash fluctuates constantly and sometimes wildly in the wrong direction. Subsistence spending, exuberance, unexpected costs, accidents, and emergencies may far overwhelm your ability to produce a surplus, sending you deep into negative territory and making your efforts seem worthless. They are not. All your contributions up to this point have added to your base wealth, as will all future efforts. As long as you get into the black again, the general drift assisted by compounding will be towards O rather than away from it.

X

COMMERCIAL NOUS

I was often described in my early years at work as "commercial," by which I think people meant "understands value and the point of the exercise and sets out to achieve it in the most efficient and quickest way possible."

Commercial nous allows you to spot a wealth opportunity and pare it off the bone like a skilled butcher with a filleting knife. It is the standout talent required in the wealth game, but what is it, and were you born commercial? I think it is something you learn by watching others and practicing. Reading books alone won't get you there, but a grasp of some basic laws of finance can help.

FINANCE BASICS

The time value of money
Money has a time value, and the first principle of finance is this: a pound today is worth more than a pound tomorrow.

You can put today's pound in a bank that pays interest. At any point in the future, it will have earned a return, making the bank balance greater than a pound. Let's say that the bank pays interest of 5% per annum. Over a year, the value of your £1 investment will grow to £1.05, calculated as follows, where r is the rate of interest:

Value of investment after one year, or future value (FV) = £1 × (1 + r) = 1 × 1.05 = £1.05.

By choosing to deposit the money rather than spend it, you have given up the opportunity to spend £1 today in return for the chance to spend £1.05 in a year's time. This is called the time value of money (TVM).

Now, let's run the same calculation over more years.

FV of £1 after 2 years = 1 × (1.05 × 1.05) = 1 × 1.05^2 = £1.10,
FV of £1 after 3 years = 1 × (1.05 × 1.05 × 1.05) = 1 × 1.05^3 = £1.16,
FV of £1 after 4 years = 1 × (1.05 × 1.05 × 1.05 × 1.05) = 1 × 1.05^4 = £1.22,
FV of £1 after 5 years = 1 × (1.05 × 1.05 × 1.05 × 1.05 x1.05) = 1 × 1.05^5 = £1.28.

After 10 years, the calculation is £1 × 1.05^{10} = £1.63. This is easy to calculate on any financial calculator.

In the second year, you earn interest on both your original £1 and the 5p interest earned in the first year. This is called a compound rate, and the interest earned is compound interest. For each year of compounding, the formula adds 1 to the interest multiplier, so after 3 years, the calculation is £1 × 1.05^3; after 10 years, it is £1 × 1.05^{10}, and so on.

While the FV formula shows how your money will grow in the future at any given interest rate, another calculation is needed to show how much a future sum is worth today. You need to be able to determine present value (PV). Do this by reversing the FV formula:

FV = PV × (1 + r)^t becomes PV = FV / (1 + r)^t.

In these formulas, t is the number of years, and r is the interest rate that, in this formula, is called the discount rate.

If a three-year investment delivers a future value of £1.16, and your target return is 5% per annum, the present value of that sum can be found with the following equation:

$$PV = £1.16 / (1+0.05)^3 = 1.16 / 1.05^3 = 1.16 / 1.16 = £1.$$

Instead of dividing future value by $(1 + r)^t$, you can equally multiply it by $1 / (1 + r)^t$, an expression known as the discount factor. In this example, the discount factor after the third year is $1 / (1.05)^3 = 0.86$, and multiplying this by FV £1.16 produces a PV of £1.

This checks to the previous FV calculation.*

*An interesting wrinkle arises when comparing the gain earned for a pound held today with the erosion of the value of a pound received tomorrow. Over the first year, the two sums correspond:

FV of investment after 1 year = £1 × $(1 + r)$ = 1 × 1.05 = £1.05,
PV of £1 received after 1 year = $1 / (1 + r)$ = 1 / 1.05 = £0.95.

A pound today is worth £1.05 in one year, a gain of 5p. A pound in one year is worth 95p today, a loss of 5p. After the first compounding year, the future-value number compounds up from a higher base (i.e., £1.05 compared with the present value number that compounds down from £0.95). So over five years, the numbers diverge slightly:

FV of £1 after 5 years = 1 × $(1 + r)^5$ = 1 × 1.05^5 = £1.28,
PV of £1 received after 5 years = $1 / (1 + r)^5$ = 1 / 1.28 = £0.78.

A pound today is worth £1.28 in five years, a gain of 28p. A pound in five years is worth 78p today, a loss of 22p. The difference is one compounding period.

Inflation

Inflation, a rise in the prices of goods and services, affects all asset values. As a simple rule, if returns for an asset are variable, its value and price will rise with inflation. If returns for an asset are fixed, its value and price will fall with inflation.

So, property, company shares, commodities, and other tangible appreciators, as a class, will rise with inflation, because their income and capital values are free to rise with it, while cash, fixed interest accounts, and bonds whose income returns are fixed and that do not attract capital growth will fall with inflation.

You should know the prevailing rates of inflation based on the consumer prices index (CPI), not including mortgage interest and the retail prices index (RPI), which does include mortgage interest. CPI is generally lower because its calculation assumes that, as prices rise, people will switch to lower-priced goods. These figures are published monthly by the Office for National Statistics and are widely reported.

In addition, you should have a view of where inflation is heading over the next one to three years. By definition, inflation is a one-way movement upward, so the question is how fast. The Bank of England and other central banks as well as the International Monetary Fund regularly release national and international forecasts, as do most investment banks, and these are all easily accessible.

Bald statistics are fine but often lag and are general in nature. Skillful players also develop a feel and sense for where prices of goods and services that matter to them specifically are heading, based on the known contributors to inflation. There are three fundamental underlying causes: demand outstrips supply (demand-pull inflation); cost pressures (cost-push inflation), and growth in the amount of money in circulation.

Indicators for the first include full employment and rising wages, consumer confidence, population growth, demographic change, plentiful credit, state spending, and economic/political stability. Cost-push inflation arises when underlying costs of raw materials, labour, and production rise. This may be overseas and the effects incorporated into imported goods and services. A weak currency also adds to the cost of imports.

Money supply, quantum, and its speed of circulation, velocity, directly drive inflation rates. If the amount of money in circulation doubles, and everything else stays the same, its purchasing power will halve: a loaf of bread that previously cost £1.50 will now cost £3. Money is created in four main ways:

1. Central bank prints notes and manufactures coins
2. Banks and other credit providers lend more
3. Central banks lend more
4. Outside capital providers, such as the IMF, lend more

Money introduced by banks and central banks into the system can be created and eliminated so that one day it exists, and it doesn't the next. Commercial banks can lend both their depositors' money and, if they have a mind to, money that they have borrowed from other lenders, subject to maintaining regulatory solvency requirements. Central banks adjust the appeal of this lent money by raising or lowering interest rates. The lower the cost, the more demand there will be for it, the more will be supplied, and the greater the inflationary pressure. The higher the cost, the less will be demanded and supplied, reducing inflationary pressure.

In extreme cases, such as after the 2008 financial crash, central banks have electronically created new money in their balance sheets and used it to buy debt assets from commercial lenders. The latter receive cash; the central banks receive debt assets. This strengthens the liquidity and balance sheet positions of commercial lenders, theoretically enabling them to lend money to businesses and individuals. When the debt assets held by the central banks become repayable or are sold back to private institutions, cash flows out of the system back to central banks, which can cancel it. This process, known as quantitative easing, is one step short of money printing, because the money can be cancelled at a later date. It is an experiment whose effects are currently under review, because none has so far been removed from the system. What we do know is that the vast influxes of newly created money have kept the international financial system functioning and the majority of its participants afloat. These influxes have also pushed up asset prices across the board.

You should pay attention to the words and indications of central banks in this regard.

Use the present value (PV) formula for calculating the effect of inflation on your cash by simply substituting the rate of inflation for your target annual return or discount rate, r. If inflation is running at 3% per annum, the spending power of today's £1 in ten years will be as follows:

$$PV = FV / (1 + r)^t = 1 / 1.03^{10} = 1 / 1.34 = £0.74.$$

Over a quarter of its value is lost!

Risk and Return
Every day, we are faced with choices, and as a commercial operator, you quickly learn ways of assessing one course of action versus another. Whether you realize it or not, when it comes to matters that have a

financial consequence, you apply some kind of risk-versus-return analysis, however primitive or rudimentary.

In finance, the concepts of risk and return are inextricably linked. Somehow, you must learn to measure returns more accurately and to identify and compare the associated risks. By doing this, you will be able to compare the performance and value of one asset against another and choose the most appealing one based on your requirements. It is one of wealth's holy grails, the key to financial success, and (unsurprisingly) impossible to master. You can only hope to get better and better over time and make fewer and fewer mistakes.

What is my cash return on an asset?

This is the cash gain or loss generated over the holding period. You can calculate it before or after the effects of taxation. The purist will argue that for strict comparison between assets, you should ignore tax that can differ from holder to holder, depending on their circumstances, and thereby distort results. The advantages of calculating your actual returns are that it is prudent and realistic, and it tailors the results directly to your circumstances. A tax-free return is worth more to a higher-rate taxpayer than to a basic-rate payer, for whom it is worth more than to a nontaxpayer. Furthermore, it encourages tax planning and a hunt for opportunities to pay less, which are helpful habits.

Whichever route you choose, remember to be consistent when comparing expected returns between assets or comparing expected returns with required returns. Treat them all as either pretax or post-tax.

In order to keep the calculation real, holding and selling costs should also be deducted:

net return = all income received net of expenses and tax + sale proceeds after transaction costs and tax – the original cost of the asset.

If an asset costs £100 to buy and generates net income of £10 plus net sale proceeds of £120, the net return is £10 + 120 – 100 = £30.

A productive appreciator generates income as well as capital growth over time. One that doesn't produce income and only returns capital growth is an unproductive appreciator.

How risky is this return?

A risk-free return is one that is fixed as to quantum and timing and fully guaranteed by a counterparty that won't default and can't go bankrupt. The only asset that fits this description is a government bond, also known as a gilt-edged security, or gilt. Governments can, of course, go bankrupt, but as long as they have the power to print money, they can pay their way.

Any other asset carries risk, but the question is how much. For any non-government asset, there is repayment, or credit, risk. The counter-party may go bust and be a default risk, or it may decide not to pay you and seek to avoid any contractual or statutory obligation. An interest-bearing loan asset with fixed repayment dates carries interest-rate risk if the rate offered is variable and not fixed. An ownership, or equity, investment bears business risk; not only is the return uncertain as to amount but also as to timing, and it may not materialize at all.

It follows that a rational investor should demand a higher return for any nongovernment asset than the rate offered for risk-free gilts. This extra return requirement is called the risk premium.

Let's say that you are asked to choose between three investment products, each priced at £100. They all offer fixed interest at 1% paid annually, with a full capital return on the second anniversary of purchase:

Asset A—a British government bond guaranteed by the state

Asset B—a deposit account with U-loan, a publicly listed, online peer-to-peer lending firm

Asset C—an IOU from Harry, someone you have just met in the pub

The least risky option is asset A, which offers a risk-free rate of 1% per annum. It carries no default risk and no meaningful credit risk. Assets B and C carry a plethora of risks, and as a rational investor, you would expect them to deliver a higher return than that offered. It is an easy choice.

U-loan and Harry, then, offer to improve their returns and ask what you require.

What premium do you add to the risk-free rate for each of A and B in order to compensate you for their extra risk? The studies on this subject are extensive and well beyond the scope of this book or the needs of the ordinary person. Nevertheless, a framework is required, and I would recommend using opportunity cost, introduced earlier, as it links together the concepts of time value of money and risk to give you a required rate of return.

For this purpose, the earlier definition of *opportunity cost* can be refined as "the expected return that is foregone by investing in an asset, rather than in comparable financial securities." Logically, you should seek out the highest return available for any comparably risky asset and set this as your required rate of return. The challenge is in finding comparably risky assets.

A bank deposit guaranteed by the government carries no extra risk to a gilt and doesn't justify a risk premium, but one not guaranteed does. In practice, you'd search across all nonguaranteed banks to find the best rate for a comparable product. Assuming that this is higher than the gilt rate, it would become your required rate of return. For a nonbank deposit, the more financially weak or unreliable the counterparty, the greater the risk.

Moving up the risk scale, the returns on the deposit accounts are no longer comparable, and you need to find another benchmark. Company shares offer this. Research indicates that since 1900, the average market risk premium of US equities over the risk-free rate has been about 7%. Throughout this book, the risk-free rate is taken as 1%, which is slightly higher than the current rate but lower than in the period before the 2008 crash. The theoretical opportunity cost of investing in an asset with similar risk level to equities is therefore 8%.

For assets riskier than a basket of all US equities, there are financial tools, such as the capital asset pricing model, but these are complex and beyond the scope of this book. Certain rules of thumb arise from transaction data and current practice, but these change with market conditions. During my career, return requirements of UK private equity on buyouts fell from 30%+ per annum to nearer to 20% and sometimes lower in very large transactions where the monetary return was significant. In difficult times, when ownership periods extended due to operating difficulties and lack of exit opportunities, returns fell due to the time value of money and investors switched focus to multiple of money invested, which took no account of time.

In practice, the 7% equity premium should be seen as a minimum and therefore increased for an individual company that does not have blue-chip status or is riskier than the market as a whole. A 9% equity premium, giving a 10% return requirement for midrisk, publicly listed companies, is not unreasonable. For illiquid private companies or risky listed ones, 15%+ is more realistic, and you should make your own commercial judgement.

Assets B and C are both loans with fixed obligations. Unlike shares, each has a legal obligation to pay interest and return the full amount of the loan, although not offering any security over the assets of the borrower. Notwithstanding the contractual protection, both carry default risk and also credit risk.

B is held in a listed company, but the loan risk is with individuals and is not guaranteed by U-loan, although it vets applicants and promises safeguards to minimize defaults. The risk falls somewhere between a corporate and personal loan, so you should look at the terms of recent corporate bond issues to the public where a number have been made at 6-7% per annum, and investigate current bank lending rates to private companies. B is riskier than these. At the other end are unsecured personal loan rates offered by banks at perhaps 10–15%. Throughout, you should keep in mind an annual equity return requirement of 10% as a sense check. Although B is a loan, not an equity, it is arguably at least as risky as certain high-quality listed company shares, if not more so.

C is quite different, and there may be no return high enough to justify the risk and no other easily comparable asset available to apply the opportunity-cost test. In this case, consider market data points like high-street bank lending at 10–15%, credit card companies at 25–30%, and payday lenders at 500%+ per annum.

Let's assume that after weighing up all available information, you decide that your return requirements are 10% for U-loan and 25% for Harry. If their terms are improved to deliver these rates, instead of the 1% first proposed, they become comparable to the government bond in that all three offer a return that meets your requirement. The gilt still pays interest of £1 per annum, U-loan £10 per annum, and Harry £25 per annum. Their risk and return are aligned. Which one you choose will depend on your appetite for risk.

What is your risk appetite?
Consider three types of risks in assessing your appetite:

1. Consider asset-specific risks of the type discussed previously, which are business or operational, default, or credit (debt-related) risks. This is also known as unsystemic risk in that it can be diversified away.

2. Wider economic or market risks that will affect values and prices are known as systemic risk. This is harder to protect against.

3. Consider your own circumstances and risk profile. Two natural and interlinked safety margins, or buffers, exist: time and liquidity. The longer your investment horizon, the greater time there is to recover from paper losses caused by market volatility and short- or medium-term dips. The more cash you hold relative to your needs, the longer you have before needing to liquidate investments, and the greater risk you can afford to take with the remainder of your assets. Your age and the amount of cash you hold are key determinants to your risk appetite. An important part of your own picture is the balance and spread of your assets, any debt you might have, and the structure of your life.

Asset concentration

If you hold only one asset—for example, shares in one company, a corporate or government bond issue, or a residential property—you are exposed to the dual risk of that asset failing in some way *and* the wider market risks for that class of asset, equity, bond, or property. Your asset is vulnerable on two fronts, and because it is the only one you hold, you are completely dependent on it. This is not a good idea.

Debt

As well as your own loans, debt can be layered into your asset portfolio. You might describe it as hidden debt.

Let's say that you spend cash savings of £10,000 to buy units in an investment fund. The investment fund borrows externally to increase its investment capacity and maintains a debt-to-equity ratio of 1:10 (common in investment trusts and hedge funds). It holds ordinary shares in quoted companies that have business borrowings equivalent to 40% of market value. For your £10,000 of units, the fund holds £1,000 of debt, and the resulting £11,000 of investment capacity buys shares carrying

£4,400 of debt. Your indirect debt exposure has increased from £0 to £5,400.

You still have net assets worth £10,000, but instead of being held as cash of £10,000 with no borrowings, they are now fund units with £5,400 of debt attached, creating a total asset value of £15,400. Your investment is 54% geared! And this is a fairly conventional structure. If your fund holds derivatives like futures and options, where a small deposit buys a large exposure, the gearing effect on that portion of its funds may rise to several hundred percent.

Clearly, it pays to investigate this hidden debt before you finalize your investment level. Instead of being a core holding, it might suit a small allocation of high-risk funds.

Personal circumstances risk
One person's or family's risk can be greater than another's because of the individual's or family's lifestyle. Can a single event upset the entire financial well-being of the family through linked pathways and contagion? This might be called personal systemic risk.

As well as asset concentration and debt, there are three lifestyle risks.

First is the dependency on a single uncertain income source, such as a working wage, or interest on savings or dividends from shares or a buy-to-let property rental. Each is like a block in a game of Jenga, whose removal causes the whole tower to collapse. This income source is, to a large extent, out of your control, yet you depend on it. Try to generate more income sources.

Second is an over reliance on a particular business that may fail. In some cases, a family's income and assets are tied up in one enterprise possibly even with personal guarantees or second charges on the home to secure business borrowings. This is not just the preserve of owner managers; it can exist for anyone whose salary, pension, health benefits, shares, and possibly share options derive from a single source.

A third and more insidious lifestyle risk lies in your needs architecture. Just as debt imposes a rigid and immovable obligation, so can needs that are cemented into the foundations or layered into the superstructure. These become requirements for the life of the family unit, demanding cash and punishing any interruptions in its flow. Once a tipping point is reached, their relentless demands not only overwhelm the available supply of cash and liquid assets but they can also imperil the entire value creation process, as pressure causes stress, underperformance, and poor decisions.

What are they? Examples are a business start-up or a house that's too large to manage, or they might be a combination of needs, like school fees, holidays, expensive hobbies, depreciators and consumables, and so on. The best remedy for these is to cut them off at the source and discard them, but failing that, allocate assets to liquid depreciators, like bonds and cash, to add some flexibility and safety to the structure.

How you view the state of the economy and the world around you contributes to your appetite for risk in financial dealings. If you misread the situation, you may become overly pessimistic and risk averse and not only miss opportunities but even fail to defend your money against inflation. Millions missed out on the largely foreseeable rise in global equity markets after 2008 because they were still in shock or looking the wrong way and overlooked the impact of global economic recovery combined with massive central-bank money creation in the United States, the United Kingdom, Japan, and, more recently, the eurozone.

One thousand pounds deposited five years ago at 1.5% per annum risk free would now be worth £1,077 (£1,000 × 1.015^5). The same sum invested in equities growing at an average of 10% per annum with dividends reinvested would be worth £1,610 (£1,000 × 1.1⁵), a 50% gain in value compared with the deposit account.

Alternatively, you may become overconfident and blind to the wider risks and make stupid wealth-destroying decisions.

APPLYING THE THEORY

One of the problems with financial theory is that it can be hard to use in practice. Another is that without the application of good sense and judgement, it can lead you into trouble. There are too many variables for it to be completely reliable, and it is best treated as a starting, rather than a finishing, point for any decision.

When valuing an asset, start by answering this question: "What is this worth?" You may be wondering, "Do you mean to me or, compared with that asset, or in itself?"

The easiest and most useful applications are in comparing one asset against another or the returns of an asset against your own requirements. It is harder to assess the intrinsic value of an asset.

"What is this asset worth to me?"
First, decide the actual return you expect the asset to deliver; next compare it with the return you'd expect for that type of asset. If the expected return matches or exceeds your required return, it is worth considering. If not, it is likely to erode your wealth.

Take an investment fund holding blue-chip company shares that offers a current dividend yield of 2% and, over the last five years, has produced an average capital growth of 10% per annum. This combined pretax return of 12% is well ahead of the theoretical pretax 8% return you require at present (a risk-free rate of 1% and an equity premium of 7%), and you would consider the investment further. If you are uncomfortable with equity risk at present, you might require an expected return of 15% to justify an investment. In this case, you would reject the proposal.

How do you calculate the expected rate of return on an asset?

Capital gain only, no income
If the gain is known and certain, you can work back from that. To do this, you need the initial cost of the asset and the expected hold period. Let's say that asset Blue costs £100,000, and you know that it will deliver back £150,000 after tax and selling costs in five years.

The net return is £150,000 – 100,000 = £50,000. Expressed as a percentage, this is £50,000 / 100,000 × 100 = 50%.

The arithmetic average rate of return per year over the five years is 50 / 5 = 10% per annum, and this is perfectly valid as a rough rule of thumb. It does, however, ignore the compounding effect and overstates the rate you would actually need to turn £100,000 into £150,000 over five years. Applying the future-value formula from earlier proves this:

$$FV = £100,000 \times (1 + r)^t = 100,000 \times (1.1)^5 = 100,000 \times 1.61 = £161,000.$$

The actual rate required to deliver a gain of £50,000 is 8% and is calculated by rearranging the future-value formula. Instead of calculating the future-value effect over time of a given compound interest rate, you now need to calculate the rate itself, given a future value. The rearranged formula that produces the compound annual growth rate (CAGR), where t is the time period in years, is as follows:

$$CAGR = (\text{ending value} / \text{starting value})^{(1/t)} - 1,$$

$$CAGR = (150,000 / 100,000)^{(1/5)} - 1 = (1.5^{0.2}) - 1 = 8\%.$$

Again, you will need a financial calculator for this one.

The lesson from this is that for greater accuracy and better decisions, use CAGR to compare your required rate of return. If your required rate of return is 10% per annum, asset Blue fails, despite producing an arithmetic average at that level.

If the gain is uncertain, you'll need to estimate it. One way is to make a prediction of future return based on past returns. For example, "This share or fund or property has grown at a rate of x% over the last three years, and I expect that to continue." Another way is to look at the forecasts of specialists in the asset class, such as equity analysts or estate agents. If the prediction is for a percentage gain over a period, rather than a rate of annual gain, say 25% over five years, a £100 asset will grow to £125. Remember that the arithmetic average is 5% per annum, but the implied CAGR is less—in this case, 4.6%.

Income only, no capital gain
Now let's assume that asset Blue is not expected to generate a capital gain and returns an income of only £4,000 after tax and costs that are paid annually. This current, or running, yield is calculated as follows:

$$\text{current yield} = \text{income} / \text{price} \times 100.$$

For net current yield, use after tax income:

$$\text{net current yield} = £4{,}000 / 100{,}000 \times 100 = 4\%.$$

Treat this as comparable to CAGR on the basis that you will reinvest it at the same rate each year.

If asset Blue is a rental property that delivers rent at £333.33 per calendar month, totalling £4,000 per annum, it is still reasonable to use the annual figure, even though the time value of money means that you will receive the cash earlier. In practice, the error margin is small and lost in the rounding.*

*To do the job properly, you need to calculate what's known as the internal rate of return (IRR), which is the discount rate at which an investment has a present value of zero. In practice, it is a more finely tuned version of CAGR that allows you to properly account for a sequence of future cash flows, rather than simply one ending value. Manual calculation is tricky, and the sum is best done on an Excel spreadsheet. The differences in this example aren't enough to be meaningful.

Income and capital gain
Finally, assume that asset Blue generates both a capital gain and income as set out previously:

total expected rate of return, or total yield = total return / price × 100.

Since capital and income returns have already been calculated for asset Blue, you can simply add them together:

total yield = CAGR + current yield = 8% + 4% = 12% per annum.

How does using debt to fund a purchase change your required return? To make the analysis more useful, factor in your funding choice, and replace required return with your cost of capital.

For a purchase 100% funded by your own cash (i.e., equity), your cost of capital is the same as your required return and is also known as cost of equity.

For a purchase 100% funded by debt, your cost of capital is the cost of your borrowing (i.e., interest cost plus any arrangement fees) and is also known as cost of debt.

For a purchase part equity and part debt funded, your cost of capital is a blend of your cost of equity and your cost of debt (weighted according to the proportions used) and is known as your weighted average cost of capital (WACC).

The cost of debt for a particular company or asset should be lower than its cost of equity, because a loan carries a repayment obligation and is less risky for the lender than an equity investment.

If, for a particular investment, your cost of equity is 10%, and your cost of debt is 7%, your WACC will vary depending on your funding mix:

$$100\% \text{ equity} = 1 \times 10\% = 10\%,$$
$$100\% \text{ debt} = 1 \times 7\% = 7\%,$$
$$50:50 \text{ debt : equity} = (0.5 \times 10\%) + (0.5 \times 7\%) = 8.5\%,$$
$$80:20 \text{ debt : equity} = (0.2 \times 10\%) + (0.8 \times 7\%) = 7.6\%.$$

The more debt you use, the lower your funding cost will be, thereby enhancing future cash flows. The lower your funding cost/required rate of return/discount rate, the less those future cash flows will be discounted, and the greater their present-day value will be to you. Each one of these factors justifies you paying a higher price for the asset, and taken together, they are a powerful combination.

This partly explains why private-equity investors try to maximize the debt component of their funding packages when buying or refinancing a business. The same applies to you, and I revisit the subject later in a fuller discussion of debt.

"What is this asset worth compared with that asset?"
If potential asset investments have similar characteristics and risk profiles, such as small-company equity funds or rental flats in the same town, a comparison can be made on expected returns alone.

If you expect them all to grow at the same rate, you can compare running yields only. Alternatively, you might attribute higher growth to some than others and can then add compound annual growth rates to the mix.

If the risk profile of assets is very different, it is better to use either the previous or following technique.

"What is this asset worth in itself?"
The financial worth of an asset lies in the cash benefits it confers, so how much cash, when does it arise, and how likely is it to come—in other words, how risky is it? The tools introduced below incorporate all three concepts.

1. Rearranging the yield equation
This shortcut involves playing with the yield equation to solve for different unknowns. Let's return to loan assets A, B, and C from earlier. Asset A is risk-free, but the others are not and were allocated return requirements of 10% and 25% respectively to match their risk profiles.

The monetary returns currently offered by these products, however, are the same at £1 per annum and the price of each is fixed at £100. The yield for all three assets is as follows:

$$\text{yield} = \text{expected return} / \text{price} \times 100 = £1 / 100 \times 100 = 1\%.$$

To find the price, the equation is rearranged as follows:

$$\text{price} = \text{expected return} / \text{yield} = £1 / 0.01 = £100.$$

Let's say that instead of asking what rate of return you require, Harry and U-loan insist that the £1 return is fixed, but suggest you make an offer on the price. You must now factor in the riskiness of the asset into the price calculation formula shown previously. This is done by substituting your required rate of return for yield:

$$\text{offer price or value to you} = \text{expected return} \ / \ \text{your required rate of return.}$$

Applying this to each asset produces the price for each, reflecting the risk you have attributed to it.

$$\text{offer price for asset A} = £1 \ / \ 0.01 = £100,$$
$$\text{offer price for asset B} = £1 \ / \ 0.1 = £10,$$
$$\text{offer price for asset C} = £1 \ / \ 0.25 = £4.$$

You offer to pay the full £100 asking price for the government bond but will invest only £10 for a £1 per annum return with U-loan and £4 for the same return with Harry.

The equation works just as well for assets bearing the same risk profile. Let's assume that you are comparing three buy-to-let flats in the same town. Each one is identical, with the same lease terms and duration, and is priced at £150,000. The assumption is that they will all grow in value at 5% per annum, so £7,500 each year.

Flat 1   rents at £375 per calendar month (£4,500 per annum), a rental yield of 3% per annum.

Flat 2   rents at £500 per calendar month (£6,000 per annum), a rental yield of 4% per annum.

Flat 3   rents at £625 per calendar month (£7,500 per annum), a rental yield of 5% per annum.

Your required overall rate of return on a flat in this town is 8% per annum, so adding the 5% annual growth rate to the rental yields tells you that all three meet or exceed this target. Flat 3 is clearly the most attractive, but how much more is it worth?

Applying the expected/required return formula gives this:

Flat 1: (£4,500 + 7,500) / 0.08 = 12,000 / 0.08 = £150,000,
Flat 2: (£6,000 + 7,500) / 0.08 = 13,500 / 0.08 = £168,750,
Flat 3: (£7,500 + 7.500) / 0.08 = 15,000 / 0.08 = £187,500.

The purchase of Flat 3 at its asking price of £150,000 would deliver you an immediate paper gain of £37,500.

2. Discounted cash flow

The longhand and more adaptable method for valuing an asset by combining cash return, time value of money, and required rate of return is to project the future cash flows and adjust these for the time value of money and their riskiness via the required rate of return or discount rate or factor described earlier. This delivers the discounted value of future cash flows (DCF).

Taking Flat 1 from the previous example and assuming a five-year hold period, the calculation is set out as follows.

Table 10.1

Discounted cash flow valuation for buy to let flat

	year 1 £	year 2 £	year 3 £	year 4 £	year 5 £
rent	4,500	4,500	4,500	4,500	4,500
sale proceeds[1]					191,442
rent+sale proceeds					195,942
discount factor[2]	0.93	0.86	0.79	0.74	0.68
present value (PV)[3]	4,185	3,870	3,555	3,330	133,240
cumulative PV	4,185	8,055	11,610	14,940	148,180

Notes
1. Sale proceeds are £150,000 compounding at 5% pa for five years so £150,000 x 1.05^5 = 150,000 x 1.276 = £191,442

2. Discount factor = 1 / (1+r)^t where r = required rate and t = time. In this example, r is 8% pa. Instead of multiplying the relevant year's cash flow by the discount factor as shown here, you can alternatively divide it by (1+r)^t to give the same result. Standard practice is to use the discount factor.

3. Present value = return x discount factor.

The present value of Flat 1, assuming you hold it for five years, is £148,180, a little short of the £150,000 derived by the previous shortcut method. The reason for this difference is that the value of the rent has eroded over time through the time value of money, and the DCF picks this up, whereas the reversed yield formula does not.

The DCF also allows more precise tinkering with other cash flows. For example, you could choose to grow your rent in line with inflation at 3% per annum and to factor in specific maintenance and refurbishment costs when they fall due.

This is the simplest possible DCF table and is here to introduce the concept. There is much skill in projecting cash flows and determining appropriate discount rates, but this rapidly reaches an advanced level of finance know-how that is not necessary or appropriate here. The topic is fully covered by Richard Brealey, Stewart Myers, and Franklin Allen in their standard textbook, *Principles of Corporate Finance*.

An asset can have different value to different holders
If either the expected or required return differs between buyers, the buyers will value the same asset differently. How might this happen?

Returns available to buyers will differ where benefits of a purchase, such as cost savings, revenue opportunities, or strategic benefits, do not equally apply to all. One buyer may benefit from the purchase more than another. For example, say company Red is being sold. Roger is a neighbour who already has an administration centre and can close Red's centre at an annual saving of £100,000. Bertolli, an overseas buyer, is new to the area and needs to retain Red's facility. Roger's expected return is £100,000 per annum higher for the same asset.

Required returns differ between buyers depending on their perception of risk and their funding structure.

An investor who needs to cash in after two years will view equities as riskier than one who plans to wait twenty and will require a higher return, thereby lowering the price he or she can justify paying.

Let's assume that Roger has a strong credit history and financial standing, and he can secure funding at a lower cost than Bertolli, who has a poor record and position. If Roger's cost of funding is 8%, and Bertolli's is 10%, and they both use 100% debt, Roger has 25% more buying power.

Roger's PV = £1 / 0.08 = £12.50
Bertolli's PV = £1 / 0.1 = £10

PRICE AGAINST VALUE

In everyday language, the terms *price* and *value* are commonly interchanged, but they are different.

Value is the material or monetary *worth* of the asset. Price is the material or monetary *payment* for sale and purchase of the asset. As a buyer, I ask, "What can I get it for?" As a seller, I ask, "What can I get for it?"

So price is the end product of a process, the outcome of an exchange between buyer and seller. It doesn't exist until the bargain has been struck. "Asking" or "list" price is no more than an invitation to buyers who may accept or turn it down or demand more attractive terms. Value, however, exists whether or not it is realized. In a world of constant change, neither value nor price can be anchored to in safety, but of the two, price is infinitely more fickle, as we'll see.

Recognition of this difference invites questions: What determines value and price? How do they behave relative to the other? Do they converge, and if so, when? And under what circumstances will they diverge most?

Price and value converge in an exchange when perfect information is available to all and the market operates efficiently.

Price and value diverge most when information is imperfect or unequally distributed and the market is inefficient.

Value is only as good as the price you can achieve when you sell, so you need a confident and supported view of both. On a sale and purchase transaction, price trumps value, because it is actual rather than theoretical. Price doesn't change value; it simply varies your wealth through its proximity to value.

As a buyer, if price is below value, you have an inbuilt wealth gain, but if price is above value, it's a loss. As a seller, if price is above value, you realize a wealth gain, but if it's below, you lose. The greater the divergence in each case, the greater the effect.

If you can buy assets at prices below their value or sell them at prices exceeding their value, you are onto a good thing. If you can do both, you have a winning formula. You can hunt the optimal circumstances for your purchase or sale—go where the money isn't to buy, and take your asset to where the money is to sell—or, if the asset is immoveable (like a house), buy when the money isn't there, and sell when it is.

The price equation has three components that are quite different to those of value: first, the level of supply versus demand for the asset; second, the amount of money circulating to fund the purchase; and third, the desire of the buyer and seller to deal.

Prices are highest when these factors combine in one of three ways:

1. Demand for the asset exceeds supply.
2. Buyers are awash with money, either their own or borrowed.
3. Buyers are keener to buy than sellers are to sell.

Prices are lowest when these factors combine in one of three ways:

1. Supply of the asset exceeds demand.
2. Buyers are short of money.
3. Sellers are keener to sell than buyers are to buy.

In practice, the three operate according to their own rules. They may all converge in one direction or another, such as in times of economic boom or bust, or head in opposite directions. The exchange between buyer and seller determines the final price.

Consider this example. Farmer Sally produces a hay bale that she doesn't need. Her neighbour Richard is keen to buy it but has had a poor year and is saving to buy a new tractor tyre. He knows that he's the only buyer around and offers her £10. Sally declines. A month later, after a wet summer, Sally has the only available hay bale in the area, and four other farmers are chasing it. Bids rise to £20, but Sally still holds on. A week later, travellers arrive with a cartload of fifty bales, selling them for £5 each. Sally sells at this price.

The following year, she produces another hay bale. After an excellent spring, the entire farming community is richer, and there is 20% more money circulating. The price of livestock has risen, and this has filtered through to hay prices. Supply of bales is just keeping up with demand. Sally negotiates with a few farmers and, well before any travellers arrive, sells her bale at £15.

You should take time to fully consider and try to understand the circumstances and drivers behind each component of the price equation in transactions that are important to your wealth.

An asset can achieve different prices at the same time
As an exchange between buyer and seller determines the price of an asset; different circumstances of exchange can produce different prices. Here's an example.

Aunt May has a painting she doesn't want.

(1) She is desperate to raise cash quickly to pay overdue winter fuel bills. Her neighbour has a friend who buys and sells art, so she invites him around. The dealer privately believes it to be worth £1,500 but offers £500. Accepting the offer, Aunt May is pleased and buys her neighbour a bottle of wine as a thank-you.

(2) The painting has just arrived as an inheritance, doesn't suit her house, and is getting in the way. Christmas is approaching, and she's very keen to get rid of it to clear some space. She advertises the painting in a local free paper with a brief description. Three people come to see it, including the dealer. She asks them to make an offer if interested, and at the end of the week, she'll take stock and reply to them. Our dealer offers £500. A private collector offers £750. At the end of the week, Aunt May rings both, and after a few rounds of private bidding, she secures a price from the collector of £1,250. She is delighted with the result and buys herself a new coat.

(3) On a whim and without any particular intent to sell, she sends the painting to Sotheby's, which researches its history and provenance and values it at £2,500 to £3,500. Sotheby's enters it in its upcoming Modern British Art Sale and advertises it online and via catalogue to its worldwide clients three weeks ahead of the sale date. A dealer has recently made a big profit on the sale of a ceramic and is feeling rich. On the night of the auction, despite lots of competition, the dealer prevails at a hammer price of £6,000. After the auctioneer's selling commission of £1,440 (20% of price + VAT at 20%), Aunt May's net proceeds are £4,560. She is over the moon and goes to Florence for a week's vacation.

This offers lessons for buyers and sellers.

Sellers

Don't be in a hurry, and never be a forced seller.

Know what you are selling and its value, or get someone who does know to help you.

Educate buyers so that they have the same knowledge as you.

Make sure that the buyer who can value it most gets to see it.

Generate plenty of competition, and run a process that delivers the highest price available in the market.

Buyers

Know what you are buying and its value.

Find a seller who doesn't understand the asset as well as you do.

Buy off market.

Learn to spot a seller in a hurry.

Don't let surplus money in your pocket colour your view on value.

Mark to market

Exploiting differences between value and price is important when buying or selling, but as a holder, you must record it in your balance sheet at a realistic level. Accounting convention for businesses requires assets to be valued at the lower of either their original cost or current net realizable value. For your personal balance sheet, use current net realizable value. If it is higher than original cost, so be it. What matters is that you can actually achieve the value recorded after tax and selling expenses.

This process of revaluing assets according to the price you know or think they would achieve if sold today is called marking to market. All professional investors and money managers do it.

Fear and greed

Sometimes called fear and hope, these two powerful human responses are important drivers behind two of the three components of the price equation, feeding most directly into the desire of buyer or seller to trade and, in turn, to supply and demand.

Fear—This is the fear of losing money, missing out on gains, being the last one holding an asset that no one wants, falling behind others, feeling stupid, looking stupid, and failing.

Greed or hope—This is the greed or hope for gathering money, making gains, being the first one into an opportunity, beating others, feeling clever, looking clever, or success.

Academic studies as well as the evidence on the ground confirm that these intensely personal sentiments are toxic, penetrating via every sense organ, and highly contagious, spreading rapidly through human contact and media. Local outbreaks and wider epidemics are common.

In the world of investment, greed and hope drive asset prices higher until they peak. Somewhere on the way, questions and doubts appear, and the spectre of fear emerges. People might say, "This market is too expensive and has to drop at some point, but who knows when?" It usually takes a surprise event or piece of news, often unremarkable in itself, to jolt the scales. Once this tipping point is reached, events can move rapidly, as informed investors and automated systems begin to sell. This promotes downward pressure on prices and reinforces the growing fears of all. A rush for the door coincides with a fear epidemic to drive prices down as sellers abandon the assets in an effort to minimize their losses.

At some point, after reflection and post rationalization, investors begin to reassess risk and underlying asset values. When prices diverge sufficiently from their view of value, the first bargain, or value, hunters reappear. Once spotted, others begin to cluster, news gets out, prices begin to rise, and the hope/greed switch is flicked on again.

This seesaw may affect an individual asset or class of assets or an entire market. The more efficient the market (i.e., faster information to more people and quick and easy ability to trade), the more pronounced the effect can be. So stock and financial markets head the list, while property booms and crashes tend to happen more slowly as owners struggle to physically sell their assets, and price information seeps out in patches.

Between fear, hope, and greed lies confidence, which occupies the broad centre ground, occasionally turning a few degrees one way or the other.

Fear and greed drive divergence between price and value. If prices are driven higher than underlying values, sellers benefit, and buyers overpay. If they plunge below values, sellers lose, and buyers benefit. Investors who panic will lose either way.

Investors love predictability. Despite the huge uncertainty, volatility, and price swings that fear, hope, and greed can cause, one thing remains predictable: the emotions themselves.

A philosophy of being different, emotional resilience, and taking contrarian positions based on sound analysis come into their own here.

PART FOUR

BUILDING THE POT

A reminder of the strategy stated earlier:

Maximize surplus cash and apply it to a mix of appreciators that you understand; use leverage (where appropriate) and compounding to boost returns while maintaining adequate liquidity throughout.

XI

WHERE TO PUT IT

Surplus cash doesn't act to feed your net worth much if you simply pile it up like a squirrel collecting nuts for the winter. The pile will grow only as fast as you add to it through your own labour and thrift. When your labour runs out or stops paying, or you become a net consumer, the stock will shrink fast, and you might run out.

You must make your cash work for you to create a self-sustaining source like the little porridge pot.

GROWTH PLATFORMS
A growth platform is a temporary home for your cash in which additional value will automatically accrue by virtue of someone else's effort or market forces. You can add more value through your own efforts, but this is optional. In the classic division of capital and labour described by Adam Smith in *The Wealth of Nations*, you become capital provider and charge for it.

Appreciators are growth platforms, and productive depreciators can also be if their cash generation exceeds their depreciation, but unproductive depreciators and consumables are not. The more effective the growth platform, and the more surplus cash you allocate to it, the faster you will build your wealth pot. In the quest for O, all your available surplus cash should be directed to appreciators.

How do they work?

Many growth platforms exist, each with its own particular characteristics, but they tend to fall into two camps:

1. A profit-seeking enterprise combining some mix of human labour, know-how, technology, process, premises, plant, equipment, and stock
2. A tangible commodity for which demand outstrips supply over time, such as gold, diamonds, oil and gas, or land and property

The first is dynamic and generates value through its own activities; the second has utility value but is primarily the passive recipient or beneficiary of value created elsewhere. There is a distinction and distance between the asset and the primary wealth-creating force. Residential property provides shelter, but its financial value is created because someone has acquired the money to buy it. It acts like a net to skim wealth generated from elsewhere. An enterprise may benefit from inflation or market forces, but the primary driver of its value is profit generation. However they generate or attract value, both types of growth platform can add to your wealth.

Your financial involvement in either type may also be active (as an owner, a manager, or a developer), or passive (as a direct investor or lender or indirectly via a fund or intermediary). You might use cash to start a business or to acquire part or all of an existing private one, you might buy shares listed on a stock market, or you might buy a fund that holds a variety of company shares. Similarly, you can take direct ownership of residential property to develop, improve, and sell; to rent out; to live in; or just to hold. Alternatively, you can buy passive exposure to it through a fund.

From the outset, you should understand how your chosen growth platform generates value and where you sit in the investor-lender hierarchy. What are your rights and obligations, and where is the scope for value gain or leakage? Are you a collector or a builder? One requires judgement, discipline, and buying skills; the other demands these skills plus many others, not least time and energy. For the ordinary person working hard to earn and save money in the first phase of the game, it is hard to do anything other than collect.

Why are they so important?

Growth platforms bring valuable outside help, whether labour and enterprise, market forces, or price inflation. These powerful allies start working for you, leveraging your own wealth-generation efforts from the moment you acquire them, and they carry on while you own them, possibly long after you have slowed down or stopped earning money from your own labour. They don't discriminate between players and are available to anyone with the money to buy or establish them.

The second reason for their importance is defensive. Over time, unless your assets grow at least as fast as inflation, they will lose value; growth platforms offer the solution.

A TEST

The universe of available growth platforms is wide and diverse, so the immediate challenge is where to start.

Here's a test.

Section A—Money

(i) Cash*
(ii) A currency of your choice

Section B—Other financial assets

(i)   Company shares, public or private*
(ii) Government or corporate bonds*
(iii) Futures and options
(iv) Structured or synthetic products
(v)   Intellectual property rights (e.g., royalties)

Section C—Tangible assets

(i)   Residential property*
(ii)   Commercial property
(iii) Farm, forestry, or oil/mineral-rich land
(iv)   Gold
(v)   Another precious metal or stone of your choice
(vi)   Art
(vii) Antiques
(viii) Jewellery
(ix)   Wine
(x)   Other collectables (e.g., stamps, rare coins, maps, books, vintage cars, etc.)

Answer the questions following for each starred asset class as well as one other from any section. The mandatory subjects are the foundations of net worth for the ordinary person. Company shares and residential property being productive appreciators are core inflation-proof growth platforms. Cash and bonds as productive depreciators provide liquidity and scope for risk management.

1. Is this asset what you think it is? (5 points)
This challenges your understanding of the asset as well as its veracity. You need to answer this question before proceeding. Accurate answers to these help you avoid buying something unsuitable for your needs or being ripped off. A typical difficulty involves overconfident or lazy assumptions that fail under scrutiny.

2. What is it worth today? (5 points)
If you can get this right, you'll recognize a bargain or avoid overpaying. Understanding worth also allows you to compare assets and make rational purchase decisions. The pushy salesman poses no risk. Problems arise here due to the absence of a valuation framework or tools, if there is a lack of skill or rigour in their application, and when candidates fall back on guess-work, received wisdoms, and qualitative nonfinancial criteria.

3. What drives its value and price? (5 points)
A "holy grail" question, this is the hardest to answer, but it is highly rewarding. Analysis informs your choice of asset and its weight in your portfolio. In limited cases, it can assist you in the timing of buy-and-sell decisions and the manner of transacting.

4. Where's the catch? (2 points)
Every asset has a catch that, although not necessarily financial in nature, can have a negative impact on building your net worth. These typically fall into three categories: selecting the asset, holding the asset, and the speed and mechanics of buying and selling it. An asset may generate issues in one or more of these.

5. Applying the principles in your answer to question three, choose an asset other than money which you expect to grow in value over time and explain why. (3 points)
This tests your ability to spot a growth platform. How commercial are you?

Your time begins now.

BRIEFING NOTES
Since each asset class merits a book of its own, a comprehensive teach-in, or model answer is unfeasible, and such detail is unnecessary for our purposes. You can research and learn about assets to fill knowledge gaps, but

what matters here is your approach, investigating and applying the commercial principles around value and price set out in the last chapter.

What follows is a starter pack of pointers distilled from theory and practice to help you on your way:

1. Cash

- Cash is available money, however it is held. It is a productive depreciator, eroded by inflation but capable of earning interest.
- As a universal medium of exchange with no intrinsic worth, its utility value lies in what it can buy: interest from a bank, dividends on shares, returns on alternative investments, goods and services, or other currencies.
- The value of cash or its buying power is therefore relative, depending on the price or terms of what it can be swapped for and so changes daily.
- You can influence the value of your own cash in the way you spend it.

   The more value you are able to buy, the more your cash is worth; the same five-pound note can buy two takeaway coffees or a large pack of fresh-filter coffee that makes twenty cups. Fifteen pounds buys a slightly worn winter coat in a charity shop, two packets of cigarettes, or a new pair of branded socks. One hundred pounds can deliver healthy family meals and household consumables for a week or a dinner for two. A thousand pounds can fund a long-haul backpacking holiday for a month or a weekend stay in a luxury hotel.

   Even the same product can be bought for different prices; the price can be low near the source of production or from a discounter, and it can be high when it has been branded, packaged, advertised, and passed through various middlemen. It is very easy to trick yourself into thinking that price equals quality and spend with impunity. Sometimes it does mean that, but most often it doesn't; it equals profit margin to the seller or supply chain or duties to the state, a direct transfer of wealth from you to them.

- A rise in interest rates adds to the return on cash and, without a corresponding rise in risk, enhances its value. A fall has the opposite effect. Central banks or governments set interest rates in order to manage money supply, using them like an accelerator to promote spending and economic growth or like a brake to slow down growth and inhibit inflation. They tend, therefore, to work in the opposite direction to inflation: they are raised to the benefit of money when inflation is too high and eating into the value of money, and they are lowered to the detriment of money when the economy needs stimulating and inflation is low.

In practice, there are periods when policy leads or follows reality, and this relationship is broken, so the two work in the same direction for a while, powerfully pushing the value of money up or down.

- Price inflation hurts returns on cash; interest paid (nominal interest) loses value against its after-inflation value (real interest). In rough terms, a nominal rate of 3% per annum is a real rate of only 2% per annum if inflation runs at 1% per annum.

Price inflation also hits the purchasing power of cash. The PV formula, $1 / (1 + r)^t$ allows you to quickly see that over a ten-year period, annual inflation of 3% reduces the spending power of £100 to £74.40, and annual inflation of 5% over the same period reduces it to £61.39. So money under the mattress is not a good strategy unless the alternative is to lose it altogether, in which case it is the lesser of two evils. Either way, over time, you'll be poorer.

If, on the other hand, your £100 is borrowed, the real value of your debt and the interest chargeable on it reduces with inflation. You are no longer a depositor but a borrower and can benefit from the erosion of value. Bear this in mind.

Deflation is rare and has the opposite effects, raising real interest rates above nominal ones and increasing the spending power of money and the real value of debt.

- Currency exchange rates affect the buying power of cash directly and indirectly. Today, one pound might buy €1.40 or US$1.60. A 5% swing either way buys you the following amount of each currency: €1.33–1.47 and US$1.52–1.68. If the prices of goods and services in eurozone countries or the United States stay the same, your pound has either gained or lost 5% of its previous buying power in those territories.

The indirect effect is on the United Kingdom's buying power as a whole. When the pound weakens, it takes more pounds to buy the same volume of imports. The same basket of goods increases in price when expressed in pounds, so a 5% devaluation versus the currency makes a chest of tea previously priced at £100 now cost £105. A 5% appreciation reduces the price of the chest in pounds to £95. If tea is included in the basket of items making up one of the United Kingdom's inflation indices, it will alter the rate of inflation.

Exchange rates are volatile and tend to fluctuate more widely than inflation, deflation, and interest rates. This is partly because they are set by financial investors who trade in and out of currencies for gain. This concentration of force is magnified by their ability to leverage their investments by borrowing at a ratio of up to 10:1, enabling a £100 stake to buy a £1000 position. The trader sells one currency and buys another to earn the interest differential between the two and, hopefully, capital appreciation. An overall expected return of 2.5% can be leveraged with debt to 25%. Strategies to take advantage of both income and capital gain are known as carry trades, and these drive currency markets.

The contributors here include a country's financial strength measured by its current account balance (the difference between the value of goods and services bought and sold between the country and its trading partners), public debt, and its political stability and overall economic performance. To invest in the currency of a highly indebted nation running a current account deficit or one that is politically unstable or has declining economic prospects, investors will want a higher return than a financially strong, politically stable one with a well-managed, growing economy. This higher return requirement will dictate a lower price for the currency.

Don't speculate on currencies to create wealth unless you are close to the currency markets and have a high risk appetite.

- Hold cash for liquidity to meet your obligations and to fund opportunistic purchases.
- Minimize inflationary erosion by hunting the best interest-paying accounts, and don't let large amounts of surplus cash lose real value for longer than twelve to eighteen months.
- Invest cash in a downturn or recession, release it when asset prices are high, and build reserves as boom times heighten.
- Develop a hunter/trader mentality to extract maximum value for your cash.

2. Bonds

- When you invest in a bond, you are lending money to the bond issuer, generally for a specified time period. Some bonds, known as perpetuals, never expire, while others, like premium bonds, can be redeemed in full at any time. In return, the issuer is legally obliged to pay interest, or coupon, at a pre-agreed rate and to repay the original amount borrowed, principal, face value, nominal value, or par value on the repayment date (maturity). Bonds are a financial instrument for funding government or corporate issuers. They are also known as fixed-income securities. As a bondholder, you are a creditor of the issuer.

- The primary utility value of a bond is as a loan instrument, and it is a productive depreciator because its capital return is fixed and therefore erodes with inflation, but it generates an income.

- Unlike company dividends that are not certain as to quantity and are not guaranteed, bond interest is certain but only as strong as the issuer, which may range from a well-funded country to a risky or near-bankrupt company.

- You can hold a bond to maturity or sell it in the secondary market if there is one at the price on the day. This determines your capital repayment. People sometimes assume that the capital invested in bonds is safe but forget that the price of bonds falls when investors seek higher yields. Unless you hold a bond until maturity, the capital repayment is at risk, and only by holding an individual bond directly can you keep control of this. Bonds held in managed funds are bought and sold at the discretion of the manager.

- Publicly traded bonds are evaluated, risk assessed, and rated by one or more specialist agencies, like Standard and Poor's, Fitch, or Moody's. The higher the rating, the less risky the bond is deemed to be and the lower the interest demanded by investors, so it's cheaper for the issuer.

- The earlier example of the UK government bond versus U-loan versus Harry's IOU illustrates how to value a bond on a running yield basis. In comparing bonds, however, investors look at redemption yield or yield to maturity (YTM). This takes into account any difference between the purchase price you pay and the par value of the bond.

    If you spend £130 in the market to buy a £100 bond that pays £5 per annum with five years to run, you will receive income of £5 per annum but only £100 at redemption. Your capital loss of £30 works out as £6 per annum for each of the remaining five years. Take this as a percentage of the price you paid, so £6 / 130 × 100 = 4.6%. This figure is deducted from the 5% running yield to produce a YTM of only 0.4% per annum.

- The price of publicly traded bonds is their market price on the day. Ordinary passive investors do not have the power to negotiate purchase prices.
- As a rule, investors require extra yield for longer-dated bonds because time increases risk. This means that long bonds usually yield more than short ones.
- Supply and demand set bond prices, where supply is governed by the number and size of issues, and demand is driven by three main variables: interest rates, inflation, and perceived credit quality or default risk of the issuer.

  Bond prices tend to move in the opposite direction to interest rates. If interest rates rise, the fixed coupon attached to a bond becomes less attractive, and the price falls until it delivers an acceptable yield. When interest rates are low, and investors are chasing income, they will bid up the price of bonds, as they accept lower yields.

  Inflation erodes the income and capital from bonds, making them less valuable. If inflation is 3% per annum, the real running yield on a 5% bond is 2% per annum. If inflation rises to 4% per annum, the real yield drops to 1% per annum. To compensate, the bond price falls, and its nominal yield rises. If investors want a 2% real return, but inflation is running at 4%, the nominal return needs to be 6%.

  Falling and low inflation are associated with rising bond prices partly for this reason and also because low inflation usually means low interest rates. Rising or high inflation is consistent with falling bond prices, exacerbated by the interest rate rises that usually accompany it.

  Changes in credit ratings directly affect the perceived riskiness of bonds. A downgrade drives prices down, as investors require higher returns to compensate for the extra risk of default. An upgrade sends prices up.
- Bonds are only "safe" if you hold them to maturity. Many of the factors that drive prices are the same as for equities, although the

effects are typically (but not always) opposite. Bonds are defensive in nature, and because they can grow in value at times of economic distress, low inflation, and falling interest rates, they are a good counterbalance or hedge for equities that tend to do badly in these circumstances.

- Buy bonds for stable income (but recognize the capital risk) and to diversify your portfolio.
- Buy bonds for protection and possible capital gain when fear stalks the market, economic outlook is bleak, and government, banks, and consumers are tightening their belts.
- Avoid bonds when inflation and interest rates are on a rising path.

3. Shares

- A share or equity is a unit of ownership in an enterprise, usually a company, entitling the holder to participate in any distributions of profit and returns of capital. Unlike a bond, neither is guaranteed, which makes this a riskier product.
- A share's primary utility value is as an investment instrument, and it is a productive appreciator because it offers uncapped income and capital returns.
- As a unit, a share is one of a number that together make up the whole. One ordinary share out of two in issue is a 50% owner-ship position of that class. One out of 1,000,000 is a 0.0001% position. For a company that makes profit after tax of £2 million, keeps half for reinvestment, and distributes £1 million as dividend, the earnings (profit after tax) per share (EPS) and dividend per share (DPS) based on the two capital structures are:

  2 shares in issue: EPS £1 million and DPS £500,000
  1,000,000 shares in issue: EPS £2 and DPS £1

- An ordinary share—the most common type traded on stock markets—occupies the lowest place in a company's capital structure. Although it generally controls voting rights and management, financially it is subordinate to all other instruments; that is, all debt and any shares with preferential rights to voting, income or capital, commonly known as preference shares. It receives dividends and capital on liquidation only after the rights of all other funders have been satisfied.

- If a company's profits are insufficient to service and repay its debt or other financing obligations, the value of equity will be impaired and possibly zero. Companies have limited liability, so shareholders can't lose more than their investment.

  Assume that a company starts trading with £100 of capital composed of 50% debt and 50% ordinary equity. It begins strongly but suffers a loss in the second year, and its overall, or enterprise, value changes.

  Enterprise value at the end of year 1 = £140:
  Debt value = £50,
  Equity value = £90 (a gain over initial investment of 80%).

  Enterprise value at the end of year 2 = £70:
  Debt value = £50,
  Equity value = £20 (a loss against initial investment of 60%).

If the company's enterprise value falls below £50, shareholder value is wiped out, and some of the debt will not be repaid. The board may negotiate with debt holders, who hold all the economic value, and equity holders—who, until liquidation, still have voting rights—to organise for a portion of its debt to be converted into shares, reducing the financial pressure on the company. The preexisting equity owners may receive a sop for their consent but will be heavily diluted, normally to no more than a 2 or 3% overall holding. The alternative is liquidation, where shareholders would receive nothing, and lenders would lose a portion of their loans. Many such restructurings have delivered huge returns to debt holders who have converted a portion of their loans into equity in overleveraged companies and seen the value of that equity rebuild to levels far higher than their initial debt position.

- In distressed situations, lenders sometimes sell their debt to professional investors for less than its face value, crystallising a loss but also delivering a return and certainty. Buyers calculate that the debt will yield more to them than they have paid, either through selling it on as the issuer's prospects improve, holding it until maturity, or using it as a tool to negotiate a swap into equity. There is an active (although opaque and largely unregulated) secondary market for stressed debt.

- Investors value companies by using discounted cash-flow analysis or applying multiples to trading metrics, such as revenues, profits, and net assets. These tools work only as well as the information fed to them, and because companies are complex and dynamic, many judgements are required, which makes the valuation process more of an art than a science.

- The most common practice is to value a business before taking account of its debt financing and any cash balances and to adjust for these after. The earnings available to all finance providers (i.e., debt providers and shareholders) are known as EBITDA (profits or earnings before interest, tax, and noncash accounting items like depreciation of assets and amortization of intangibles like goodwill). EBITDA is projected for the current and upcoming year, and a multiplier is applied to give total enterprise value (TEV). From this, the company's net debt is deducted, or net cash is added to produce the equity value available to shareholders.

For publicly listed companies, multipliers are often applied to the profits available only to shareholders, known as profit after tax, or PAT (profits after debt financing costs, tax, and accounting items have been deducted). The resulting equity value, also known as market value, is commonly used for comparing listed companies.

Companies that make no profit, such as start-ups or early-stage Internet or high-tech businesses, are sometimes valued on a multiple of current revenues/sales. This can quickly become fantasy, as many never become profitable.

These multiples are known respectively as TEV/EBITDA, price/earnings (PE), and revenue or sales multiple.

Multipliers are derived in two ways, often blended:

I. The reciprocal of an investor's required rate of return—If an investor's required rate of return for a share is 12%, the multiplier is $1/12 = 8.3\times$. Required returns of 10% and 15% deliver multiples of $10\times$ and $6.7\times$, respectively. EBITDA is pretax, so the comparable return requirement should also be pretax. Earnings are post tax, so you would use your after-tax return requirement. For this and other reasons, EBITDA multiples tend to be lower than PE multiples for tax-paying companies.
II. An average of the multiples at which comparable quoted companies trade or an average of the multiples at which similar companies have recently been bought and sold—the latter approach is commonly used to value residential property as we'll see later.

Consider Company White. Company White makes EBITDA of £4 million and PAT of £2.5 million. It has net debt of £5 million and 10 million shares in issue giving EPS of 25p (£2.5 million / 10 million).

Investors have a pretax return requirement of 13.33%, giving an EBITDA multiple of 7.5× (calculated as 1/ 0.1333 =7.5), and an after-tax return requirement of 10%, giving a PE multiple of 10× (1 / 0.10 = 10). Let's assume that these multipliers are consistent with comparable company trading and transaction multiples and are the ones chosen to derive price:

$$\text{total enterprise value (TEV)} = \text{EBITDA} \times \text{EBITDA}$$
$$\text{multiple} = £4 \text{ million} \times 7.5 = £30 \text{ million},$$
$$\text{equity value} = \text{TEV} - \text{net debt} = £30 \text{ million} - 5 \text{ million} = £25 \text{ million},$$

or

$$\text{equity value} = \text{profits after tax} \times \text{PE multiple} =$$
$$£2.5 \text{ million} \times 10 = £25 \text{ million}.$$

Price per share is calculated in two ways:

$$\text{price per share} = \text{equity value} / \text{number of shares} =$$
$$£25 \text{ million} / 10 \text{ million} = £2.50 \text{ or}$$
$$\text{price per share} = \text{EPS} \times \text{PE multiple} = 0.25 \times 10 = £2.50.$$

This is all an application of the yield / required return formula from before where

$$\text{yield} = \text{return} / \text{price} \times 100,$$
$$\text{price} = \text{return} / \text{yield}.$$

Where required, return substitutes yield to derive price:

$$\text{yield} = \text{EPS} / \text{price} \times 100 = 0.25 / £2.50 \times 100 = 10\%,$$
$$\text{price} = \text{expected return} / \text{required return} = \text{EPS}/$$
$$\text{required posttax return} = 0.25 / 0.1 = £2.50.$$

Dividends are not typically used to value companies, because they don't capture the entire profits, but they are used to compare income yields between different companies.

If Company White pays a dividend per share of 12.5p, a 50% payout ratio based on an EPS of 25p, the dividend yield at a share price of £2.50 is as follows:

dividend yield = return / price × 100 = 12.5 / 250 × 100 = 5%.

If the share price rises to £3, the yield falls to 4.17%, and if the price falls to £2, the yield is 6.25%.

Remember that this type of multiple-based valuation doesn't take account of capital employed by the business or the returns earned on it. A company can destroy shareholder value by earning a lower return on its assets than its cost of capital, even as it increases earnings.

- A wide range of ratios and multiples exist to measure the financial strength and solvency of a company using balance sheet and profit-and-loss data. Most common are net gearing, calculated as net debt / net assets; debt / EBITDA; and interest cover ratios, such as EBITDA / interest due. These are used by lending banks to assess repayment risk and by equity investors to assess bankruptcy risk, so while not directly used in valuation, they feed into the calculation via required returns.

   In practice, net gearing of over 50%, debt / EBITDA of greater than 3× and EBITDA / interest of less than 2× would give both lenders and equity investors cause to delve deeper.
- When running discounted cash flow–based valuations, investors also use financial data from companies to project future cash flows, which they discount back to present value using the methodology

described earlier. This is notoriously unreliable and best suited to companies with highly predictable cash flows. The range of variables that are easy to misjudge and the sensitivity of outcomes to even small changes frequently leads to buyers overpaying when their assumptions are too rosy and turn out to be flawed.

- For companies whose shares are listed on a stock exchange, the price is the price and not up for negotiation. The better established and regulated the exchange, the more protection investors have. Value/price divergence remains, however; information seeps out into the hands of few, some buyers investigate harder and more effectively than others, and company boards disclose to different standards.

- Company values are driven by their operating performance. Investors like revenue growth, implying a growing market or capture of market share; profitability (high EBITDA/sales margins), indicating valuable goods or services; defensiveness to price cuts; and predictability from either contracted or repeat business, as well as high conversion of profit into cash. Analysing this is impractical for all but experts and company insiders.

- Share prices frequently detach from underlying company values, presenting risks and opportunities for investors.

- Supply versus demand and the availability of money drive prices. Supply into an otherwise finite pool is set by the aggregate number of new shares issued less shares cancelled following buybacks or take-overs. Demand is the variable to watch, and being a human sentiment coloured by fear and greed, it has many influences:

    a. The relative attractiveness of equities versus other asset classes—in other words, how much do investors want to hold equities now versus cash, debt securities, real property, or other assets?

        Given the vast amounts of money circulating the globe, if a greater proportion of this suddenly starts to funnel into shares, the price tide for all shares would rise. If there is a mass exodus, and investor money drains out of shares, the price of the entire asset class falls. This rising or falling tide lifts or lowers all boats on the water. The financial performance and underlying value of a company may not change an iota, but its price will.

This great rotation typically involves a move from less risky assets, like cash and bonds, into more risky assets, like shares and property, or vice versa. It explains why many financial academics and investors believe that the asset allocation between classes of risk assets is more important for returns than your choice of specific assets within a class.

b. Interest rates

Interest rates are the base for investor return expectations, as explained earlier. When they rise, return requirements (cost of capital) also rise, and share prices fall. At the same time, the higher financing costs for companies deplete their profits, creating a doubly negative effect. A drop in interest rates has the opposite effect.

c. Inflation

Equities offer inflation proofing. If companies can pass on rising costs to customers while maintaining sales, the nominal value of their sales and profits rise, as do their share prices and enterprise values. Company borrowings that are fixed in value depreciate in times of inflation compared with its assets that rise in value, reducing gearing levels and strengthening balance sheets. Growing or high inflation carry the risk that central banks will raise interest rates, depressing share prices.

Low or stable inflation enables companies and funders to invest confidently; businesses grow, and investors lower their risk premia to the benefit of share prices.

d. Availability of money

Easy bank credit at low cost fuels share price growth. Both companies and their investors have more to spend. The same applies when central banks expand the money supply by printing money or pursuing quantitative easing, as demonstrated by share prices between 2009 and 2013.

e. Fear and greed

Nowhere is this better seen than in stock markets. Fear and greed drive herd-like behaviour one way or another, with dramatic effects on share prices. They creep up slowly but, at a tipping point, accelerate rapidly. At first, fear and tumbling share prices can leave underlying values unaffected. When they reach critical or sustained levels, real damage can occur as debts are called in, customers stop paying or go bust, and confidence evaporates. At times of "irrational exuberance," when confidence is unchecked, and investors borrow to chase equity gains, the underlying values of companies can be held back or eroded, because managers allow cost bases to balloon, ignore risks, and make reckless, value-destroying decisions.

f. Currency exchange rates

A weak local currency makes shares cheaper for foreign buyers, increasing demand and pushing prices up. If, at the same time, a company is exporting products or services to stronger currency areas, its products are cheaper, and it will sell more. In addition, the foreign currency proceeds of these sales, when converted back to local currency for accounting and reporting purposes, will boost profits further. A strong local currency has the opposite effects.

This is one of the reasons that there is a race to devalue between countries at times of economic weakness and that a one-size-fits-all structure like the euro is problematic for user nations that are forced to trade at a currency level that may not suit their particular circumstances.

g. Rotation within equity classes

Investor tastes are fickle, and money often flows strongly to one type of company or another—for example, blue-chip dividend payers, small growth stocks, or midsized value players. Individual countries and regions go in and out of fashion, as do industry sectors. Learn to watch and anticipate these trends.

h. Mergers and acquisitions activity

Benign or positive economic conditions and available finance encourage expansionist behaviour by trade and private equity buyers. Public company take-overs deliver selling shareholders a chance to crystallize short-term gain, because offers tend to be at a premium to the target's market price. The prospect of possible take-over sharpens the focus of company managers, spurring them to deliver better returns to shareholders so that they don't lose their jobs. If there is a bout of activity in a particular industry sector, the share prices of other companies in the same space may benefit from a halo effect. Data on mergers and acquisitions activity is widely available, and large accounting firms have produced much analysis on the topic.

- Buy equities for inflation-proof income and capital growth, but only for the medium or long term, so with a minimum hold period of at least three years and preferably more.
- Avoid DIY single-share analysis and buying unless you have the information, skill, and time to do it properly.
- Buy shares through managed funds that hold many companies or trackers, which follow entire markets. I address this later.
- Consider value and price drivers carefully when making buy, sell, and hold decisions.
- Buy shares in times of economic recovery or stability and when fear stalks markets and prices have fallen due to panic selling. Avoid buying when markets are frothy. If you have enough spare cash, hold in tough times, and avoid what traders call "trying to catch the falling knife," selling and crystallizing real losses. Stock markets have always bounced back.

4. Residential property

- Residential property differs from cash, bonds, and shares in that its primary utility value is not financial but as a dwelling, yet it also offers uncapped, inflation-proof rental income and capital growth. Cash income is generally paid monthly and without tax deductions at the source. The attractiveness of residential property is further enhanced by the owner's scope to influence and negotiate prices, improve or develop the property, gear up with cheap mortgage debt, and utilize tax breaks. These unique benefits make it a productive appreciator and growth platform par excellence.

- A residential property's status in the wealth game, however, depends on how you use it. It can be used as anything from a luxury to a pure investment.

    If you use the property as your home, you forego the rental income opportunity but save yourself the cost of paying rent to live there or in a similar house. The benefit and the cost cancel each other out. If you could rent out your house for £20,000 per annum but live there instead, your potential income of £20,000 per annum is offset by its £20,000 per annum effective cost.

    In order to gain, you need to reduce your accommodation cost to less than £20,000 per annum. You might let out a room and, by reducing your usage of the house, capture some of the available rental income. Alternatively, you can move out completely, let the house, and rent a home that costs less—the difference between the rent you pay and the rent you earn is upside.

    As a property owner, the income cost of your accommodation is foregone rent.

    The capital return on your property is captured whether you live in it or not, but there is a rub: it helps you reach O only if you release some or all of it into your pot. By living in the same home until you die, your accommodation need cancels out any gain.

To release gain, you could borrow cash against your equity in the property, sell it and buy somewhere cheaper, or rent. It follows that the capital cost of your accommodation is unreleased gain.

"On costs" is a term is typically used for measuring the true cost of employing staff or the costs of running a facility of some kind. In the case of staff, it is not uncommon for a £30,000 salary to become a total charge of £50,000 by adding the cost of recruitment, training, share of office space, employer's national insurance, pension provision, computer and mobile phone contracts, and benefits, such as car, canteen, childcare, sports club membership, and health insurance. None of these costs would be incurred if the person were not employed there. The on costs in this example are £20,000, or 67% of the salary.

The associated costs of insuring, protecting, maintaining, and running a home and the lifestyle that goes with it grow in proportion to its size, gardens, age, and style, as well as the value of its location. Large, old, grand country houses with elaborate gardens attract the highest on costs. Outgoings for all homes are magnified in a wealthy area. The range of on costs for a family house can easily range between £5,000 and £150,000 per annum. What are yours?

It gets worse because on costs are value straight out. They have no corresponding financial benefit like rental income potential or capital gain to offset them. They directly erode your surplus cash and wealth.

An owner who treats the property purely as an investment will only incur essential on costs related to insurance and maintenance but not those related to lifestyle.

Finally, foregone rent and on costs are cash that you could have invested in growth platforms to generate extra wealth.

Putting all this together, the true cost of your accommodation is foregone rent + on costs + potential returns given up on these + unreleased capital.

By identifying the true or opportunity cost of your living arrangements, you can consider this separately against your needs and decide whether it is a luxury or subsistence cost. Do you need to spend this much on your accommodation, or is it an indulgence, a reward to be enjoyed as such? How does this choice affect your path to O?

- The combination of financial and nonfinancial benefits offered by residential property also clouds the value assessment.

Pure financial analysis is based on the now-familiar techniques of income and capital yield versus required return equation and comparative pricing. Price per square foot is a commonly used benchmark, particularly in tightly packed cities. Qualitative features, like architectural interest, beauty, build quality, environmental standing, location, peace, and rarity, however, are impossible to value consistently, and there can be an element of "the emperor's new clothes." You should factor these into your assessment, but with the cold eye of an investor rather than through dewy eyes behind rose-tinted spectacles.

At least someone on the buying team should focus uncompromisingly on defects and blights, because few properties are free of them.

For town houses or flats, there is a limit to the range of problems: damp, rot, subsidence, infestations, leaks, neighbour disputes, unauthorised building works, upcoming developments, and so on, but in the countryside, the scope for defectiveness rises exponentially.

Title is often a mishmash of various register entries, some full and some qualified; boundaries, if they exist at all, may bear little relation to maps; and rights of way, covenants, restrictions, way leaves, and easements may not be documented, registered, or apparent. Utility services can be patchy, particularly gas, water, and broadband. Surveyors exclude large parts of houses that they can't access and limit liability for those they can. And how can you tell if the fifty-year-old trees that shape the grounds are diseased and will soon die and fall over?

"Caveat Emptor" or "buyer beware" has struck fear and a sick feeling in the stomachs of plenty of house owners who have made unpleasant discoveries after purchase.

I worked with someone who competed to buy an expensive, beautiful country house with grounds. The marketing took place during spring and summer, when the trees were in full leaf, and the air was warm. The following February, he told me that once the trees were bare and the air cooled, the roar from the motorway, previously inaudible, was almost unbearable. I've known people who instruct agents to show only after 11:00 a.m. They claim it is "a more civilized time," but in reality, it is a ruse to avoid rush-hour traffic.

Unexpected noise is one of the most complained-about problems according to agents, and not just road traffic but also planes, trains, or perhaps off-road motorbikes, land rovers, or fox hunts. It takes a fortunate viewer to encounter all of these on one visit. Ordnance Survey maps are useful but not infallible. The same issues apply with footpaths across land, particularly in new national parks, where the usual trickle of hardy enthusiasts can turn into busloads of ramblers with too much time on their hands on a pub or tea-shop circuit.

When people buy in flood zones, near rivers, or on cliff edges are other classics where "picturesque" or "cheap" overcomes good sense, it shouldn't come as a surprise when the garden either becomes a lake or a lot smaller overnight and insurers rebel.

A final challenge is illiquidity. Residential property takes time to sell in a bad market (possibly years) and can't be relied on for ready cash like bonds or shares. To maximize liquidity, buy a "standard" property with a wide and well-funded buyer community.

• Beyond rental income potential and projected capital growth, where information is readily available from many local agents and market commentators, the drivers of value are largely subjective and therefore unreliable. You should not, however, ignore their impact; many buyers lead with the heart and the wallet, and appealing to them can pay dividends.

- The lack of a regulated and uniform exchange for buying and selling homes makes the process a free-for-all. Agents are lightly regulated, and codes of ethics and practice vary widely.

  Asking prices for residential property are set by agents with reference to comparable sales. This is imperfect; not only are some homes hard to find valid comparators for, but statistics become dated and irrelevant quickly, so when the number of transactions falls and stays low, there is little recent data. Further distortion arises when selling agents push the envelope and overprice new instructions. The Internet has helped open up property markets, but many remain highly localized with imperfect or unequally distributed information and random, ad hoc approaches to marketing.

  These inefficiencies allow large disparities between prices and values, as well as scope for buyers and sellers to gain or lose value, depending on their skill, patience, and judgement. You should practice the tips mentioned so far and investigate all possible negotiating strategies to gain maximum advantage.

- Supply versus demand and the availability of money drive prices.

  The supply channel is fed by two sources: new builds or redevelopments of previously uninhabitable property and existing homes being put up for sale. A supply shortage versus demand drives its price up. Your prospects for gain are, therefore, best in a place where there is no room for new homes and where owners hold the property for a long time. Prime Central London is an example; there is virtually no room for new homes, and developers have to convert commercial buildings or build high-rises. Many continental buyers, particularly Europeans, buy for life and pass property on to the next generation, further reducing the circulation of available stock.

As you continue along the spectrum, the least-appealing investment prospect is a place with almost infinite building land and fickle owners who have unsteady funding. Examples are Middle Eastern development hot spots like Dubai, a mix of desert and speculators and fashionable coastal Mediterranean holiday home centres like the Costa del Sol and Algarve, where the coasts are long and the hinterland wide, and there is an unremitting drip of homes for sale as moods change or money dries up.

Think carefully about these factors before buying any property.

On the demand side, human appetite for a safe, functional, appealing home is unwavering. The more people gather in a particular place, the greater the demand. And whether they rent or buy, their hunger drives demand and delivers investment returns, either income yield, capital value, or both. The first and main demand driver is, therefore, demographics—not just how many people but who: students, sharers, single dwellers, first-time buyers, newlyweds, starter families, established families, people upsizing or downsizing, retirees, second homers, investors, locals, overseas buyers, and so on.

Understand who the buyers are in your area and what influences their behaviour and funding. What are the social trends? There are a number of current forces:

- a growing number of single-person households and need for separate dwellings
- urbanization—the magnetic appeal of cities over countryside
- regeneration of inner-city areas to create appealing living spaces near to work
- rise of rural hub towns and villages that combine the best of country living with modern connectedness and amenities over disconnected areas or urban sprawl
- focus on eco-friendly, cost-efficient homes rather than over-sized, old drafty ones
- the boomer generation of 1946–64 downsizing to release cash for their children, top up their pensions, or avoid inheritance taxes

- "generation rent," seeking better quality, long-term solutions
- high-quality assisted-living communities for the elderly

An aging population and wider shifts from larger to smaller, energy hungry to efficient, isolated to connected, and solitary to community are changing the supply-and-demand dynamic and seem likely to accelerate over time. There is no certainty of a return to the old ways and no reason that swathes of the current housing stock should exist at all in the face of better replacement product.

The second demand driver is appeal, so location, size, quality, and connectedness of the home. Although some of this is subjective and particular, much is universal and easy to spot if you are looking. Skilled buyers find potential appeal hidden below the surface and missed by others. Bigger and clearer appeal at the time of sale equals greater likely demand and a higher price. Lesser or invisible appeal has the opposite effect.

Confidence is the third factor. Without it, people won't or can't safely commit to purchases or rentals and make do where they are. Consumer confidence indicators abound; look at unemployment levels and trends as well as spending and confidence surveys. All build to give a picture of the state and likely direction of home-buying appetites.

For homes, availability of money is a tap that switches on and off. It directly and powerfully fuels prices. You can anticipate it by watching the economy and beat its effects once it starts to become apparent. Acting on this is one of the most powerful wealth-generating techniques in the wealth game.

The money tap is fed by borrowing or mortgage lending, wages, and released savings. Watch mortgage-lending statistics and commentary about banks' appetite for releasing cash. The cheaper it is, the more people can afford to borrow; their cost of debt falls, translating into a lower return requirement and higher price. When credit tightens and interest rates rise, the tap shuts. Wages are important but move more slowly and without the high volatility. Released savings are becoming a greater influence as boomers pass money to the next generations, but they represent a small part of the overall picture. The dominant force is supply and cost of credit.

- Buy residential property first for its investment potential, and second for its use as a home. In the beginner and central phases of the game, it should be the cornerstone of your portfolio, and its unique advantages over cash, shares, and bonds make it a must-have asset.

- It's easier to predict a sustained price rise for residential property than for shares, bonds, or other assets with more complex or less clear price drivers. The clues are economic growth (particularly after a slowdown or recession), stable or rising employment, improving consumer confidence, low or stable interest rates, and competition amongst mortgage lenders.

    Also look for times when people have been unable to buy or sell for a few years and get on with their lives. This generates pent-up demand for change, which is released like the cork from a champagne bottle when the funding tap is switched on and confidence returns. Buyers waiting on the sidelines for signs of market improvement are quick to jump in, so as not to miss the boat, accelerating the upturn.

    Predicting house price falls within a twelve- to twenty-four-month period is harder, because credit doors shut suddenly and consumer confidence turns to pessimism without as much advanced warning, and economic statistics lag rather than lead. The danger in selling early and sitting on cash or holding back from entering the market in the hope of a property crash is that you can miss years of growth.

- Residential property offers a natural hedge against economic downturn, because we all need somewhere to live. In broad terms and ignoring localized factors, when buyer demand and prices are weak, more people rent, and income yields improve; when owner occupation returns, prices rise, but the availability of rental stock reduces to match lower demand, thereby maintaining rent levels.

XII

USING DEBT

As a lender or creditor, there's something solid and reliable about debt. You can tether to it for a while, safe in the knowledge that you've fulfilled your side of the bargain and that it'll deliver a set return over a certain time frame, as long as the borrower doesn't default. It's a perfect asset if you want low or no risk and certainty of financial outcome for minimal effort.

For a borrower or debtor, the tables are turned, and instead of paying now to receive later, you receive now and pay later. Your obligations begin with the loan, rather than ending with it, and disappear only when you have repaid the entire advance and all interest accrued during its term, which may run for years. Generating enough to do this is in your court alone.

In terms of effort and obligation, it is a one-sided contract loaded in favour of the lender, who can relax in the sun and live off the interest while the borrower toils to repay it. Of course, if the borrower lends the money to someone else at the same or a higher rate of interest, then the obligation to toil passes to that person.

Let's say you borrow £1,000 at a cost of 5% per annum interest for two years. You could spend the money on a holiday and work to pay off the loan from employment income over the next two years. Alternatively, you could lend it to someone at 8% per annum for two years, pocket £30 profit each year, and repay your original loan without needing to work for it. Either you work to repay the loan, or you make the loan work for you. One approach is a recipe for hard work and pressure; the other, a basis for wealth creation.

This chapter addresses the borrower's tale: What is debt, and how can you use it to enhance your wealth? If you owe money, it is almost certainly the single most important liability in your personal balance sheet. How it arrives there, what it's for, and how you get rid of it are questions that you need to have clear answers for. Lending, on the other hand, is simply a form of asset.

EIGHT FEATURES OF DEBT

Debt is unfairly maligned, and its providers are widely misunderstood. It is an incredibly powerful tool in the wealth game but, like any tool, needs to be used with care for a clear purpose. Gasoline is great for powering the car, and without it, you'll need a horse and cart or bicycle, but if you throw it onto a barbecue to speed up the lighting process, the whole thing may go up in flames. Food is indispensable, but too much of it or the wrong sort will make you unwell, and while an axe is useful for splitting logs, it becomes a dangerous liability in the hands of a five-year-old. Fortunately, unlike compounding, which happens naturally without any input from us, you can choose whether to pick this tool up and use it or leave it alone.

Lenders are in business to make a profit from lending. Their job is to lend as much as they can at the highest possible price above their own cost of funds to customers who will pay them back. There is no mystery in this, yet many consider them somewhere between bloodsucking monsters, unethical purveyors of toxic products to innocents, and a failed public service. Are their practices any less wholesome than big chemical, pharmaceutical, tobacco, food, or media companies—or any other business, for that matter? It doesn't matter. What should concern you are the answers to these questions: Who are they? Is the debt package the best available solution for your needs? Can you buy better elsewhere?

Before borrowing, consider the following features of debt. They appear obvious, but their simplicity is deceptive:

1. It must be repaid.

    Unlike equity, debt represents an obligation that must be repaid. It is the easiest test of whether an instrument is debt or not. If there's no repayment obligation, it's not debt, and for a taker of funds, this is important.

    Imagine that a funder advances £1,000 to help you start a business. If you offer a share of the venture in return, your backer gives up any right to demand repayment until the venture is sold or the business is wound up, and will then get only a share of what's left after all debts and other obligations have been met. This may be more than £1,000 if the business has prospered, but it may be nothing. If, on the other hand, the money is advanced as a loan, the funder can demand repayment of £1,000 in accordance with its terms—for example, at the end of the loan period or earlier—if you default on your obligation to pay interest.

2. The nominal principal (i.e., the amount of the initial loan) doesn't increase during the term. It reduces only by the amount of any repayments.

    This constancy caps the amount you have to pay back, which is great for future planning, but it makes no concession if your means of repayment disappears.

3. Interest not paid when due compounds.

    A lender is entitled to receive interest of an amount, either fixed or variable, and at times agreed at the outset. It is baked into their returns. If you fail to pay this, it rolls up alongside the principal outstanding and itself attracts interest. Punitive rates and penalties may be incurred, which exacerbates the compounding effect.

4. The present value of the principal loan erodes with inflation (i.e., it reduces in real terms).

   If inflation runs at 3% per annum, the real value of the loan erodes by this amount each year. The compounding principle works in reverse to your advantage, because each year that passes, the 3% reduction applies to an ever-decreasing balance.

   Lenders will, if the market allows, charge interest at a rate that exceeds inflation.

5. If the cost of debt is less than the return generated on the money borrowed, value is added. If it is greater, value is destroyed.

   The cost of debt for this purpose is the interest charged plus arrangement fees. The return is income and capital gain on the investment generated over the period of the loan. In the earlier example of financial engineering, you borrow at a cost of 5%, earn 8% on the money, and make 3% per annum profit. If the numbers are reversed, you make a loss of 3% per annum.

   The inflation effect compounds any profit and mitigates any loss. A profit of 3% per annum becomes 6% per annum when 3% inflation erodes the loan principal. A loss of 3% per annum is offset to nil when the inflationary benefit is factored in. Use the resulting rates to work out future or discounted present values, to compare geared and ungeared returns for the same asset, or to compare geared returns for one asset (e.g., property) with ungeared returns of another (e.g., shares).

6. Debt magnifies returns or losses when added to a project.

   Whereas compounding works slowly to grow or destroy value, debt turbocharges results, whether good or bad.

   The proper use of debt enables the ordinary person to act as a private-equity investor and create the equivalent of leveraged buyout structures around particular assets, creating maximum effect from minimum effort—or in this case, minimum equity.

How does it work? Since debt remains constant, all gains and losses of an investment go to the value of the equity. Debt acts as a multiplier.

For example, assume that Sarah and Tim have £100,000 each to spend on residential property. Sarah gears up by borrowing an additional £400,000, giving her a total spending power of £500,000. Tim does not borrow and has £100,000 to spend.

Sarah's debt-to-equity ratio is 4:1. Her gearing, also known as loan to value, is 80% (debt / total assets × 100 = £400,000 / 500,000 × 100 = 80%).

First, let's look at the capital gain for each over five years, assuming that the values of both properties chosen rise by 5% per annum:

Table 12.1.1

Sarah's capital gain over five years using debt

	year 0 £000	year 1 £000	year 2 £000	year 3 £000	year 4 £000	year 5 £000
property value	500	525	551	579	608	638
less debt	(400)	(400)	(400)	(400)	(400)	(400)
surplus	100	125	151	179	208	238

After deducting the initial £100,000 cash, she has generated a capital gain over the period of £138,000 equivalent to a CAGR of 18.9% and a money multiple of 2.38×.

Table 12.2.1

Tim's capital gain over five years with no debt

	year 0 £000	year 1 £000	year 2 £000	year 3 £000	year 4 £000	year 5 £000
property value	100	105	110	116	122	128

After deducting the initial £100,000 cash, Tim's gain is £28,000, with a CAGR of 5% and money multiple of 1.28×.

Before factoring in borrowing costs, Sarah has generated £110,000 more value and doubled her initial stake in less than four years. The price for achieving this is the cost of servicing and re-paying £400,000 of debt. We'll see later whether this is financially prudent or not.

The gearing effect on income is more complicated. The input is any rent received, and the outputs are the cost of any borrowing and any tax on rent.

If both players choose to live in their properties rather than let them out, the only adjustment will be for the cost of Sarah's borrowings. To be properly comparable with Tim, the total interest payable over the five years must be deducted from her gain. For simplicity, let's say that Sarah has a five-year, interest-only fixed-rate mortgage costing 3% per annum. On borrowings of £400,000, this is £12,000 per annum and £60,000 over the period.

Sarah's gain reduces to £78,000 (£138,000 – 60,000), equivalent to 12.2% compound annual return on equity and a money multiple of 1.78×. She is still £50,000 better off than Tim.

Where the numbers become interesting is when both players rent out their property. Assume that both properties earn a rental yield of 4% per annum as well as capital growth of 5% per annum, giving a combined pretax return of 9% per annum.

Table 12.1.2

Sarah's income and capital gain over five years using debt

	year 0 £000	year 1 £000	year 2 £000	year 3 £000	year 4 £000	year 5 £000
investment value	500	545	594	647	706	769
less interest		(12)	(24)	(36)	(48)	(60)
less debt	(400)	(400)	(400)	(400)	(400)	(400)
surplus	100	133	170	211	258	309

Her total extra return over the period before tax is now £209,000, equivalent to a CAGR of 25.3% and a money multiple of 3.09×.

Table 12.2.2

Tim's income and capital gain over five years with no debt

	year 0 £000	year 1 £000	year 2 £000	year 3 £000	year 4 £000	year 5 £000
investment value	100	109	119	129	141	154

After deducting the initial £100,000 cash, Tim's extra return before tax is £54,000, with a CAGR of 9% and money multiple of 1.54×.

Factoring in tax will enhance Sarah's position further against Tim's, because she can, at least at present, offset loan costs against rent for income tax purposes, while Tim has no loan costs and will pay the full marginal rate.

The example illustrates the power of gearing positive returns. Its multiplier effect works in the same way for negative ones. On the 4:1 or 5× debt structure, a 20% fall in house prices wipes out Sarah's entire equity base, and any more leads to negative equity.

7. Debt adds financial risk to an investment.

   A fixed, immovable object whose interest costs compound if you default is placed into a pot of variable, uncertain, and moving parts. Unless your investment provides a certain and risk-free return, which is certainly not the case for company shares and bonds or property, or you have a guaranteed method of repaying the loan and its interest, debt adds risk to the equation.

8. The riskier the loan (i.e., the greater the likelihood of default), the higher the cost or interest that will be charged by the lender.

   Risk is mitigated by offering valuable and realizable protection or security, such as a guarantee or charge over an asset or by demonstrating a low chance of default.

WHAT'S IT FOR?

In November 2013, UK personal debt including mortgages passed its September 2008 peak. The number was so large as to be almost incomprehensible: £1.43 trillion, which is £1,430,000,000,000, or £1,430 billion. By March 2015, it had grown by another £44 billion, and the UK Office for Budget Responsibility forecasts that by 2020, the number will reach £2.5 trillion.

That's a lot of debt—so much so that the Bank of England has warned that the "household-debt hangover" must be prioritized as the "holiday period" of low borrowing costs comes to an end and that a "modest increase in interest rates could render almost 25% of UK households in severe financial stress." Of these, 1.1 million UK households could be in "debt peril" by 2018, meaning that they spend more than 50% of their income on debt repayments.

It would seem a good time to ask why we borrow.

There are only two reasons:

1. To enable us to buy something now that we couldn't otherwise afford
    Instead of waiting until you have saved enough money to pay for an item, you buy it now and pay later. It's the commonest purpose.
2. To increase our wealth through financial engineering

So far, I have discussed the importance of creating surplus cash and putting it to good work in appreciators. Wasting your own money destroys wealth. Borrowing someone else's money and wasting that is the equivalent of committing financial suicide.

Here are two very simple golden rules. Spend borrowed money only on assets that (1) will not fall in value below the amount of the loan and (2) will produce a return higher than the cost of the borrowing.

Your asset is allowed to fall in value but not below the loan principal, so unless you have a rare asset whose value will never fall below a certain amount, create a safety margin by borrowing less than its purchase price.

If you follow these rules, provided that you can service the cost of the loan and aren't forced to sell the asset at a low value point, you will be okay.

It is clear that spending borrowed money on depreciators and consumables is folly. You should borrow only to fund appreciators (preferably productive ones).

This raises the question of whether you appreciate what you are borrowing for. It is a concept that I call disguised borrowing. This is a common pitfall in the game. The minute you borrow money, you have an obligation to repay it at some point in the future. Most people treat this as a deferred liability, one that arises only when the cash repayment is required and, in doing so, mistakenly forget that it is a liability from day one. A kind of rapid amnesia sets in, similar, I imagine, to that of women after childbirth, where the pain is forgotten. This condition is exacerbated by the tendency to associate debt with a particular asset or purpose, say a home or car or new kitchen. In reality, a debt in your personal balance sheet is a liability, no matter what it's for or when it is repayable.

Think about this: anything you buy while you still have any debt outstanding is effectively being funded with borrowed money.

You might think that because you are comfortably paying the interest on your mortgage or other debt and can see a way to repaying it in the future, surplus cash is yours to spend. It is not yours; it is borrowed. Only when all your borrowings are repaid is it yours. Every pound you choose to spend rather than to repay debt is a borrowed pound. You are borrowing to spend.

Now reread the two golden rules. Are you behaving prudently?

A further golden rule emerges: in order to reach O in the quickest time, apply all surplus cash flow to repay borrowings or to investments whose returns exceed the cost of those borrowings.

This ratchets up the spending bar a little further.

A simple example illustrates this:

Tom and Lucy each have a home and identical repayment mortgage (where interest and some principal are repaid each month). The monthly interest and repayment charge for each is £500. They both generate surplus cash flow of £500 per month. Tom spends this on socializing, holidays, and clothes. Lucy spends £100 on luxuries, invests £200 in shares that are expected to return more than the cost of the mortgage, and puts £200 towards repayment of the mortgage. Tom is borrowing £500 each month and spending it on consumables, so the net effect is value loss of £500 per month with no reduction in the loan size. Lucy is borrowing £100 per month for consumables, repaying £200 of loan, and borrowing a further £200 to engage in financial engineering through return arbitrage.

Another player, Sam, who is in the same mortgage position, uses his surplus £500 to take on and service another mortgage to buy residential property to let. Sam's overall debt position has increased, but so has his asset base and income-generation capability.

Tom gets credit for owning a property and having a mortgage in the first place, but whether a hedonist, misguided, or simply lacking self-control, he is doing nothing further to promote his cause in the wealth game. Lucy is following a middle path that should allow her plenty of sleep at night as value accretes steadily and O moves closer. Sam may crash and burn, but if all goes to plan, he will have gained a march on both of the others, albeit at greater risk and possibly with less sleep.

Whether it is better to repay debt or invest in higher-returning assets depends on the circumstances of the day. When standard mortgage rates jumped from 7% to 13% per annum in a few short stages during the early 1990s, it was an easy call to repay debt quickly. When interest rates dropped to 0.5% per annum after the 2008 financial crisis, if mortgages could be had for anything near this rate, it was worth holding the loan and investing in recovering assets.

A point to bear in mind when making the comparison is that personal loan interest is paid from taxed income, so the effect of repaying debt charging 5% per annum is equivalent to a pretax saving or return of 6.25% per annum for a 20% taxpayer and 8.3% for a 40% taxpayer.

Where else can you earn a guaranteed, risk-free, tax-free return that consistently beats bank deposit rates? A mortgage or other loan secured against an appreciator is a superb investment and savings vehicle. First, borrow money to purchase a higher returning asset, and next, divert spare cash to repay part or all of the debt that cuts your financial risk and earns you lenders' rates, tax-free and compounding monthly if the borrowing is a mortgage or typical personal loan. Repayment also creates capacity for future borrowings, opening the door to buy and hold or build strategies discussed later. It's a complete no-brainer.

The case is even more compelling for repaying unsecured loans taken to purchase lower returning or non-returning items. Here, there's no question of positive-value arbitrage between asset return and borrowing cost, so it's all downhill, while at the same time, loan costs will undoubtedly be higher, given the absence of security. Repaying a personal loan or a credit card debt costing 28% per annum delivers a return that even private-equity investors would get out of bed for.

To bask in the illusion of financial comfort, feeling and behaving rich, yet packing away your debts into a box marked "later" and mindlessly spending borrowed money is one of the greatest value-destruction strategies known to mankind. It's like drug abuse—bliss and altered mind states hide the underlying corrosiveness.

And who or what is the cause of this unhappy situation? Is it debt itself, lenders, the government, money, or is it the user? I'll leave that one to you. All that counts in the wealth game are your own choices and actions and the natural consequences that flow from them, and thankfully, these choices and actions are your gift to determine. In a free world, only you can say yes and no.

Playing the private-equity game
In my early days of work, a constant source of frustration and sense of personal failure was that I was simply a paid hand with no stake in the business. Looking around me, it was the same for a junior analyst or a managing director, barring a few share options granted along the way. "It's an income game," the head of the business told me at appraisal time. The income was indeed good relative to national averages, and it made plenty of my colleagues feel rich, or at least spend as if they were, but to me, it was just income—and heavily taxed at that.

How could I compete with partners in their own firms or owners of businesses who could earn the dividends of ownership as well as a capital gain when their business or share of it was sold? The glamour and kudos of working in a well-paid job seemed superficial and pointless in comparison, as I had no interest in showing off or feeling superior because of my chosen career. In fact, the years of study and training to gain professional qualification seemed more like a mental chain, holding me down and demanding that I put in the time and sweat to reap adequate financial rewards for all these efforts. To take a risk and become an entrepreneur now seemed foolhardy and unjustifiable. If I had left school early, learned some practical skills, and had a few more years in hand with less fear of losing if it all went wrong, now that would have been different.

The challenge was simple: how to reach O when I didn't own equity in the business, and the profits of my hard work were going to others. I had no interest in thinking and behaving rich when I was clearly not, resigning myself to a working underclass and giving up completely, or getting bitter and twisted with frustration.

The solution slowly dawned and now seems as clear as day:

- Get paid as much as possible, given the structure of the firm.
- Use salary to borrow money to buy residential property.
- Add company shares to the pot.
- Feed cash from earnings to service and repay debt.
- Watch the virtuous circle begin as assets begin producing and debt capacity grows.

Suddenly, I had an equity base. All my efforts in buying, funding, and managing assets were for my own benefit, not someone else's. The equity base was simply a separate business from my day-to-day workplace.

In this way, use your day job to fund a private-equity strategy. Private-equity, or venture-capital, investors make money by buying businesses, incentivizing management through an ownership share, and gearing up with debt. Cash from the business services debt and repays part or all of it, while equity value grows, benefitting the owners. If the business can be made to perform better, or if its prospects for future profitability can be improved so that it can attract a higher price multiple on sale than on purchase, even more value will be added for equity holders. When it works, the model is entirely self-sustaining without the need for more equity to be added.

Instead of buying private businesses, buy productive appreciators, residential property, and quoted company shares. You have the added benefit of a steady source of equity from outside your growth pot, as well as that generated by the assets themselves.

HOW MUCH AND WHEN?

How much?
Debt adds purchasing and gearing power but also cost and risk. You must weigh and balance these forces, taking account of your overall financial position and circumstances. How much can you borrow in the market, and what's a prudent amount?

The first can be answered by market testing. Present your case to a range of lenders, directly or through an intermediary, and see how much they'll advance you. This sets the outer parameters as well as provides details of loan terms. You'll certainly need to do this before securing finance.

The second requires desktop analysis. Assemble the relevant information, and prepare a cash flow forecast, run it through a set of affordability ratios, review risks, and decide on a sensible level. Adopt a banker's mindset and focus on default risk, not upsides. Put yourself in the lender's position, and look at the proposition objectively and critically.

On the cost side, set out the interest rate and repayment schedule. If the rate is variable, assume it will go up. How much you factor in for rate increases depends on your view of economic conditions, inflation prospects, and likely central bank action.

On the sources side, list all the income sources available to contribute to the loan servicing and repayment: salary, rent, dividends, interest, state benefits, and so on. The more sources there are, the less reliant you'll be on any single one. Now, add up your total after tax income from these sources, allowing for any interest offset from the loan itself. Do not include discretionary bonuses unless you have a history of receiving them, and your employer is performing well enough to afford them, and even then, scale back your expectations to the bare minimum. Include all relevant deductions for property rents, and allow for at least one month of void every year. Roll this number forward for at least three years with no increases.

Next, project forward your outgoings for the same period, factoring in any known increases, such as start-of-school fees, and inflate the total annually at a rate exceeding RPI inflation. The outgoings figure should be realistic, not simply aspirational, and allow for an element of spending on luxuries as well as all subsistence expenses.

The first year should be in monthly intervals; the second, quarterly; and the third and beyond, annually. At each measuring point, you now have three important numbers:

1. Loan interest and repayment costs
2. Cash available to service the above
3. The difference between 1 and 2

Having modelled the cash flow effects, consider how you will repay the principal. Do not rely solely on selling the asset, as this may not be achievable or desirable. How much can you repay from your own means over the next three to five years?

Affordability ratios are finance tools to help you evaluate credit default risk. Lenders will certainly be performing their own versions, and so should you. The two most important affordability ratios are cash interest cover and net gearing, or loan to value.

The first is a cash flow test that assesses your ability to service the loan. The formula is as follows:

cash interest cover = cash available to service interest and repayment of borrowings / loan interest and repayment cost.

If you have available cash in the year of £10,000, and loan costs are £5,000, the cash interest cover is 2×. You can cover the costs twice; in other words, your costs can double before you have difficulty. Alternatively, you can survive a halving of your available cash.

When companies borrow, they usually set 2× interest cover as the bare minimum, and lenders generally want to see over 2.5×. For individuals, particularly early in the wealth game, these cover levels are very limiting. Try turning the calculation around and asking what size of loan £5,000 per annum interest implies. For this purpose, let's assume that the £5,000 is all interest and no repayment and that the loan interest rates on different products are 4 to 6% per annum.

Loan size = annual interest payable / annual interest rate

Maximum loan at 4% interest = 5,000 / 0.04 = £125,000
Maximum loan at 5% interest = 5,000 / 0.05 = £100,000
Maximum loan at 6% interest = 5,000 / 0.06 = £ 83,333

In order to borrow more, you need to pay a lower interest rate or reduce your interest cover. If you reduce this to 1.25×, your available cash income increases to £10,000 / 1.25 = £8,000 per annum.

Available loan sizes now will be as follows:

at 4% = 8,000 / 0.04 = £200,000,
at 5% = 8,000 / 0.05 = £160,000,
at 6% = 8,000 / 0.06 = £133,333.

The closer you move to 1×, the less margin for slippage you have. Less than 1×, and you are insolvent.

The second affordability test, loan to value, is a balance-sheet test. It measures your overall indebtedness relative to asset base—in other words, how much debt risk is included in your wealth—and is a useful indicator of your ability to repay the loan. Loan to value is commonly used in the property world to assess the ratio of debt on a particular property or portfolio. The formula is as follows:

$$\text{loan to value} = \text{total debt minus cash} / \text{total}$$
$$\text{asset value (i.e., total debt + equity).}$$

Continuing the example, assume that you settle on interest cover of 1.25× and borrow £160,000 at 5% per annum. To add a further margin of safety you chose to borrow only 80% of the property value and contribute £40,000 of your own savings to buy a house for £200,000. (£160,000 / 0.8 = £200,000).

If these are your only asset and liability, your loan to value multiple is as follows:

$$\text{loan to value} = £160,000 / (160,000 + 40,000) = 160,000 / 200,000 = 0.8×,$$
$$\text{loan to value as a percentage} = 0.8 \times 100 = 80\%.$$

The property value can fall 20% before it reaches the loan amount. Any further fall creates negative equity. Lenders have, in the past, offered debt up to the property's value or even beyond to sweep up a borrower's other, more expensive debts or allow funds for refurbishment or development. Borrowing to this level is one of the factors behind the US subprime mortgage collapse in 2007–2008 and the associated repossessions.

Cash flow and ratio calculations provide the data and framework for decision making but are not safe to rely on without a commercial assessment of the risks.

This is your responsibility. Examine each source of your income, every category of living expenses, and the risk of interest-rate increases and asset-value falls. Assume that they will all turn negative. Setbacks tend to group together in a vicious spiral; the economy goes south, stock markets and property prices fall, bonuses and overtime disappear, jobs are lost, tenants go into arrears, and cash dries up. Whoever has cash to meet his or her needs is in a strong position; surplus cash opens the door to buying cheap and building an asset base for the future, but in a realm where cash is king, the overindebted and short of cash become slaves to it and are forced to sell fast at whatever depressed prices are offered.

It's impossible to predict with certainty the timing of downturns and bad things happening; the trick is to construct a debt package that builds in a comfortable safety margin for a realistic worst-case scenario, and, if at all possible, to keep some cash aside. In the early days of the game, the latter is often impossible, making the safety margin all-important.

Stress test your proposed borrowings for different worst-case scenarios to see how long you could survive. You should build in at least three months of available cash flow (preferably more) to give yourself time to solve or deal with whatever problems have arisen. Self-evidently, if you are in transition, without stability or a clear view of your financial and personal circumstances for the coming one to three years, do not commit to something as fixed and uncompromising as debt.

When should you use debt?
Over time and with practical experience, you'll develop an instinct about debt. This can be helpful, provided it doesn't override careful analysis. Before this instinct has a chance to develop, you are reliant on analysis and best guesses, plus whatever outside help is available. Attempts at timing the market will necessarily include an element of trial and error, and

in the early days of wealth creation, borrowing is likely to be borne more of necessity than opportunity.

As with any sense arrived at after the assimilation and processing of too many data points to label or count, instinct around debt can't be fully described. In simple terms, it means that conditions feel propitious, the purpose of the borrowing is attractively value enhancing, it is affordable within your risk tolerance, and market conditions feel right. There's a lot in that pot!

Instincts also develop for asset values. There are times when the opportunity to buy an appreciator is so compelling, either due to its quality, price, or both, that you can stretch boundaries. Assessing genuine cases rather than imposters requires skill and effort but is possible. With experience, you will also learn to detect frothiness in asset prices and tread carefully.

In terms of market conditions for taking on debt, you should look for

- promise of stable or growing economy with unemployment steady or falling;
- stable or rising asset values—borrowing to buy assets on the way down is risky;
- interest rates that are stable, falling, or likely to rise only slowly;
- moderate but stable inflation sufficient to erode the real value of the loan and to inflate asset values but not on such an upward trend as to risk unmanageable interest rate rises; and
- low borrowing costs relative to available returns.

In the recovery period after the 2008 financial crisis (broadly, 2010–2015), these conditions have applied, making it an excellent time to gear up if the financing could be found.

Getting the Best Deal

Securing debt on the best terms is another form of negotiation—you versus the lender. It's a mixture between a courtship and a battle. You will both be living together for some time, but rather than seeking happiness, your only objectives are avoiding unhappiness and making money. To this end, the terms agreed to at the outset are vital; get these wrong, and unhappiness and financial loss will follow.

Understand your opponents—your future relationship partners—before you deal. Who are they? What do they want? What are their values? How are they likely to behave when things go awry? The days of relationship lending are gone. Power resides with head offices, systems, and procedures, rather than local managers, so this due diligence is on the banks as institutions, rather than the people you deal with.

Certain universal truths apply to all banks and lenders. These leave limited scope for institutions to genuinely differentiate. All are in business to maximize profit, they need money to lend (this either comes from depositors or has to be borrowed from elsewhere), and this money costs—depositors require a return, and so do lenders to the lender.

How do they profit?

Lenders profit by charging more to lend money than it costs them to procure it. This is called margin or spread. Lenders also need to factor in the cost of interest and loan defaults and all business expenses.

Lenders like the highest margin relative to the risk of the loan. Remember the value equation works only when risk is factored in. A lender would rather lend at a margin of 2% over its cost of funds to a no-risk borrower than at 4% over to someone with a high default likelihood, where the lender would lose some or all of its money. Lenders like to give safe loans to customers who pay interest and make repayments on time and who are predictable and reliable.

Lenders do not like having to chase after borrowers or losing money. Yes, certain lenders do target high-risk customers and price their loans to reflect the higher default rates and costs of chasing people, but it's a very different business from healthy mainstream lending.

When do they lend?
Lenders lend when they have funds to lend and when margins are high enough. Deposit takers are highly regulated, because they hold our money; lenders are less regulated—most mainstream lenders (i.e., banks and building societies) are deposit takers and limited in the amounts they can lend relative to their assets. These solvency rules have been tightened, and the bar has been lifted since 2008. Only if they have lending capacity can they lend. Look at the published capital ratios of different banks to assess their financial strength, and take care to compare like for like, as the tests are being toughened to comply with the European rules in Basel III. Clearly, as a borrower, you are not so much interested in whether the lender will go bust but more how much it can lend and whether it may get into trouble and need its money back.

If lenders don't have the available funds, then they'll ration new lending to even the most valuable borrowers. Lenders run short of funds like anyone else. Perhaps deposit levels fall because customers aren't saving as much, or maybe the lender can't borrow on terms that work or at all. Another reason is that their assets (i.e., loans) become impaired because customers default and become less valuable to them, so they don't meet the solvency tests required for lending. When lenders are really struggling to meet solvency requirements or prevent losses, they will take every opportunity to recover loans already made; overdrafts are called in, renewals are rejected, and loan-arrangement fees multiply. This creates a perfect storm for customers who need loans most when times are toughest and invokes a hail of protest against the "unfair" or "immoral" behaviour of banks.

Think about these reasons for a moment, and you'll notice that they may all flow from the same cause—a weak economy in which businesses underperform, wages stagnate or fall, and unemployment rises. If these conditions combine with individuals and businesses being too indebted or with particular banks being mismanaged, the effects can multiply. From 2007 to 2009, money evaporated. Creditors called in their loans as confidence and asset prices collapsed, creating a vicious downward spiral that was only halted by massive injections of liquidity by central banks as lenders of last resort. Commercial lenders did what they could to raise funds; they ratchetted up interest rates on deposit accounts in a desperate attempt to attract money, and they borrowed from whomever they could, often at very high prices. They also stopped lending. To some degree, this is exactly what happens in every recession.

The margin issue is different. If a bank can't make enough margin to cover its overheads and selling costs and deliver a profit, it might as well close down until the situation improves. In effect, this is what happens. The lending tap is switched off, overheads are cut, and any remaining staff are left to manage existing accounts. Fund providers set their lending rates for customers by reference to central bank interest rates and competition. Those that want to gain market share sharpen their rates to attract more business; others for whom profit is paramount will seek opportunities to lend at higher margins.

When do they put their prices up?
If lenders' own borrowing costs rise, they'll pass these costs on to customers if they want to maintain their profit margins. Irrespective of market rates, lenders will also raise their interest charges to customers if they think that they can make more money; that is, not lose more income from

departing customers than they gain in higher charges from the remainder. Key to this decision is whether there are other lenders who may offer cheaper loans to attract customers. Low competition leads to higher charges.

Lenders also change their strategies from time to time and decide to focus more on one type of borrower than another. For those existing or potential customers who fall out of favour, charges are often raised in order to encourage them to move elsewhere. When you stand back and consider banks and lenders as the commercial creatures they are, none of this should be a surprise.

So first, find a lender who is keen to have your business, and then present it with the safest possible proposition. The first is easily done by market testing a range of lenders to test their appetites.

Your commercial proposition combines three elements: financial background and credit history, current circumstances, and the terms of the particular "ask."

Financial background self-evidently evolves over time, but, like compounding, it builds automatically. The trick is to gently steer a course that generates a blemish-free history. At worst, it should be neutral, arising from caution and prudence; evidence of good judgment and a track record of loans repaid and wealth generated is a bonus that can be layered into the storybook over time. A catalogue of overreaching, overpromising, missed targets, broken agreements, and county court judgements—or even a hint of financial irresponsibility—will turn lenders off, or at best cause them to harden terms and conditions.

As for your current circumstances, lenders look for stability and predictability as risk indicators. A school leaver or college graduate just starting a first job and sharing a new, rented flat is a different proposition than someone who has been at the same job for three years and has a stable, proven home setup. Since debt is an obligation, those who can demonstrate life commitments, work ethic, and proven staying power in tough times are seen as better risks than disengaged loners with dropout tendencies or reckless greed merchants and gamblers.

Finally, would you lend yourself this amount on these terms? One of the reasons for stress testing your own package before going to lenders is that it highlights risks that any commercially minded lender will pick up. What can you offer to mitigate these risks? More security, outside guarantors, more safety margin, evidence of job security, or prudent financial behaviours?

Prepare yourself and your proposition just as if you are packaging an asset for sale.

XIII

Compounding

Compounding is as natural as time itself, a spiralling escalator that never stops. Whether you stand on it and effortlessly glide upwards or take some extra steps to boost the process, it offers a unique advantage to travellers over those who choose to plod up the staircase alongside it. It's a free service, without age threshold or limit, available to you twenty-four hours a day, 365 days a year, every year. There's always room for you, and there's no need to book. You just need to turn up and get on board.

Why spiralling? Because it tracks a virtuous circle of wealth building, adding force to the natural upward motion of this wheel of fortune. How does it add the force? By applying returns to assets *and* to their previously accumulated returns.

Picture an asset wheel where all the returns on assets, both income and capital, are removed and spent on depreciators and consumables or given away. The only propellant to this wheel is new cash from outside. It still spirals upwards but very slowly. If this feed is removed, the wheel will stop and begin to reverse as the drag of inflation overpowers it. This is a setup without compounding, a downward spiral towards zero value.

With compounding present, some or all of the income and capital gains generated by assets is kept inside the wheel, and as it rotates, further income and capital gains accrue to the enlarged vehicle and so on, generating exponential growth. The wheel becomes a self-sustaining wealth-creation machine.

Albert Einstein referred to compounding as "the eighth wonder of the world; he who understands it, earns it, he who doesn't pays it."

To make compounding work for you, examine it more closely in different scenarios. This will help you make sound choices.

TIME

The slow, deliberate nature of compounding doesn't inspire grand news headlines in a world of speed and action, nor does it tend to grab the attention of the ordinary person. By its nature, its effects are glacial, like watching the movement of the minute hand on a watch. Add to this the knowledge that it happens naturally, without your doing anything. The watch can stop, but time continues regardless, and so does compounding.

Powerful, yes, but is it exciting to the ordinary person? No. We all understand that time passes inexorably and that our quota of it is limited, but our tendency is to recognize and perhaps act on this only when it begins to feel as though it is running out—perhaps in our midforties onward. The issue for compounding is worse, since, unlike time, many do not even register its existence. The first we might hear of it is towards the end of a working life, around retirement time, when a financial adviser produces an illustration of future pension payouts and the monthly contributions needed in the meantime to fill the gap in expectations. Perhaps twenty to thirty years of previous compounding opportunity may have been squandered through ignorance, and getting the point now is not much help, as time has run out.

The "campaign for compounding awareness" has a big job to do—to somehow help people link outcomes twenty to thirty years into the future with actions now and to appreciate this particular example of cause and effect and its place in the financial well-being firmament.

Why not start with this question: "How long does it take for compounding to make a difference?" At least this gives time periods to work with, to overlay onto your own life. The easiest way to answer this is to look at some numbers. Since we are all different, the amounts that we think make a difference will vary wildly, whether we look at them in absolute terms or as percentages. Better to have the tool kit so that you can do the calculations and make your own mind up.

For simple compounding calculations, such as the effect of compounding returns on an asset, the future value (FV) formula from before can be used:

$$FV = \text{starting value} \times (1 + r)^t.$$

This works for annual compounding but needs adjusting for more frequent compounding, such as quarterly or monthly. It also doesn't help you to calculate the future value of a pot you are adding outside funds to as well as allowing to compound.

To do this, you can either build your own spreadsheet by inputting all the cash flows as they arise and applying the growth or interest rate to the growing balance, or you can use one of the many online calculators. I would recommend the latter, unless you have a complex scenario or need a lot of detailed output information and have the necessary skills. Financial spreadsheets should carry a health warning: they require technical skill in building, an understanding of the underlying financial concepts, accounting and taxation rules, reliable inputs derived from correct data, and reasonable assumptions. In the wrong hands, they can deliver a large volume of rubbish dressed as accuracy.

Fortunately, our purpose here is limited—to illustrate the effects of compounding in different scenarios—so either our FV formula or online calculators will suffice. As to the latter, I suggest searching "online compounding calculator" and playing with various ones until you find one that suits.

To shed light on the starter question, I've used the FV formula and my calculator to produce a ready reckoner which compares the effects of simple versus compound interest at 5% per anum on an investment of £1,000.

Table 13.1

Compounding ready reckoner

	0 years	5 years	10 years	15 years	20 years	25 years	30 years
FV compounded	1,000	1,276	1,628	2,079	2,653	3,386	4,322
absolute increase every 5 years		276	352	451	574	733	936
total return over entire period %		28	63	108	165	239	332
average annual return %		5.6	6.3	7.2	8.3	9.6	11.1
FV simple interest		1,250	1,500	1,750	2,000	2,250	2,500
extra value compound FV versus simple FV		26	128	329	653	1,136	1,822
% value increase compound FV versus simple FV		2.1	8.5	18.8	32.7	50.5	72.9

The first thing I notice is that with compounding, I'll double my money in fifteen years and double that number again in less than fifteen more years—fourteen years and seventy-three days to be precise. That would take me from age twenty to fifty. Simple interest takes an extra five years for the first doubling alone, and a further doubling is some way off the chart.

It appears that the effects of compounding start to become pronounced after ten years and ramp up from there, with the average annual return increasing by about 1% per annum for every five years that pass. At the five-year mark, the results are uninspiring. By compounding simple interest of 5% per annum, the arithmetic average return reaches 6.3% per annum at ten years, which is 26% higher than the simple interest rate. At fifteen years, it is 7.2% per annum, and by thirty years, it exceeds 11% per annum. These are worthwhile increases, particularly as the only requirements for their achievement are to deliver 5% per annum every year and reinvest the entire return from the outset.

Absolute increases tell the same story, growing over 27% in each five-year period. By year ten, the extra value generated by compounding has begun to run away from the simple interest scenario and generate worthwhile sums.

The ten-year theme emerging here is convenient, because, personally, I feel that fifteen years is too long for any kind of detailed personal planning. The end date is too far away to properly visualize, and it gives only two instalments in a thirty-year career. I prefer ten-year intervals, as they sit well with life periods—for example, from twenty to thirty, we are getting started in a career and home, single or married but without major overheads; from thirty to forty, we spend on a mortgage and children, if they come; and from forty to fifty, we are in peak earnings and spending, but costs tail off as we head to O. This is a loose framework, and start and end dates will vary. At some points earlier in my career, I projected in five- or seven-year slots to reflect rapid life changes.

This raises a further question relating to time: What annual rate of return will double my money in a particular time frame, say ten years or even five years? Using some trial and error with the FV formula, the answer for ten years is 7.2% per annum, and for five years, it is 14.9% per annum. The first of these looks realistically achievable, with a modest amount of risk, while the latter is clearly challenging, year on year, for five years. To plan to achieve this return, one would need to take significantly higher risk or fund asset purchases with borrowings to leverage returns.

Anyone who has ever played backgammon understands the power of doubling dice on the outcome. The more doubles played in a game, the higher the result is ratcheted for the winner. In the wealth game, you're the only player, so the more often you can double, the better.

FEEDING THE MACHINE
What happens if you add cash or assets to the compounding pot?

So far, I've just looked at the change in a fixed-size pot over time. This doesn't mirror life in practice where we tend to add savings to our pot either at regular intervals or as occasional lump sums. We may also dip into the pot for spending on consumables or depreciators, but ignore this, because it makes the calculations unnecessarily complicated and clouds the picture without good reason.

At this point, I recommend that you reach for an online compounding calculator and plug in some numbers yourself. Our FV formula as it is won't help.

Using one of these calculators, I have updated the ready reckoner above using the same start investment of £1,000 and simple interest rate of 5% per annum compounded as before, to show the future values of your investment if you add cash of different amounts from outside the pot each month. The results are instructive:

Table 13.2

Compounding effect of adding cash each month

	0 years	5 years	10 years	15 years	20 years	25 years	30 years
FV compounded	1,000	1,276	1,628	2,079	2,653	3,386	4,322
£20 pcm		2,602	4,648	7,259	10,589	14,841	20,267
£40 pcm		3,929	7,666	12,437	18,525	26,295	36,213
£60 pcm		5,255	10,685	17,615	26,461	37,750	52,158
£80 pcm		6,581	13,704	22,794	34,397	49,204	68,103
£100 pcm		7,907	16,722	27,973	42,332	60,659	84,049

Note that different online calculators can deliver different results depending on their set up. These numbers are taken from the official US Government Securities and Exchange Commission calculator and assume annual compounding.

A danger with this table is that you focus on just the large numbers and overlook the investment made over the period. For example, over ten years of adding £100 per calendar month (or £1,200 per annum), the extra investment is £12,000 on top of your initial £1,000, leaving a gain of £3,722. As the power of compounding begins to work, the results improve dramatically, and the gain more than doubles over the next five years to £8,973.*

$$*£27,973 - (1,200 \times 15) - 1000 = 27,973 - 19000 = £8,973$$

Increasing contributions to the pot creates significant extra value over time, because these additions generate returns that are themselves compounded.

Adding cash to the compounding pot is like changing to a higher gear on a bicycle on a gentle downhill slope. Gravity alone allows you to cruise, but by changing up a gear and pedalling, you go faster and travel farther. If the track levels or turns uphill, the extra momentum you have generated will carry you on, possibly until you reach another downhill section. A year of weak or negative investment returns will slow wealth gains or reduce net worth for the player who is relying solely on compounding, whereas the player who is feeding the machine with cash as well has a better chance of staying ahead. This is extraordinarily important because when investment gains return, both players will start from a completely different place. One's assets may be 10% up, and the other's may be 10% down, a difference of 20%, and it is these assets that begin compounding again.

TIMING

How does the timing of contributions affect future values?

As a variation of the last exercise, let's look at the effect of making contributions either at the beginning or at the end of a period. Given the nature of compounding, it is clear that earlier contributions will be more valuable than later ones, because they will have longer to compound, but how much more valuable?

Table 13.3 shows the future values of an initial investment of £1,000 and monthly contributions of £60 per calendar month made at different times in the period.

Sienna makes extra contributions of £60 per calendar month for the first five years and nothing thereafter.

Charlie makes extra contributions of £60 per calendar month for five years (years sixteen through twenty).

Edward makes extra contributions of £60 per calendar month for the last five years of the period.

All three players invest the same overall, £4,600 (£1,000 + (720 × 5) = 1,000 + 3,600 = 4,600). As before, interest compounds at 5% per annum.

Table 13.3

Effects of different investment timings on compounding

	0 years	5 years	10 years	15 years	20 years	25 years	30 years
FV compounded	1,000	1,276	1,628	2,079	2,653	3,386	4,322
Sienna	1,000	5,255	6,706	8,559	10,924	13,942	17,794
Charlie	1,000	1,276	1,628	2,079	6,632	8,464	10,802
Edward	1,000	1,276	1,628	2,079	2,653	3,386	8,300

Note that all compounding is annual not monthly. These numbers are taken from the US Government Securities and Exchange Commission calculator.

In year zero, all scenarios show the initial £1,000 investment. Over the first five years, Sienna adds £720 per year, totalling £3,600, which, combined with her initial investment and accrued interest, delivers a balance of £5,255. Charlie and Edward make no contributions over this period, and their end-of-year-five balances are £1,276, which is their initial £1,000 compounded at 5% per annum.

Sienna's base for future compounding is now over four times higher than that of the other two, placing her at an unassailable advantage. Every year that follows, compounds from that higher opening number deliver a final balance after thirty years of £17,794.

At the end of year fifteen, Charlie adds £720 each year for five years, so by the end of year twenty, he has built a higher compounding base than Edward, who doesn't start making additional contributions for another ten years.

Over the thirty years, Sienna makes an overall gain of £13,194 (17,794 − 4600), or 287%, an arithmetic average of 9.6% per annum. Charlie's gain is £6,202 (10,802 − 4,600), or 135%, equivalent to 4.5% per annum. Edward gains £3,700 (8,300 − 4,600), or 80%, equivalent to 2.7% per annum. By investing her additional £3,600 early, Sienna gains over twice as much as Charlie and 3½ times as much as Edward.

To show the compounding effect on annual returns over the entire period, use the compound annual compound annual growth rate (CAGR) formula to calculate CAGR:

$$CAGR = (\text{end value} / \text{start value})^{(1/t)} - 1,$$

$$\text{Sienna's CAGR} = £17,794 / 4,600^{(1/30)} - 1 =$$
$$3.87^{0.033} - 1 = 1.046 - 1 = 0.046 = 4.6\%,$$
$$\text{Charlie's CAGR} = £10,802 / 4,600^{(1/30)} - 1 =$$
$$2.35^{0.033} - 1 = 1.029 - 1 = 0.029 = 2.9\%,$$
$$\text{Edward's CAGR} = £8,300 / 4,600^{(1/30)} - 1 =$$
$$1.80^{0.033} - 1 = 1.020 - 1 = 0.020 = 2.0\%.$$

This highlights two things: first, as seen before, the compound interest rate required to deliver a given FV is lower than the simple interest rate required. Be careful not to overlook the power of compounding when comparing the two rates. Sienna needs to earn 9.6% per annum simple interest to deliver the same outcome as 4.6% per annum compound interest. Second, the later you make additional contributions, the greater the drag on the effective CAGR. Remember that all players are earning 5% per annum compound interest, but Sienna's £3,600 contribution misses out on some of this during the first five years, because she invests monthly throughout rather than as a lump sum at the start. Charlie and Edward miss out on far more, because they start contributing their £3,600 from years sixteen and twenty-six, respectively.

REAL-LIFE SCENARIOS

So far in this chapter, three fuels for value gain have been identified:

1. Time—the earlier you begin investing, the longer the compounding opportunity.

2. Extra contributions—the more assets you add to the pot along the way, the greater the compounding benefit.

3. Investment returns—the higher the annual investment return, the quicker you double the value of your assets, allowing you to achieve more doublings in your lifetime.

The first two, as long as you are earning more than subsistence, require effort but are in your control. The third depends on your risk appetite, the level of returns you target, and the actual return you manage to deliver, which is a function of your skill and judgement as well as factors outside your control.

Leaving risk appetite and returns aside (because I've addressed them already), the first two elements point to a single course of action: direct all surplus cash as soon as it is available to savings, productive appreciators, or appreciators by deferring spending on depreciators and consumables.

This is a tall order, of course, and unless you are an ascetic or robot, there will be some leakage for luxuries. The point, however, remains that even if you can't plug the holes completely, you should do our utmost to minimize value leakage so that compounding gets the chance to work. Failure to do that is like throwing assets from the up escalator to the down one.

Which areas of spending can be deferred? While any luxury can be resisted altogether, deferred, or, in some cases, substituted for a cheaper version, four stand out: cars, homes, children, and exotic holidays. I have discussed cars and home purchases, so let's continue with home improvements, where the cost-benefit analysis is often misconceived.

Home Improvements

During my married life, we have refurbished every property we ever bought, spending hundreds of thousands on extensions and upgrades, in part for our own pleasure and in part for investment, but anything other than an extension depreciated. After ten years of hard use, any kitchen or bathroom will start to show its age, and decorations, roof tiles, woodwork, wiring, and plumbing will deteriorate. Tenants will start to haggle, and buyers will factor in the cost of replacement. An estate agent friend in London summed up the problem: "People in this area tend to buy houses, spend a fortune on doing them up, and sell them ten to fifteen years later, at which point they need doing again."

Aside of any extra space created by the works, all the extra value has been utilized along the way. The message is simple: to maximize financial gain, refurbish as near to the point of sale or rental as possible.

Consider this example. John spends £100,000 on interior refurbishments (kitchen, bathrooms, redecorations, and carpets) to a newly purchased home. Terry makes do and waits five years until spending on the same work. In each case, the cost adds an equal amount of value on the day that it is completed.

Let's assume that the refurbishment depreciates at 10% per annum on a straight-line basis and that Terry is able to invest the £100,000 at 5% per annum compounding.

The future value for each person after five years is as follows:

Terry—using the FV formula, he has a future value of £127,628 ($100,000 \times 1.05^5 = 100,000 \times 1.276 = £127,628$).

John—depreciation is 10% of the original cost each year, so £10,000 per annum. Over five years, this reduces the value of the improvements to £50,000.

After five years, Terry is £77,628 wealthier than John simply by waiting. John has effectively spent £50,000 of depreciation and £27,628 of foregone investment return.* This is the effective or true or opportunity cost of spending on personal use, a luxury, rather than selling its benefit to a buyer. A rational player considers this cost (or at least an estimate of it) before doing the work. The choice is simple—spend the money now for your own pleasure, or invest it to build wealth and reach O sooner.

*This analysis is oversimplistic, because in practice, the cost of the specified home improvements will rise. A rise won't affect Terry's wealth position; the pot available for refurbishments will still be £127,628 after five years, and he can spend up to this level, but it will affect John's wealth total. Let's say that the costs rise 5% per annum over the five-year period to £127,628. The depreciating effect is 50% (5 × 10%) leaving a value of the work for John of £63,814, a small improvement compared with costs staying the same. Even a 10% per annum cost rise delivers only £80,525 when depreciated back.

There is a funding shortfall for Terry if costs rise faster than investment returns. A 7% rise in costs would generate a bill for the improvement works of £140,255 after five years, compared with his pot of £127,628, leaving him £12,627 short. This is not a problem—he can either trim the improvement specification to match his pot size or find the extra money from elsewhere, in which case the extra cost is offset directly by the value obtained. Both options leave him with net value of £127,628.

Children

Our first daughter was born when I was thirty-five. There was no design in this; it simply happened at that point. I was ten years past the age at which I'd mentally pencilled in "family" as a youngster and had been long overtaken by most of my friends. From the age of twenty-three, when I began proper work, to thirty-five, I benefitted from twelve years of compounding before subsistence expenses began to multiply. I didn't recognize quite how helpful it was until I was into my thirties and began to notice the increasing volume of noise about financial strains coming from my friends just as I was finally beginning to feel some elements of early wealth. Seeing cash drain away to fund the paraphernalia around children confirmed that a halcyon period for my finances had just ended.

The lesson is simple: delay having children as long as you can.

Luxury holidays

Luxury travel is great, but it ceases to be luxury if it becomes everyday. Furthermore, to overdo it on children denies them the opportunity to discover it for themselves later in life and sets an expectation level that is hard to exceed. Travel and exploration, however, is something that everyone should do if they can. As something of an expert on shoestring travel as well as having savoured the odd dip into luxury, I can recommend a ratio of about 80:20 (20% being luxury) as being very satisfactory at middle age. As a younger, single person into my midthirties, I was more than happy with 99:1, but I have softened, although as the prospect of travelling light without children enters the horizon, I think the pendulum will swing back.

From a financial and compounding perspective, this works perfectly. The trick is to keep all thoughts of guaranteed easy luxury at bay for as long as possible and develop the courage, resourcefulness, and resilience necessary to step into the different worlds of ordinary people. Not only is this more interesting and stimulating but it also rewards with the most vivid and vibrant experiences and memories. Value leakage is minimized, and compounding builds options for untold luxuries in the future.

Status pressures in some social groups almost dictate terms for the required number and type of holidays. This kind of pack mentality is clearly to be avoided in a serious quest for O. There's a time and place for opulence, and our net worth is a better determinant of when and where that is than our family, neighbour, or friend.

Doubtless you get the picture, so I won't continue with gadgets, dining out, designer clothes, accessories, or any of the other luxuries that tempt precious cash away from the compounding escalator.

XIV

The Art of the Pot

There is no finished product in the wealth game, only a series of working models with short life-spans. At no point do you sit back, say, "It's done," and switch off. You design, make, hone, and adapt your pot in a process of constant evolution as your needs and resources change. What starts with sweat, grit, and determination is soon supplemented by rewards and the wherewithal to build using your capital and the efforts of others. But nothing is rigid and fixed for long; yes, there are elements of structure and solidity, but these are on shifting foundations. Everything is fluid.

You should recognize this, stay flexible, and not cling to things as if they are permanent or can deliver any lasting security. This will tie you in knots and cause suffering. Over the course of the game, your job is to commit wholeheartedly to phases of play, complete tasks, and move on, leaving behind the props and materials previously required and all the time evolving and improving with all your available physical and mental energy. You gain material weight, you lose material weight, the job grows, it shrinks, it grows again, and it shrinks; you shift from simple to complex to verging on chaos back to simple again. Stepping back from this ebb and flow allows you to see more clearly with detachment and equanimity, make sounder decisions, and act wisely—behaviours that naturally create a virtuous circle of improvement.

After lots of discussion about cash, assets, and financial techniques for wealth building, it is worth asking what exactly you are trying to create. The objective, O, should be clear and fully absorbed by now—"I can live the life I want without needing to work for money again"—but what are the steps before this working model is reached? After all, O is just another staging post, and the pot needs to be fit for its purpose from the start.

A current buzz phrase in personal finance is investing for outcomes, which, like many freshly badged concepts, is a rehash of old ones. At O, the purpose of your pot is to provide you with money—not an indeterminate amount for general, unspecified future needs but a very precise measure: enough to allow you to live the way you want without needing to work for money again. If, in practice, it delivers a bit more, that's fine. If it delivers a great deal more, you've spent too long making something that is partly redundant. If it delivers too little, you haven't reached O and never did.

Before reaching O, the pot can't be relied on to meet all future needs. It isn't big enough. Somehow, it must support your current needs where necessary and grow to sufficient size to see you over the finish line. This challenge takes you straight back to the question of where to put your cash or, more particularly, how to allocate it between different growth platforms. Even in the early stages of the game, when capital is small or nonexistent and funds are tight, there are more choices than you might think. Later, the need for asset management becomes apparent.

This chapter starts to consider the art of using the raw ingredients—cash, shares, bonds, and property—with the help of debt and compounding, to make a pot that is fit for your purpose. It is neither too big nor too small and is a worthwhile product of your efforts rather than one that is not fit for purpose, is over- or undersized, or is not a worthwhile product of your efforts. The key to this is attribution.

ATTRIBUTION

Attribution, or hypothecation, is a refinement of mere accumulation. It is gathering for a specific purpose and flows naturally from the exercise described earlier of listing what matters to you.

The verb *attribute* means "to regard something as belonging to, made, or being caused by something else." I use it here to mean particular assets belonging to particular needs. The concept is well understood by governments that direct certain tax revenues into a general pot and earmark others for specific spending. Similarly, savers often put money aside into a separate place for a particular future use. The idea is to preserve the resulting asset pot from being ransacked by competing needs.

Imagine two people setting up vegetable gardens from a plot of tatty scrubland. The area is full of rubbish, grass, weeds, and stones that need to be cleared. After a few days of hard work, this is done, and they can begin to dig the beds.

Arthur is very organized and has already decided to grow only plants that his whole family likes, don't take up too much room, and are worth the time and effort (i.e., they are expensive to buy in supermarkets). The chosen short list is selected premium vegetables: broccoli, celeriac, fennel, runner beans, salad leaves, spinach, tomatoes, and tender vegetables, such as okra and aubergine. Arthur plans ahead several years and also adds some perennials, like asparagus, artichokes, and rhubarb.

He digs three separate beds to allow rotation from season to season, each big enough for phased planting during the year and to provide adequate growing room for individual plants. A brick pathway divides each and allows easy access. He then checks the quality and type of the soil, adds green manure, and plants the first crops.

Marianne, meanwhile, digs one big bed, adds some manure, and then goes to buy a selection of seeds, deciding in the shop to buy packets that look good or are on special offer. Returning to the patch, she plants all the seeds.

As the first season progresses, Arthur harvests, plants, and harvests again, utilizing all the produce and saving many trips to the supermarket. Marianne also harvests what can be used, but much isn't wanted and goes to seed. As the large bed becomes tangled and chaotic, she loses track of what is growing, tires of the effort, and gives up and goes to the supermarket instead.

Over the next two years, as his family gets bigger, Arthur refines and extends his garden, with new areas dedicated to herbs, berries, and fruit trees, and the kids are given a space to grow what they want. A wildflower area is added, along with two beehives. Marianne revisits the idea of starting again but loses heart in the face of Arthur's glorious production empire. Her sad plot has been taken over as part of the children's play area and will require complete reshaping to be productive again.

Eventually, Arthur's needs shrink, and the growing area is cut back to one bed. The garden has provided self-sufficiency and more; it has done its work. Marianne also needs less now and looks back on her years of hard work earning the money to buy fruit and groceries.

The lessons are clear: By planting and nurturing crops for specific needs at set times, Arthur has designed and created a garden that delivers on track throughout the year, and its rewards justify the effort. Marianne's cavalier attempt without any clear plan or purpose produces an abundance of unwanted stock and fails to provide varieties that are needed or any consistency of supply. Not surprisingly, the incentive to keep working at it is lost. Her lack of attribution isn't the only cause of this disappointing performance, but it has played a part.

In finance, conventional wisdom is that during his or her working life, the ordinary person should buy a home with a mortgage, pay down the loan, and contribute to a pension scheme that will supplement the state pension on retirement. Remaining cash is spent on living and, if lucky, a few luxuries. The logic is that by the time you stop work, all being well, you will have a home that is bought and paid for and a satisfactory income for life. On paper, this sounds reasonable enough, but it conveniently glosses over two major flaws: first, it takes too long and consigns the healthiest and most active years of your life to working for money, and second, it delivers the bare minimum, if that—a small reward for a near lifetime of work. Somehow, you must up the ante.

Adopt the home and pension elements, but add further growth platforms; shares in a tax-free wrapper, like a private pension or Individual Savings Account (ISA); a rental property or two; more shares; and so on. With finite wages, the only way to fund these additional assets is to divert income away from wasteful spending and to save and invest without stopping until you reach O. Attributing funds to particular near- and far-term needs and badging assets to match them helps.

An insight into my own experience illustrates this. At the beginner phase of the wealth game, I identified three future needs: home, school fees for any children I might have, and retirement living expenses. Attributing assets at this stage was easy, as I had none to start with. Without savings or inherited wealth, my only route to build assets was to save and invest. At the age of twenty-three, I borrowed £1,500 from my mother for a deposit (later repaid) and bought an apartment in Clapham with a school friend. This was attributed to "home." I also started paying into a pension to provide for retirement income. Within three years, after a rise in property values, my friend found another to buy me out, and with £12,000 of equity gain, I bought a place of my own half a mile away.

Step number three on the property ladder was to set the modus operandi for future purchases. Holding on to my Clapham home, I bought a very old and run-down semidetached cottage on the Isle of Wight for not very much, funded with savings and some money borrowed from a friend. It was unmortgageable, and the surveyor recommended complete demolition. Two years later, having saved some money, I hired tradesmen to gut and restore it to habitability. As well as providing a much-needed bolt-hole near the sea, this was to pay for school fees. It didn't matter that I had no girlfriend at the time or any near-term prospect of producing offspring. To me, it was an each-way bet: if I was lucky enough to have children, I'd have choices for their education by being able to fund private schools, and, if not, I'd be able to buy a yacht and go travelling. From that time on, it was always the "school fees" pot.

Sixteen years later, the cottage was sold at six times the total cost of purchase and refurbishment, representing a pretax compound annual growth rate of 11.9% per annum over the period.* After capital gains tax, the multiplier and return were 4.8x and 9.8% per annum. We put the proceeds into a small house in Southsea for my mother, who had run out of funds. By this time, junior school fees were underway and being met from salary, and a new equities pot had been set up for secondary school and university fees, so the house was redesignated "retirement income/next generation." Two years after that, it morphed again when my mother died suddenly. Unable to sell, we let out the house for a while and sold when the market picked up, putting the proceeds into the schooling and university pot. The original "school fees" pot was united with the new one.

*The compound annual growth rate (CAGR) formula is (end value / start value) $^{(1/t)}$ − 1. In this case, the purchase and renovation cost was £40,000, and the final selling value was £240,000:

$$CAGR = (240{,}000/40{,}000)^{(1/16)} - 1 = 6^{0.0625} - 1 =$$
$$1.1185 - 1 = 0.1185 = 11.85\%.$$

My "retirement income" pot got off to a dreadful start, because for its first four years, I contributed to Equitable Life, a widely respected pension firm that offered guaranteed returns but managed to go bust, unable to meet its obligations. I put the paltry proceeds from that debacle into a scheme with Allied Dunbar, which I now know literally siphoned money out of my pot into their pockets through excessive fees, many of which were hidden. The third pension disaster was following my work colleagues into a Schroder-managed pension fund that, for five years, delivered fourth-quartile returns, woefully underperforming the FTSE and, after costs, returning less than I had put in. Overall, I lost ten to twelve early and precious years of compounding growth.

The good news was that I put all surplus cash into repaying the original £73,000 mortgage on my London flat, in small lumps here and there, completing the task in just less than ten years. The flat's value had fallen 15% in the early '90s, wiping out my equity, but by 1998, the ten-year anniversary of my ownership, it was well into positive territory and heading higher as the new millennium beckoned. In need of a change and mortgage-free, I held on to my flat, mortgaged up, and bought another flat, now my third property, near the Portobello Road, and moved there to enjoy a few more years of bachelor life. I mentally designated Clapham as a growth platform to meet future living expenses or luxuries, while the new one was to be home. It felt like starting again on a new mortgage mountain, albeit this time with an equity cushion.

We still own the Clapham flat, now in its twenty-eighth year of ownership, which delivers inflation-proof retirement income as hoped. The pension pot is healthier and still growing after I took control of investments, challenged managers on costs, and made some more contributions. The "school fees" pot provides dividends and chunks of capital for the girls' education, and, as things stand, it looks healthy enough to help fund university or college studies. Other pots for specific property renovation projects have come and gone, but home, education, and retirement living have continued as the constant themes. Over the next eight years, education costs will end, and anything left in that pot will be repatriated into "living expenses and luxuries," leaving us with this and two other pots: "home" (bought and paid for) and "retirement income."

How fast you can create an asset pot for a need and how far you can grow it depend on your focus and determination and your level of contributions. Racing others isn't the point; however much fun it might be when you're ahead, the real race is against time. If you are to have any free time in life, you need to get on with the game and not waste a second.

Currently, it is hard to get onto the property ladder, and, according to mortgage lenders, the average age of the first-time buyer is now over thirty. Buy with friends or family and with whatever help you can muster, but do what you can to start younger than this. Until you are on the ladder, pay as little rent as possible, and find the best returns for your savings in other growth platforms.

Attribution is, of course, entirely optional and offers no guarantees. There is no requirement to attribute assets to needs in the way I did, and most people don't.

It's for you to decide whether and how it might help. I found it helped in three ways.

1. It raises your productivity.

    By demanding an asset solution for every future need, attribution constantly keeps the pressure up, reminding you of what's still to be done and forcing you to fully commit on every front with all the discipline, energy, and stamina you can muster. The mission doesn't end until O is reached, so you instinctively raise productivity to meet this challenge.

    This is a substantial and meaningful activity; it is not insubstantial and pointless. Every step towards its end, however small, helps make the hard work worthwhile. Instead of chasing quick-hit pleasure substitutes, like statement wardrobes, the latest gadgets, expensive cars, jewellery, or an intimate knowledge of the Caribbean islands, these rewards really count: a home bought and paid for, children given the best education possible, and all future living needs met, plus entry into a new phase of life free from the drag of financial worry. There's no contest.

The promise of these rewards powered my performance through many long nights, weekends, days, and years in the office, which in turn increased my contribution and value as a worker and the personal financial benefits that consequently flowed.

2. It enriches.

In responding to the gauntlet thrown down by attribution, you are more likely to direct the maximum possible free cash to appreciators and not waste it. Only when all the required pots are full is the job done, and this denies you the chance to rest on your laurels for more than the shortest respite. Without attribution, a seemingly large pile of assets can offer the illusion of security and riches, even though it may be woefully short of the level actually required. Similarly, just as humans are good at mentally spending a windfall several times over, even though it was actually all spent on the first purchase, a single asset heap can also be spent many times over. Attribution cuts through the fog and trickery to reveal a state of affairs as it actually is.

Separating assets to match needs also promotes the formation of diverse growth platforms that can be individually managed. You can nurture and direct an asset pot according to its own needs and the prevailing market environment, tailoring it to the time horizon of its original purpose. For example, a two- to three-year pot will have a large cash component; a three- to five-year pot may include liquid productive appreciators, like listed equities; and a five- to ten-year pot offers scope for investment in less liquid appreciators, like rental property or venture capital funds. Each pot essentially has its own mandate and becomes a self-contained mini enterprise.

From time to time, in cases of buying opportunity, such as market mayhem and tumbling prices, or difficulty, such as job loss or unexpected cash needs, strict rules against dipping in can be temporarily waived, and the cash in one pot borrowed to invest or spend, as the case may be. By forcing you to hold cash for nearer-term needs, attribution creates useful flexibility to the whole—a kind of liquidity buffer. Once the opportunistic investment has delivered or the cash crunch and forced sell-off avoided, the borrowed cash can be returned to its lending pot in one lump or over time. Either way, you emerge richer.

Finally, establishing these mini enterprises with their varied asset types and mixes naturally leads to a variety of different growth platforms and assets, helping you to manage overall portfolio risk.

3. It directs your actions.

Attribution can't fail to provide an element of structure and purpose to your life. It creates an overall sense of being in control financially, even if your asset pots are far from complete. You know what you need to do and are getting on with it, even if the prospect doesn't delight you, and you are more likely to battle on, regardless of setbacks and difficulties.

It has parallels with a studying timetable for exams. Faced with a two-month study slot followed by final exams, someone who gets the calendar out and divides up the available hours and days between study, sport and activity time, and relaxation will feel in control and able to enjoy time off without guilt and worry. The same person charging at it with no advance time allocation may or may not cover the ground but will certainly have less balance and peace of mind on route to the exams.

Also, by shining a light on how much more money you must put aside to meet your needs, attribution forces you to directly challenge the nature and scale of those needs versus the struggle to fund them. In many cases, the equation doesn't balance. Your time is more precious. Attribution forces you to decide what really matters and declutter, allowing you space and time to appreciate the subtle and profound satisfaction of a simple, utilitarian existence.

FURTHER BUILDING TECHNIQUES

Some of you may begin to tire at the prospect of this slow, unremitting quest for the perfect pot and yearn for some action and excitement on the way. There is no escaping the fact that self-control, patience, knowledge, and hard work are all essential skills for a successful player, but somewhere in the process, alchemy or good fortune arises. It might be an insight of extreme high-definition clarity, a flash of brilliant inspiration, or simply a deep sense of contentment and optimism. This fortune can, in a single moment or over time, like the grit in an oyster, irretrievably change the course of your financial well-being.

I believe that it exists in all of us, sometimes buried beneath layers and hidden from light but there nevertheless. Playing the wealth game creates the conditions and space for its release. The physical and mental discipline needed to banish poverty-promoting behaviours clears the path, allowing mindfulness and focused investigation to reveal things as they are, not as we have previously seen them through our own particular prisms.

Any fool can be led by the first thought that enters his or her head and daydream his or her way to wealth or any other prize, but this is no more than a delusion born of ignorance and desperation, a blind hope that somehow things will turn out well. Such infatuation springs up and vanishes just as quickly, but the kind of hard-won good fortune that I'm discussing is made of sturdier stuff and really does make good things happen.

Trying to describe it accurately is impossible, but some examples of building techniques where financial alchemy can and does arise can be helpful.

Buy, hold, and buy again.
Gear up your personal balance sheet through residential mortgage secured against quality property to the highest level you can comfortably and safely afford, and pay down the debt as rapidly as possible, allowing for investments in tax-free equities like pensions and ISAs. Don't sell your assets unless you can recycle the after-tax proceeds into higher-returning appreciators. Releverage as soon as you are able to buy more property or appreciators. Continue for at least two or three cycles.

Contrarian investing
This technique is more often the subject of bar talk and daydreams than hard action, but in fact, it is one of the easiest and most reliable methods of boosting your pot.

The target is a good quality appreciator that is out of fashion, unloved by the market, and not attracting much buyer interest. How you find it doesn't matter; you might spot an out-of-favour property region or stock-market segment and then hunt out a suitable asset, or you might find the asset first and then wait for it to become overlooked. As you become more commercially and market attuned, you naturally begin to notice pockets of market weakness, and your antennae tune in to interesting opportunities.

Once you think you have found the right contrarian investment opportunity, evaluate it against the earlier exam questions to be sure that it's sound. The key to success in this technique is buying fundamentally good assets, ones that can deliver income and capital growth over a long period without too much effort and that won't fall down or disappear. If an asset passes this, test your view that it is unloved by offering a low price while at the same time making yourself the most attractive possible buyer on every other count—have ready funding, the ability to deal quickly, and so on. Revisit the buyer tips from before, and stay emotionally detached. Wear down reluctant sellers with charm and persistence.

For the ordinary person, this works best with residential property, where you can see and understand what you are buying, check out the surrounding area, value it, and deal directly with a private seller. The signposts for these situations may be quite well hidden. Half the battle is being awake and mindful, because contrarian means exactly that—doing the opposite of others. The chance may be no more than a yet-undiscovered area next to a popular one or an upcoming infrastructure or regeneration project that isn't yet reflected in prices. Artists and craftspeople are excellent barometers of where to look. They have a knack for spotting cheap but convenient areas to inhabit, and over time, their presence alone can stimulate buyer demand, new investment, and price increases.

In the case of quoted company shares, the opportunity arises when markets succumb to fear and forced selling; the share prices of excellent, well-managed companies or funds get swept along in the current and can start to offer great medium-term value.

This strategy is as old as the hills but often forgotten in the rush for instant gains. It does require the luxury of liquidity, but you can achieve this in the central and final phases of the game and beyond. It changes your perception of economic downturns, currency or debt crises, bank failures, wars, and other contributors to market mayhem. As long as you maintain a cash buffer to ride out the storm and are not overindebted, these are times of great opportunity. The assets you buy now will jump in value and deliver mouth-watering returns when stability resumes.

It is easy to get drawn into a debate about timing, but this is best avoided. In contrarian buying, you don't look for the top of the market but the bottom, and it doesn't matter if you miss the absolute bottom and buy one side or the other, as long as you're reasonably close; prices may fall a little further, or they may already have bounced slightly. It is sheer luck whether your timing is spot-on or not, but the trick is to be there or thereabouts and not buy too early. Wait for prices to be at least 20% below their peak—preferably even lower.

Stock markets tend to break these loss barriers very quickly and then pause for breath before deciding what to do next. Bounces on the way down can be short lived and trick you into buying early, so patience is called for. If in doubt, wait, because genuine buying opportunities are more frequent than you might think. In my working life, there have been at least four: 1987, 1992, 2000–2001, and 2008–2009. I missed the first two, lacking confidence and cash, but by the third, I was standing by for action.

Residential property prices are slower to respond and more predictable. According to Halifax Building Society, average home prices in greater London have fallen in only seven out of the last thirty years: 1990–1993 and again in 1995, 2008, and 2009. The biggest single annual fall was 11.8% in 2009. This has taught me to buy in the third or fourth year after a fall, by which time sellers of quality properties tend to have accepted a lower price environment, but buyers at large aren't reentering the market. Earlier opportunities can arise from overgeared, distressed sellers, but, particularly with speculators or those who got into the market late, their products are often poor. Real quality generally takes time to shake loose.

Never confuse this kind of contrarian investing with the completely different strategies of buying distressed assets and then fixing them or buying ordinary assets and somehow making them more valuable; these are the preserve of experts.

Go where the money is to earn it, and go to where the money isn't to buy depreciators and consumables.

I love this method; it is so simple and effective. In a world of connectivity and globalization, this is easier than it first seems. London's magnetic quality to workers is testament to this, as are thousands of immigrant workers throughout Britain and other developed nations who send money home to their families. Where you live and work can have a greater effect on your wealth than what you do and how well you do it. All these factors set boundaries to your earning potential as an individual.

Conversely, your earnings go much further when spent in places where money is in short supply and prices are low; you can live like royalty and indulge. Internet shopping has opened up a world of opportunity.

Buy assets where the wealthy buy them.

You won't get far in the game by buying assets that those with money don't want and aren't likely to in the future. The notion of spotting the next big thing and getting in ahead of the pack is romantic but hard to achieve, and it is too opportunistic to be relied on as a core strategy. You are better to monitor the movements of global capital: to what cities, countries, and asset classes the money flows or has flowed historically. Go there in pursuit of quality assets. Information on this subject is easy to obtain from wealth managers, international estate agents, and stockbroking firms.

Proactive tax planning

Knocking the wealthy is a national pastime in Britain. It might stem from our innate sense of fairness, justice, and support for the underdog, or perhaps it's just chippiness. There's a two-way process going on here, and, as we saw earlier, many of the fortunate people with serious money make themselves hard to like. If it's not self-obsession and distorted values, it's unscrupulous or antisocial behaviour that harms people or the environment. And nothing antagonizes the populous more than those with power and means finding ways to pay taxes at lower rates than ordinary working people—or, in some cases, avoiding them altogether.

The trap for the ordinary person is succumbing to grumbling inactivity, which is pointless and distracting, rather like bemoaning banks and bankers. It is negative and dispiriting and achieves nothing. A better approach is to adopt one of three universal options when faced with something you don't like: make a stand and fight it, join the other side, or ignore the issue completely.

In the game of pot building, taxes are an enemy to be fought, and it will serve your financial interests better to become a clever tax planner than play the victim and moan about others who do take up arms and defend themselves. Remember that value gains and losses begin with your own actions, and if you don't pay attention to your money, no one else will.

Tax legislation and practice is fiendishly complicated, and no ordinary person should seek to go it alone. Just look up *Tolley's Tax Guide* or spend some time searching the HMRC website for guidelines, rulings, and practice notes. Either exercise will quickly reveal the scale of the issue. Our tax system, like our legal one, has evolved over many years and combines statute and case law. It changes every year when the finance bill becomes law and so compounds through piecemeal political intervention rather than any kind of master plan.

After a lifetime of ignoring the subject or muddling through, I started taking tax advice only in the last year or two before reaching O, as part of a complete system overhaul and spring-clean. A lawyer friend introduced me to a former tax partner of one of the big four accounting firms, who had recently left to advise the partners of a national law firm on their personal affairs and who was also taking on a limited number of outside clients. Able to tap into the resources of his clients to stay up-to-date and seeing more real-life issues in a week than I might in ten years, he has been a gold mine.

Every autumn, we meet for an hour or so over coffee to have a creative brainstorm. The meeting always begins with my updating him on changes in the family finances or circumstances over the year and raising a few questions if I have any. Sometimes I turn up with no agenda and almost doubting whether the trip will be worthwhile, but since I have grown to like him, it's always an easy one to diarise. He then questions, probes, and suggests until I am tired of talking and writing, and we part for another twelve months. The trip home is spent summarizing my notes into a short list of possible tax-planning actions that I mull over, sometimes for months. The whole process is absorbing and fascinating, rather like seeing a specialist medical consultant to jointly plan tailored ways to improve one aspect of my health.

During the year ahead, we might have one or two e-mail exchanges when I seek advice on specific issues, but no more. I keep all my own tax records and file my personal return and limited company accounts, VAT, and corporation tax returns online, at no cost other than my time. Long ago, I learned to keep all low-level administration away from expert advisers. It is not interesting for them or cost-effective for me. Outsourcing such tasks can also lead to disconnection from the issues and the habit of passing responsibility to others, which impedes self-improvement. On some things, you say, "Trust experts," and on others, you say, "Trust myself."

I have never calculated the actual financial benefits of his advice, but a quick "back of the envelope" confirms gains of well over ten times the cost of his very modest fees over the last six years. It is telling to note that independent financial-adviser firms are now waking up to the fact that tax planning and advice is the greatest value add to private clients who already have some level of investing knowledge, and they are beginning to develop offerings in these areas to meet latent demand.

The areas that have been most fruitful to me have been splitting assets with my wife and children; using all our annual reliefs, pension, and ISA allowances in full; managing assets to minimize income and capital gains tax; accounting for all expenses I can offset and utilizing all available losses; and, more recently, since giving up employment, channelling any business activities through a limited company with a simple bank-account structure to make reporting easy; utilizing trading expenses and capital allowances; and managing distributions to stay below higher-income tax thresholds. Beyond tax-efficient wills, I have not yet started actively planning for inheritance tax, but it is creeping onto the agenda.

This book is clearly no place to delve further into the subject of taxes, but I include it in this section rather than in a roundup of miscellany for completeness, because for me, it has been a hidden gem amongst pot-building techniques and is completely available to the ordinary person. My overarching practical guide to the subject is as follows:

- Set as a cardinal obligation the duty not to pay more tax than is required. It is incredibly easy to overpay without realizing.
- Find a genuine expert on tax with the resources to stay up-to-date, and build a long-term relationship.
- Have at least one tax-planning meeting each year.
- Spend time playing with different scenarios to optimize all-around benefits.
- Read around the subject to fill in gaps or raise further questions for the tax adviser.
- Do all tax filings online.
- Keep impeccable records, and archive paper ones from the cabinet to the attic every few years.

- Use every relief and tax-saving method offered by government that fits your situation and that doesn't direct you to areas of investment that you don't understand.
- Utilize all costs and losses that can be used to offset tax, if necessary, creating income to utilize them by turning an asset into a productive one.
- Declare everything—a clear conscience is priceless. No brown envelope from HMRC will ever cause the slightest heart flutter.
- Avoid nonstandard tax-saving schemes that are entered into for the prime purpose of reducing or avoiding tax. These are a recipe for worry, moral recrimination, and adviser fees. Additionally, in cases where the tax authorities challenge or overturn schemes, you will avoid real financial pain as interest plus penalties adds to the original sum due.
- Avoid complexity wherever possible—trusts, offshore companies, and other such vehicles can tie people in knots, wasting years of their lives. They rarely work fully as intended and are always high cost.
- Challenge the tax authorities if they get it wrong, which they frequently do. They are public servants and human.

Maintain perspective, and don't lose sight of what really matters: peace of mind born of a clear conscience, knowledge that you have contributed fairly, and freedom to live your life the way you want. The world's tax havens have been dubbed "open prisons" and are populated by large numbers of self-imposed exiles able to spend only limited nights in their home country. What a bizarre setup! Who values keeping money away from the tax man more than freedom to travel freely in the world and spend as much time at home as they'd like?

Understand skimming versus overall wealth creation, and apply each appropriately.
Skimming is a zero-sum game. This means that any gain or loss you make is matched exactly by an equivalent loss or gain by other participants in

the game. For example, a buyer makes £100 profit on a share sale, while the seller has lost the opportunity to make that profit by selling. Great wealth can be derived by redirecting assets from others to you. Look at the former Soviet Union. To do this, you need to know where the wealth is and how to access it. Similarly, service providers, agents, brokers, or other intermediaries can amass large sums by skimming a small portion of capital as it flows around the system.

Overall wealth creation, on the other hand, is a not a zero-sum game, because the total amount of utility or usefulness in circulation increases as a result of your action. This route, too, can deliver great wealth, as proven by many inventors and business builders.

How does your wealth-generating activity split between each category? Take some time to investigate game theory, and think hard about how and from whence your wealth can be derived.

Game changers
These are big opportunities that arise maybe once or twice in your lifetime and change the course of your finances for the better. The scale of these moves is intimidating, but the potential rewards are enormous.

The wealth game sharpens your senses and skills, enabling you to spot these titans when they come. They generally don't appear with a sign marked "gigantic financial opportunity," and it's easy to miss them if you are looking the other way or are too busy to notice.

Spotting game changers is one thing; grabbing them with both hands is quite another. Fear, stubbornness, pride, overanalysis, and indecision or inertia are just a few of the powerful enemies of opportunity, and I have seen people beset with these pass up game changers and never quite get over it. Not only have they missed the chance to move the dial financially, but they also know they missed it.

Where do these gifts come from? They are tailor-made for you; they are not off-the-shelf products fit for all, and they are born from the personal circumstances that you, in part, create. Thomas Jefferson is reported to have said, "I'm a great believer in luck, and I find that the harder I work, the more of it I have." An opportunity that you can't take is called fantasy, so the trick is to get into a position to take it. Herein lies the other great enemy of opportunity: not creating the conditions for it in the first place.

Most of this involves money, and, perhaps not surprisingly, given their scale, these bets stretch you to the outer limits, where the margin between a deal happening or not is wafer thin, a tiny proportion of the overall cost. At a different time, it would seem like pocket money. Whoever tells you that the small things don't matter—and a surprising number of financial experts do—is overlooking the power of cause and effect compounded over time and forgetting the fine line between success and failure.

A motivational speaker once said that "winning is a game of inches," and I often reflected on that as I crawled along the slow lane, being passed by all and sundry. Any Olympic medal winner or musical virtuoso is testament to hard yards not only putting them in the game but also enabling them to grab the prize. When you pull off a great wealth-generating deal, observers generally focus on the transaction itself: "How did you find that?" "What luck!" "What a great price!" "You'll make a fortune out of that one!" It is easy to overlook the slow, inch-by-inch progress you have made over years to get into the position where you could pull it off.

For many, shortage of money isn't the only problem. Reaching out and grabbing the biggest opportunities requires nimbleness, flexibility, and speed. Those weighed down by lifestyles, clutter, convention, and obligation or who are unfit through prolonged inactivity can only watch helplessly as the boat sails by. If you want an argument for travelling light, here it is.

And what are these deals? For me, they were residential property with development potential. For others I know, they have been the opportunity to own a meaningful stake in a valuable business.

XV

ASSET ALLOCATION

Whether you attribute or not, asset allocation is hard to avoid. It's the sharp end where asset choices must be made. What types, which specific ones, and in what quantities? Do you follow an opportunist and piecemeal approach, a strategic one, or a mix of both? And how much outside help do you need, if any?

The scale of asset choice within classes, now magnified by the Internet, creates two immediate problems for the ordinary person. First, it takes a lot of time, both up front and continually, to understand and evaluate assets, and for the working person in the beginner or central phases of the game, this is one commodity that is in constant demand. There simply isn't enough time to build a career, maintain a social life, have relationships, stay fit, feed the creative spirit, learn new skills, *and* become an expert in asset picking and portfolio management. And that's before children or other dependants appear on the scene. Something must be put to one side until later, unless you want to deliver half-baked outcomes that satisfy no one.

The second problem is fear. The world of financial instruments feels like a dangerous, alien place, an unknown territory full of myths and legends, heroes and villains. For the ordinary person with any care for consequences, stepping into this can be scary or at least unsettling. How many times have you heard or read someone saying words to the effect of "I don't touch shares, because I don't understand them" or, echoing Woody Allen's sentiment, "a stockbroker invests your money until it's gone"?

People fear loss, making a mistake, or being cheated by a vendor, salesman, or corrupt, unregulated market. Wall Street insider of the late 1920s Jesse Livermore boasted of owning six yellow Rolls Royce vehicles, two yachts, a private railway car, and five homes, including an apartment on Fifth Avenue he bought as a place to change clothes before the theatre. The game at that time was promoting a company as the next great thing and stirring up a frenzy of buying interest, during which the early-investor club would quietly sell at a vast profit before reality dawned, and everyone rushed for the door. Groucho Marx, who lost $240,000 on October 29, 1929, later quipped, "I would have lost more, but that was all I had."

Even if you can find the time and overcome your fears, more and different assets mean complexity: paperwork, records, accounting, taxes, and regulatory filings. This is a world of spreadsheets, ring binders, cabinets, and, worst of all, administration, a force of nature that mushrooms and spreads if not tended to.

WHY ALLOCATE?

Why enter such a world? Wouldn't it be better to hold just one or possibly two straightforward and understandable assets, like cash or residential property, or perhaps hand your money over to someone else and pay that person to manage it for you? The answer for many is probably yes, and it is certainly yes if you aren't constitutionally suited to the task, but before deciding, it's worth considering the case for spreading wealth between assets and the various ways of doing it.

The primary decision point is cash versus other assets. Here, the trade-off is liquidity (i.e., having enough money available to pay your way) versus watching the value of that money decline inexorably over time as inflation erodes its spending power. You must set aside enough cash or income to stay solvent but, at the same time, at least preserve the value of what remains. If you don't, you will either go bankrupt or get poorer. The first reason to allocate is therefore to balance liquidity with growth.

This conundrum argues for at least a rudimentary allocation between cash and less-liquid appreciators. Available assets offer a wide range of income, growth, and liquidity characteristics, allowing you to pick and mix a selection that suits.

The second reason to allocate is to manage risk. Earlier, I suggested that you consider three types of risk: asset-specific or unsystemic risk, wider economic or market risk (also known as systemic risk) and the riskiness of your own personal setup, age, income sources and needs.

The subject of risk in finance occupies many volumes of academic work and, perhaps because it is so complex, is too easily oversimplified. Financial advisers and wealth managers baffle clients by asking questions like "What is your risk appetite?" They sometimes offer a scale from one to ten or from low to high to assist, but the problem remains that in the absence of a detailed and holistic consideration of your own circumstances, future needs, and temperament, any answer is likely to be faulty. It's not the same thing as guiding a doctor to your pain threshold, where you can instantly retrieve all the data needed to give a very accurate answer.

For many, the question itself is unintelligible, and the alien environment in which it is asked merely encourages uncomfortable clients to offer up glib responses in order to move through the process as quickly as possible. A better way is to flag and discuss the big risk areas of personal circumstances, debt, and asset concentration that apply to an ordinary person's financial condition.

The third reason to allocate is to actively enhance portfolio performance. Good risk management in itself leads to better performance by protecting against downsides. The other side of the coin is investing in a class of assets that you believe will outperform others or in specific assets with better-than-average value growth potential. Over the last thirty years, finance academics have intently studied the drivers of portfolio performance. In 2010, a group of US academics led by Yale School of Management's Roger Ibbotson published "The Equal Importance of Asset Allocation and Active Management," in which they identified three parts to the total return on a mixed fund or portfolio: (1) the return from the overall market movement; (2) the incremental passive, or beta, return from the asset class allocation policy; and (3) the active, or alpha, return from specific asset selection, timing, and fees. Their conclusion was that, "In general (after controlling for interaction effects), about three quarters of a typical fund's, variation in time series returns comes from general market movement with the remaining proportion split roughly evenly between the specific asset allocation and active management."

By separately identifying market movement as the principal value driver, it dispelled previous folklore that 90% of returns are driven by your choice and mix of asset class alone. For the active and confident investor, the logical conclusion is to shift funds from asset classes that you think will underperform to ones that you expect to outperform. Here, practicalities like transaction costs, speed, and tax weigh in, so in practice, these shifts are easier implemented at the edges.

HOW TO DO IT

The wealth game is most rewarding when you take charge of decisions and actively engage. You learn and exercise skills and use commercial judgement to achieve clear goals. This is stimulating and empowering, a prize in itself. During the phases of play, your personal involvement in choosing and managing assets can graduate from slight to significant, depending on your abilities and circumstances. Like a novice sailor, you may begin with an unsteady hand on the tiller, setting course and direction while others provide the seamanship and handle practicalities, but as your skills, experience, and confidence grow, you can evolve into a single-hander, capable of running all departments in the toughest of conditions.

1. Allocating funds between asset classes

Most personal finance books apply a top-down view to create model portfolios determined by risk appetite, personal needs, and time horizon. A low-risk structure will be weighted towards bonds and cash; medium risk, a balanced mix of cash, bonds, equities, and property; and high-risk, more equities and property. This is fine for a player who has the luxury of already owning a variety of assets or sufficient funds to buy them but is of limited practical help to the ordinary person during the beginner and central phases of the game, where the job is to build and develop the pot from scratch and prioritize which assets to focus on. In the final phase of the game and beyond O, asset stewardship and allocation take over as the main tasks, and conventional theory becomes more useful.

For all players, the starter question is this: "What classes of assets do I hold?" The following table provides a framework for funds allocation at each stage of the game.

Table 15.1

What assets to hold at each phase of the game

asset type	property		equities				bonds	cash
	home	rental property	private pension	ISAs	outside a tax wrapper			
type	A	PA	PA	PA	PA	PD	PD	
beginner phase	yes	no	yes	yes	unlikely	no	minimum for liquidity	
central phase	yes	yes	yes	yes	yes	perhaps	minimum for liquidity	
final phase	yes	yes	yes	yes	yes	yes	yes	

Notes
A = appreciator
PA = productive appreciator
PD = productive depreciator

The next question is this: "How much of each class do I hold?"

In the beginner and central phases, your home is likely to dominate. This begs the question of whether you should follow traditional wisdom and stretch to buy the biggest, best-located property you can afford, even if it constitutes the bulk of your noncash assets. Personally, I support this strategy—but *only* after starting a private pension plan and allowing for regular monthly contributions. A pension should be your first long-term financial commitment and, for compounding reasons, started as soon as you can.

Property and equities are the two most powerful wealth motors, and as soon as you own them, they will start working for you. The mix between them will change over time, depending on relative performance, any value you can add to specific assets, and future cash allocation. As long as you have a mortgage or other debt, your priority should be on paying it down fast for the reasons discussed earlier. Only where there are higher-returning asset opportunities in classes that you want to build should you divert surplus cash flow away from debt repayment. In practice, therefore, your ability to shift the mix between asset groups is extremely limited or nonexistent, and talk about top-down asset allocation is academic. This is not a problem to worry over; you are on the escalator, and your options and choices will grow.

After your loan-to-value and cash-interest cover tests, which help you determine how much debt to take on and how much cash to set aside to service it, there are three tests that you can use as the game progresses.

Test 1—Liquidity, or solvency, ratio

This is an expanded version of the two debt tests and is the ratio of liquid to total assets. It is only likely to appear on the horizon in the central phase, when you have a greater asset base and more funds to spread, but, usefully, it helps you fine-tune your allocations, perhaps between ultra-liquid assets capable of being cashed in a few days and others that might require one or two months' notice.

Let's say you have the following assets:

£300,000 home equity after mortgage; £30,000 pension (invested in equities); £15,000 equity ISAs; £10,000 other equities; £10,000 bonds; and £5,000 cash on instant access and £5,000 on thirty-days' notice.

Your total assets are £375,000. For a tough tier-one ratio, exclude ISAs and cash on thirty-days' notice or longer, so your liquid assets are other equities, bonds, and instant cash, totalling £25,000. Your tier-one liquidity ratio as a percentage = tier-one assets / total assets × 100 = £25,000 / 375,000 × 100 = 6.7%.

If you define tier-two assets as including ISAs and all cash available within sixty days, your total tier-two base is £45,000, giving a tier-two ratio of 12%.

You might wonder where these ratios should be at each phase of the game, but this depends on your indebtedness, goals, time horizon, and risk appetite. I introduce the tool as nothing more than that: an implement for planning. Looking back on my own experience in the game, the ratios were near zero throughout the beginner phase, crept up to in the central period (but probably never reached double figures), and began to grow only in the final phase and beyond O.

Test 2—Asset class weightings
Whatever your asset holdings makeup, assuming that you hold more than one type, you should calculate the contributions of each. The assets in test 1 show the following contributions:

Property—80%
Equities—14.6%
Bonds—2.7%
Cash—2.7%

Total—100%

This is a growth-oriented portfolio with limited downside protection.

Test 3—Asset classification ratios
Here you can use the classification of appreciators, depreciators, and consumables. In practice, these are the most illuminating and apply to every phase of the game. Even at the start, there is no reason, in principle, why you shouldn't make your home produce income by letting out a room or outbuilding. Later on, the tests challenge you to be more active and less comfortable or complacent, and they challenge you to keep luxuries in their place.

There are any number of permutations, but there are three useful ones:

1. Productive assets / total assets
   What proportion of your assets generates income? For this purpose, treat appreciators as productive only if they are actually

generating income, not just capable of doing so. Unless you rent out or sell depreciators or consumables as a business, your only other producing assets will be bonds or cash. Phrasing it another way, this ratio shows how much income-generation assistance your chosen asset base provides.

2. Appreciators / total assets

    How much of your asset base is in assets that you expect to grow in capital value, rather than decline?

3. Appreciators + productive depreciators / total assets

    What proportion of your asset base generates growth or income or both? By definition, the remainder is doing neither.

Let's apply these to three asset mixes, each totalling £500,000.

Table 15.2.1

Example asset portfolios split by classification

asset type	portfolio 1 £	portfolio 2 £	portfolio 3 £
home (A)	200,000	220,000	250,000
holiday home (A)		130,000	
rental property (PA)			150,000
equities (PA)		50,000	55,000
bonds (PD)	25,000	50,000	
gold (A)	5,000		
cash (PD)	25,000	10,000	20,000
car (D)	60,000	10,000	10,000
boat (D)	40,000		
caravan (D)	15,000		
furniture (D)	45,000	15,000	5,000
art works (D)	25,000	5,000	
media equipmemt (D)	15,000	7,000	5,000
jewellery (D)	30,000		3,000
clothes and shoes (C)	15,000	3,000	2,000
total	500,000	500,000	500,000

Notes
1. Letters in brackets indicate asset classification.
2. Assets may be held in a variety of wrappers, such as pensions, ISA, etc, or independently.
3. Art, furniture and jewellery are treated as depreciators, as very few examples ever appreciate.

Applying the three tests generates the following results:

Table 15.2.2

Analysis of example asset portfolios

asset type	portfolio 1 £	portfolio 2 £	portfolio 3 £
productive appreciators	0	50,000	205,000
appreciators	205,000	350,000	250,000
productive depreciators	50,000	60,000	20,000
other assets	245,000	40,000	25,000
ratio 1 - income (%)	10	22	45
ratio 2 - growth (%)	41	80	91
ratio 3 - income + growth (%)	51	92	95

In portfolio 1, almost 60% of assets are declining in value, and only 10% generate income. Portfolio 2 is growth oriented, but the luxury of a holiday home limits income generation to 22%. Portfolio 3 is highly efficient, with only 5% of assets neither growing nor producing income. Cash generation is good at nearly half the total assets. If this is reinvested and the returns compounded, it will have a powerful boosting effect on the overall value of the portfolio.

Running numbers in this way helps you understand how your lifestyle choices are helping or hindering wealth creation, and it provides targets for you to aim for. To reach O in the shortest time, you should keep all ratios as high as possible by minimizing nonperforming assets.

2. Allocating funds within asset classes
Which specific assets do you buy in each class?

Residential property is one for you to decide on yourself. Follow the guide in this book, follow your own nose, and enlist wise counsel from those who have made money here. In buying bonds, you should work with an expert manager in the field who specializes in fixed-income products to select the right package for your needs. These might be individual issues or funds, and cover government and corporate loans.

Long ago, I stopped buying specific company shares; insufficient time, the evaluation challenges described earlier, and tough disclosure and dealing rules in our firm made it impractical and risky. You should hold a basket of shares in actively managed or passive funds—unit trusts, investment trusts, or index trackers. It is worth paying for the time and expertise of a professional manager who evaluates companies for a living and is held accountable for it. Or avoid asset picking completely by choosing an index tracker. Researching and buying individual shares is time consuming and risky. You should do it only if you have expertise, time, and enjoy doing it.

A quick guide to the options

A. Buying the market—passive funds or trackers
This is an extremely low-cost way of accessing equities. The costs of active managers and researchers are removed in favour of sophisticated tracking systems that mirror as closely as possible an underlying market or index. By gaining exposure to the entire basket of shares in that group, individual stock-picking risk and reward are eliminated.

Competition between providers, such as Fidelity, Vanguard, Deutsche Bank, Legal & General and Blackrock is fierce—costs are falling, and the range of products is increasing.

Whether for index trackers or exchange-traded funds (ETFs), you should understand four things: first, the index being tracked; second, how closely the manager is able to track the index; third, whether or not underlying securities that make up the index are owned or whether the tracker is a synthetic version that holds rights through derivative contracts; and fourth, how all charges work. The answers to these questions are easily found with some digging.

Many academics and market practitioners believe that this kind of passive investing triumphs over active stock picking over time and that the edge that active managers claim is either illusory or offset by their higher charges. Furthermore, actively managed funds often comprise a large weighting of the same companies in their chosen market index—for example, blue-chip UK income producers—simply because they are the best-quality companies in the index. This effectively relegates a proportion of the fund to tracker status, albeit with high fees and limits its scope to outperform the benchmark. Watch out for these closet trackers.

Active managers argue that, over selected periods, they can and do outperform passives after costs. They also point out that funds geared to benchmarks and indices, whether active or passive, are forced to follow the market up or down, buying when prices are rising and selling when they are falling—in other words, the direct opposite of a smart contrarian investor strategy. Whilst certain managers do consistently outperform over given periods, Nobel Laureate William F. Sharpe, in his short paper, *The arithmetic of active management*, argues that taken as a whole, active managers seem just as prone to herd mentality as any other investor.

Lars Kroijer's 2013 book, *Investing Demystified: How to Invest Without Speculation and Sleepless Nights*, presents the case for buying the market and covers the practicalities.

B. Buy actively managed funds

The key here is to understand what the fund is set up to achieve and what it owns. At one end of the spectrum, balanced or mixed investment funds set out to offer a broad portfolio of assets across classes chosen to meet certain risk and performance targets or benchmarks. These are aimed at investors who want to hand over all decision making and responsibility to a third party. At the other end are pure equity funds that hold only company shares and cash. They may specialize in certain countries or regions, industry sectors, or sizes, and they may be tied to a benchmark—or they may be unconstrained and free to roam wherever they choose. Within these groups, some funds are "long only," meaning that they buy and hold assets; others include short positions, where shares are borrowed and sold in the hope of buying the shares necessary to fulfill the bargain at a lower price later.

I have a natural bias against generalists of any kind, and funds are no exception. Hundreds of conglomerate funds set up by household-name pension and insurance firms languish at the bottom of the performance charts, victims of poor management and excessive costs, and they are rarely held accountable by investors, who are asleep on the job. They tarnish the reputation of the many excellent and high-performing active funds.

If you want to include a portion of active-managed funds, you should seek out the best-managed, pure equity funds and build a portfolio of these. I apply a fairly methodical approach to choosing funds, which allows me to make more choices than I can under the previous strategy but leaves individual stock analysis and selection to the fund manager.

I choose which country or region I think will deliver over my time frame, based on its current economic performance, outlook, and where it is in the cycle; the longer my investment horizon, the greater risk and volatility I tolerate, pointing towards a higher weighting of less-developed fast-growth nations. Politics plays a part, particularly around election time, as does the impact of central bank interventions and future policy indications. Local currency strength or weakness also impacts share-price performances. Finally, I'll look at the recent stock market performance and valuations of the country or region. A period of strong performance and high-price multiples indicates confidence in future profit growth and vice versa. Sometimes, investor buying or selling creates momentum of its own, and markets become detached from underlying economics. A country that has been overbought is worth watching for a while (or dripping money into slowly), while one that has been oversold may be worth a greater portion of my portfolio now. Many FTSE 350 companies have substantial overseas earnings, giving international exposure through an apparently UK fund.

My next decision is whether to seek income, growth or a blend of the two. Some funds are specifically aimed at generating capital growth, and they hold companies that reinvest most of their profits to fund new projects. Others aim to deliver income and target companies with stable and predictable cash flows and high-dividend payouts. Such companies are often in mature or regulated industry sectors, such as tobacco, health care, or utilities, which offer defensive qualities as well as diversification through international exposure.

Both are growth opportunities, because income can be reinvested in extra units of the fund, creating a compound-growth effect. My choice of one over the other depends not so much on my income requirements but on my sense of the market. In times of investor fear and uncertainty, I tilt towards defensive income, but as confidence returns, I shift emphasis to growth. Studies show that the power of dividend income reinvested is great, so most of my portfolio is income generating, at least to a degree.

Size matters, and I pay close attention to this, as it can make a real difference. On the whole, small companies grow at a higher rate than large ones, because they start from a lower base. Their prices also tend to fall further and faster; they are more volatile. Volatility creates uncertainty, which adds risk to investing. If I need to sell my small-company shares in a certain time frame, and the stock market has fallen, their prices are likely to be in a trough deeper than large-company shares at the same point. I like the growth that small companies provide over the medium to long term, so I always hold some and increase or reduce the holdings in the same way that I switch between growth and income stocks.

Midsized companies are often overlooked, and some of the best special-situations funds mine this area for value. Very large multinational groups with market-leading positions in growing markets can provide an excellent mix of capital appreciation and income as well as geographic diversification.

Next I consider which industry sectors I feel will perform well. By definition, cyclical sectors are more volatile than defensive ones. The highs are higher, the lows are lower, and they gyrate more. Fund managers all take their own decisions and populate their holdings accordingly. One may like mining and basic-goods industries tied to commodity prices; others may favour financial services, retail, consumer products, business-to-business services, advanced engineering, IT and telecoms, or media. Whether or not one has a particular view on an industry sector, it pays to know where individual fund managers are investing. I stay away from highly fashionable areas, such as commodities and mining. For a time, I avoided funds with high financial-services exposure. Healthcare products and services for a growing and aging population has generally performed well as a sector, as have established consumer brands, particularly drinks companies.

A final question before choosing specific funds is whether to buy an open ended company or fund, which creates and cancels units as customers buy and sell them, or a closed ended listed investment trust, which has a finite number of issued shares that investors buy and sell on the stock market.

Although I hold a balance of both, I prefer investment trusts for four reasons: First, they can take longer views because they aren't forced to sell underlying stocks when investors redeem fund units. Second, they can borrow to gear returns. Third, they can retain income in good years to pay out in poorer ones, thereby offering smoother, more consistent income flows. And finally, their cost structures are generally lower than open-ended funds. The case against them is that gearing adds risk and that unloved trusts can trade for long periods at sizeable discounts to their underlying net asset value. Spotting a well-managed trust trading at a large discount can deliver a burst of gain if the discount closes, as discounts often do.

Despite their advantages, investment trusts attract a tiny fraction of the money invested directly by private individuals. They have never paid commissions to introducers, like investment platforms and financial intermediaries, and historically, have not been promoted by these powerful seller groups.

The reasons for buying open ended funds include choice (there are many more of them offering greater range of opportunities) and quality of fund manager. Some managers can be in two places at once and manage an open-ended fund and an investment trust, but many aren't. An excellent fund manager will outperform an average or poor one, whatever the fund structure.

Finally, I arrive at percentage allocations for my chosen categories and start to pick funds for each. Let's say my categories include smaller Asian companies, Asian income, global income and growth, North America, smaller UK companies, special UK opportunities, and UK income.

At this point, the mist clears somewhat and form cards become very helpful. *Money Management* magazine reproduces FE Crown Fund ratings and rankings over one month to ten years by fund, split into each category for both investment trusts and open ended funds. It is one of several independent fund-comparison sources. Fund-comparison sources indicate pretty clearly which the consistently high-performing funds are and which should be avoided. After producing short lists of funds for further investigation, I then look at their own websites and download fact sheets and fund information to make final decisions.

Every so often, fund managers leave, and this prompts me to review the holding. Aside from these one-off events, I tend to review fund performance every quarter. Two consecutive quarters of underperformance puts a fund on a watch list. There may be a good reason for it (some strategies need time to develop), but, if not, I will consider switching to another fund. Even star managers can go off. Here is another area where independent market experts may have helpful insights that are worth paying to.

Because I create different investment pots for specific needs, the time frame for each need and resulting investment horizon dictates the level of risk that is acceptable in any given pot to an extent. The "pension" pot is in medium- to high-risk investments, because I don't expect to touch it over the next ten years. The "education" pot has a three-to-eight-year time frame and a medium risk weighting, composed of smaller-growth companies, midsized opportunities, large multinationals, and a good layer of defensive income producers. The "living expenses" pot has an evergreen feel, because it is designed to pay out and grow at the same time and contains lower-risk income producers.

OUTSIDE HELP

Harbours and ports of the financial world are brimming with captains and crew for hire, a few worth their weight in gold, plenty of lazy journeymen and incompetent fools, and a clutch of charlatans. From the outset, you should decide what you want from three broad options.

1. Execution-only services
These are the basic tools for asset management, execution of trades, custodial services, account and market information, and administration, including tax-return data. Stockbrokers like Barclays provide these services for company shares and investment trusts, and fund providers like Fidelity and Hargreaves Lansdown do the same for open-ended funds.

They all provide tax-wrapper accounts, such as self-invested personal pension (SIPP) and ISAs. You make the decisions and take all actions and have no comeback to the providers if your investments fall. By and large, these plain services are efficient, low cost, and fit for purpose.

2. Advice

This is where the problems start. The only advice you can consider relying on must come from someone who charges clear and transparent fees for it, irrespective of what actions you subsequently take. They must convince you that they do not receive any income related to you from other sources, such as companies whose products and services you buy—in other words, when the adviser's business model is wholly dependent on having satisfied clients like you. Only in these circumstances can the advice be genuinely impartial and oriented solely to your needs. You also need someone who is a clear expert in the field, and has recognised and worthwhile professional qualifications, lots of first-rate experience, and the resources and team support to stay fully up-to-date with changing rules and products.

3. Advice and execution

This is the realm of the discretionary fund manager (DFM) or wealth manager. There are two types of DFMs:

1. Traditional—someone who manages your money in line with bespoke, preagreed risk-and-return targets, aiming for a mix of income, growth, and capital protection. These managers take on funds only above a certain size, typically £250,000.
2. Ready-made model portfolios—these have no minimum investment size and are essentially off-the-shelf products. You choose the one that most closely fits your requirements.

DFMs charge a percentage of funds under management. They are only as good as their managers, and many are not good.

Wealth managers come in various forms; some are no more than glorified relationship managers sitting in the private banking departments of high-street or merchant banks; others are independent, sometimes orphan sole traders from larger institutions. These people charge you a percentage of your funds under management for their expert investment guidance. Execution, custodian, and administration fees are usually payable on top.

Look carefully at charging structures for all these types, particularly the layering effect of hidden costs. Their fees are in addition to management and administration charges of the funds they put you into. They can build quickly into several percent that, compounded over time, takes a massive chunk out of your portfolio value.

This group is fraught with danger, as evidenced by a long list of Ponzi schemes, fines, and investor rip-offs since the Industrial Revolution and the dawn of modern banking. Because many trade under premium brands, old family names with cache, and are generally marketed quietly through introductions to those in the know, this group is a snob's charter, and it preys on the naïve, trusting, gullible, lazy, unconfident, greedy, proud, and foolish. There *must* be a compelling financial reason to entrust any of this group with your money instead of using low-cost execution-only services.

As a basic rule, relating to all categories of outside help, dismiss all advertising and selling propaganda originating from the seller. This includes brochures, flyers, planted newspaper editorials, published performance figures and market position statistics, competitor analysis, and so on. Smart suits, handsome or pretty executives, plush offices, and slick presentations also cloud the decision process and are best ignored. Treats and incentives are no better than worm- or fly-covered fishing hooks. You must set and apply your own measurement criteria quite independently from anything the seller wants you to know or think.

Accreditations from industry bodies and qualifications are no more than first-round entry requirements to the selection process and don't guarantee good service. Personal recommendations from sources, whether trusted or not, are only as good as those recommending and their genuine intentions. Cold callers should be dismissed out of hand.

Checking up on track records requires detective work, access to reliable data, and possibly discussions with other clients—the more external verification, the better. The finance industry is increasingly regulated, so advisers, intermediaries, and product providers are bound to keep records, file returns, and make full disclosure. If what they reveal isn't enough, ask them to reveal more. If it's not clear, ask them to explain. I recently asked my insurance broker to disclose her commission. My relationship manager wriggled slightly and said that she'd need to check, because this isn't a usual request. About a week later, after getting permission from their compliance department, she revealed that their share of my £4,000 annual property insurance bill was £1,500, or 37.5%, of the total. This is a sobering amount, and I will be looking at their service and value adds very carefully before renewing.

It is frequently the case that fee and commission structures promote behaviours from product or service providers that are diametrically opposed to those that best deliver your objectives. Consumers have become wiser to this in recent years, and regulators do their best to catch up after scandals erupt, but problems do and probably always will remain. If you want maximum performance, you should weight remuneration to the product provider or introducer towards this, rather than deliver them a fat profit whether or not the asset performs. Nothing sharpens the mind more than knowing that the only way to make decent money is to meet or exceed a client's expectations. Push back on standard charges as a matter of course (they are invariably negotiable), and avoid the desire to please or not offend an adviser/salesperson who has been helpful and worked hard on your account, creating a sense of obligation to buy. The natural tension between their desire to make profits from you and your desire for the right products and services at the best possible price is unavoidable. Get used to walking away.

At the root of all good decision making around choosing outside help is understanding their value proposition. What are they doing that you can't or don't want to do, and how much is that worth to you? A fund manager who, together with a support team, sifts the market for valuable investment opportunities, researches and analyses them, meets the senior management teams, and buys when the price is attractive is offering a valuable service, as I don't have the time or current expertise to do that. By selling that service to a large number of fund investors, the manager creates an economy of scale, and the cost to each investor is minimized by spreading overall costs across a larger number of people. An independent financial planner who is not only up-to-date with all the latest rules, regulations, taxation, and allowances relating to pensions, savings, and inheritance-tax planning, but also knows who provides what and where the best deals can be found is a valuable resource in the wealth game.

Paying a fair price for this kind of value makes a lot more sense for the ordinary person than trying to do it all yourself or getting "free" help from someone who is no more than a glorified product salesman claiming to be acting in your best interests.

It is easy to come unstuck by overrating your expertise and knowledge on a subject and not listening to or even seeking wise counsel. Industry-wide rip-offs, misleading materials, hidden charges, and self-serving advice from participants breeds justified cynicism, but this is dangerous if it puts you off the game altogether or stops you buying the really good advice and help that is available with careful searching and due diligence. The trick is to learn the principles and the language of finance before taking advice; you will get a better result at lower cost.

PART FIVE

WHERE'S THE CATCH?

XVI

OBSTACLES TO REACHING O

In any game, some players achieve the objective; others fail. Analysing failure and its causes helps us and future generations of players improve our skills, tactics, and win rate. In the wealth game, we are fortunate to be surrounded by players to observe and an abundance of failure. In fact, so many people fail to master their financial situation that money worries consistently top the surveys of discontent at all age ranges of adulthood. Think about it for a minute: How many adults do you know who are completely satisfied with their financial position and don't worry about money? Perhaps an elderly relative or two?

No doubt some never get into the game because they don't generate enough income to create the vital surplus cash to fuel the early stage of pot building. The vast majority in developed economies do earn enough income to make a material difference, yet they somehow fail to deliver it, consigning themselves to years of financial constraint and paid work that could be avoided. In a curious substitution, the industrialists and robber barons of the past that created vast wealth for themselves through organizing and exploiting labour and resources have been replaced as taskmasters by us, the workers. Despite earning power on a different scale than the Victorians, people manage to create their own financial straightjackets by wasting money on artificial needs and misplaced obligations.

Fatalists contend that humans are predestined to win or lose, that external forces are pulling strings, laying traps, and directing them to choose certain paths. Whether or not this is the case, such a view leads you away from personal responsibility and from direct action to improve your lot. It denies human and natural cause and effect, and it snuffs out action, like landing on a square in the game marked "switch off, and see where you end up." Some of these players assuage the resulting feelings of helplessness and failure by claiming it was meant to be and paying homage to their chosen power source in the hope that, although unproven and without scientific basis, it will deliver them to a better place.

Hard-nosed pragmatists argue that anyone can become wealthy with determination, hard work, and a positive attitude. The evidence of life suggests otherwise, as there are too many people with these qualities who have remained poor or beset with money worries for reasons beyond their own control, and there are others with no such qualities who have become wealthy beyond dreams.

Placing all your money on either camp to win is clearly risky, so the better thing is to follow a middle path, take charge of all the areas that are within your power and control, and position yourself for the best possible outcome, recognizing that bad things do happen and that no one has yet found a way of stopping them. This approach leads you to a systematic analysis of what you can do, and it leads you away from endless fear and speculation of what you can't. Interestingly, the ledger of wealth-affecting items is weighted heavily in favour of the former, isolating the real out-of-the-blue disasters to a small section at the back. Once the tasks are clear, all that's left is to implement them, which, of course, is where much of the trouble starts and ends.

MATTERS WITHIN YOUR INFLUENCE

There are two causes of failure that you have the power to influence or determine: (1) not following the strategy and (2) playing unskillfully.

This is the strategy: maximize surplus cash* and apply it to a mix of appreciators that you understand; use leverage (where appropriate) and compounding to boost returns while maintaining adequate liquidity throughout.

*To maximize surplus cash, one, by definition, manages needs.

The first problem is not doing the above; the second is trying but not doing it very well and getting it wrong. At the risk of repeating earlier messages, the point needs to be made because it strikes at the heart of the problem. There is no other way of winning at the wealth game without random or exceptional good fortune, which none of us can plan for.

Maximize surplus cash—you can influence your income, not control it. But you can determine your spending. The net effect gives you huge power to get this part of the strategy right.

Apply it to a mix of appreciators—you now know what they are and where to find them.

That you understand—the information is there if you look for it, and the necessary level of understanding starts low, increasing naturally with experience and further study. Different entry points to equities and bonds can be chosen to match your knowledge and confidence at every stage.

Use leverage (where appropriate)—granted, if banks and other providers aren't lending, there's not a lot you can do, but nothing stays the same for long in finance, and they soon will be. Basic safeguards around the use of this tool are there if you choose to use them.

And compounding—all you need to do to benefit from this natural force for wealth creation is make investments, small or large, as soon as you can and as continuously as possible, and wait.

To boost returns—this is the automatic consequence of leverage and compounding. Whether returns are positive or negative depends on the direction of values for the assets you have chosen to buy.

While maintaining adequate liquidity throughout—although easier said than done, this is entirely possible, even if it does require you to provide more for unexpected, out-of-control events and to go slower than you might like.

If you have the necessary income to join the game, you are free to follow this strategy if you wish. It is entirely voluntary. Full time, part time, or no time, the choice is yours, and cause and effect will play out.

Skill is a slightly different matter, and if you're looking for catches, here's one. Maximizing surplus cash and maintaining adequate liquidity require discipline more than skill, but choosing assets and using debt are different. Attribution, allocation, and other techniques around the art of pot building are further complementary skills, but great progress can be made without them.

Problems arise where you make a poor judgment and choose to buy an asset that (either good or bad to begin with) is bad when you want to sell. Problems also arise if you take on debt that is too expensive, inflexible, or just too much. If you are too cautious, you miss out on returns and lose purchasing power, as inflation erodes value, but if you take too much risk, there is a chance of catastrophic loss. Such challenges in executing your strategy are just part of the game, and every game has them. Like learning to ski, sail, garden, or paint, no amount of theory and planning alone will get you there. You must engage and take on these challenges. As novices, the trick is to take one step at a time, watch, learn, and tread carefully, building skills and judgement through practical application.

This analysis may be accurate, but is it helpful? Is it any different from saying that the reason there is an obesity problem is that people eat too much and exercise too little? At one level, it's all we need to know—a simple, accurate diagnosis of the problem with equally simple remedies. At another, because it is so self-evident, it leaves us slightly unsatisfied and curious to investigate the underlying causes and the contributors to those causes. Analysis paralysis can develop and with it, the risk that we forget the simple causes and cures or fail to act.

It's for you to decide how far to analyse, but there are six underlying causes to start with.

1. Forgetting what O is and why you are pursuing it
No goal can stay front of mind at all times. Once adopted, it joins the pack, and your affection for it will ebb and flow as others jostle for attention. O suffers from being so distant. At age twenty, it is over twenty-five years away, which seems like a lifetime. How many twenty- or thirty-year-olds want to put restrictions on their lives for a reward so far off? The skill, as you'll see, is to convince yourself that you can have your cake and eat it; instead of putting anything on hold, you are travelling light, unburdened and free to enjoy simple things, and at the same time speeding towards O.

You can meditate to visualize the point of arrival or blissful afterlife, or perhaps you can say it as a mantra every day, like US salesmen and traders who stand in front of the mirror each morning bellowing, "I am great. I am the best," over and over again. Or perhaps you can learn it like a language. Whatever your technique, O and your reasons for pursuing it need to become ingrained and part of your default setting, so much second nature that any behaviour to the contrary feels instinctively wrong. Like a piece of DNA or a stem cell, this small, potent idea begins to shape your entire being.

Interloper risk remains, however, and none is as dangerous as the curse of comparison, which, like a wily serpent, subverts and replaces O with something that, on its face, looks like a helpful aid to your quest but is, in fact, a major obstacle.

Competitiveness, like the human immune system, can turn from promoting positive and beneficial outcomes to becoming a destructive force—toxic and corrosive. What is this unhelpful competitiveness? "I want a bigger pot than you," or "I want the biggest pot," or "I want to build my pot at the expense of yours," or "I want to see you fail whether I succeed in reaching O or not." Quite apart from the fact that these sentiments are fuelled by ill will, which isn't good for you, none is a goal in the wealth game, so pursuing them merely distracts and wastes valuable time and energy.

Yet they are beguiling and habit forming; we seem to be programmed to measure achievement and success against that of others, particularly those closest to us. For many, if they get paid more; have a better-looking partner; have brighter, sportier, or more musical children; have a nicer house; are healthier; have more hair and fewer wrinkles; have longer holidays; have more exotic interests; have a livelier social life; or have a newer car than their family, friends, or work colleagues, they're happy. The scope for one-upmanship is virtually endless.

I have a friend whose new wife "adopted" mine when they moved to London. She was an ex-banker who had previously been married for ten years to a New York lawyer and often told Jessie how "wonderfully unthreatening" she was. Children were arriving for both women, and there was much discussion about playgroups and socials. Every time she visited us, this friend bought chocolate pastries that she generously offered around, never taking one herself. Over time, the evidence of her mission to promote fatness in all others became humorously transparent. Oh, the meals she cooked us and the time we spent watching her move food around the plate without eating it and bemoaning her unhealthy lifestyle, while all the time she was secretly doing boot-camp training in Hyde Park! Was she happier that we were getting fatter? Maybe.

Another wolf in sheep's clothing even more insidious and harder to spot is the friend who is always there for you and ready with advice and solutions for your endless problems, shortcomings, and failures. With palpable enthusiasm and passion, he delves into your misery like a terrier with the scent of blood, showering advice all over the place and, at the end of the session, leaves feeling thoroughly worthy and uplifted. There is a fair chance that his advice is not entirely dispassionate! Your overenthusiastic friend may either be trying to escape his own sorry situation or engaging in some kind of power play. It's best to enjoy his soothing words but treat his advice with caution.

In my experience, there is no corner of human existence where this doesn't take place. Industry is fraught with it, and some corners are far worse than others: financial services, media, and the professions—for example, where the value resides in individuals and a firm's brand. It is no coincidence that king makers in these industries are so often dissatisfied. They work with each other and live with themselves. Think also about government and the civil service, a twilight world of games and manoeuvres; the public sector, with managers presiding over vast budgets and empires; and the military, where rank is emblazoned on clothes, and postings and privileges, if not money, define status. Are the clergy any better? I don't know. How about farmers? Maybe they are an exception. I know a few, and perhaps there is something about the grimness of trying to harness nature for profit that creates a rare solidarity.

How about "I want to reach O before you"? Reaching O early certainly is an objective, so is this competitive sentiment helpful? Some players, though inherently loving and generous hearted, thrive from outdoing others; they simply can't help it. While understandable, this too is wasted effort, and any satisfaction arising is no more than temporary delusion. It just doesn't matter if, when, or how another person reaches O. That's their story, and you have your own to write. Shed ill will, and you can devote all your resources to worthwhile endeavour and reach O sooner.

What are examples of helpful competitiveness? "I will not give in to cravings," "I will put up with this discomfort," "I won't be beaten by tiredness or lethargy," "I will master these skills," "I will understand this concept," "I will do these things I don't want to," "I will follow the strategy," and "I won't be overcome by setbacks and difficulties." The competition here is against our own frailties, not other players, and it's the toughest game there is.

Healthy competition, however, is essential in knowing your commercial value and position in your industry and organization. You need to understand what your skills and services are worth and price yourself as high above that level as you can negotiate at any given time. You also need to know what people in your industry with your skills and experience can and do earn. If you work in a firm, measuring pay and grade, performance, and output against others in the same firm is a primary requirement. This kind of comparison is no more than intelligent commercial research to maximize your earnings on route to O.

What about portfolio theory and the zero-sum game, where each person's gain is equivalent to another's loss, so the net overall change in wealth or benefit is zero? Surely as skimmers rather than wealth creators, we only gain at another's expense? First, you don't have to just skim; you can create, even in a small way, without ownership. By adding some value to a product, process, or service through your work, you add to the size of the overall wealth pot, creating more to go around and enabling a win-win scenario. Second, even if you are only skimming, the field of play is so big, and wealth resources are so huge that there is a lot to go around. Are there enough wealth and resources on planet Earth to allow everyone to win at the wealth game, at least theoretically? I suspect there are.

On that basis, it's incumbent on everyone to compete for their share. "I will go to where the wealth is," "I will work harder or more creatively or productively than others," "I will push to be recognized," "I will demand to be paid appropriately for my contribution," "I will buy my share of good assets," "I will make smarter judgements than others," and so on. All these competitive actions help you reach O.

The fundamental problem is that other people represent the easiest targets for our competitive zeal. Whether playing the wealth game or not, they are weak like us, prone to the same cravings and frailties, getting it wrong, and failing all the time. To set your sights on vanquishing such fickle and wretched competition is to aim at the wrong target completely. How often though do we set our course by reference to others, justifying all sorts of poverty-promoting behaviours in the process?

2. Impatience
Patience, so often interpreted as weakness or submission, is strength and, like other human qualities, can be trained and exercised to maximum effect. Like the power of silence in a room of babbling voices, it stands apart, exuding confidence and wisdom born of self-control and mindfulness. It creates the space and time for you to see things as they are and not as you might first have perceived them. This gentleness and calm allows equanimity to develop—not weary resignation and inaction where events and circumstances have beaten the life and resistance out of you, but a positive chosen mind-set.

These skills benefit you in all areas but are particularly useful in the wealth game, where the results of your actions and inactions ripple out throughout your entire life, sometimes noticed and other times appearing only when they converge with others. Taking the time to observe all these small consequences creates a sense of achievement and fulfilment that balances the disappointment of setbacks and mishaps. The bigger picture is always clear and offers refuge when your will is fading.

The very opposite of this health-and-wealth promoting state of mind is one that allows unfiltered access to external data sources, creating a miasma through which virtually no clear independent thought is possible and where one is pulled and jerked in all directions at the whim of unrestrained senses and cravings. We are tested to the full in this current age of information overload, 24/7 connectivity, and demand for instant results.

Those who are driving their way to success, jumping or swerving to avoid obstacles, traps and enemies, and accumulating points all the way as if playing a computer game may ask, "What's wrong with full-on activity? Surely that's the way to success." This isn't a question of wrong or right but cause and effect. Greater activity creates more ripples but doesn't necessarily get you farther—just watch competitive swimmers versus their splashing, puffing recreational counterparts. One is graceful, fast, and efficient, combining skill and strength earned from training; the other is enthusiastic and determined but fairly ineffective in comparison. It is the combination of activity and skill that counts.

Patience and equanimity help you overcome the inevitable pain and setbacks of endeavour and skill building and give you staying power to get the job done.

There are some traps they help you avoid: one is overtrading. In the business world, this term is applied to firms that grow too fast and run short of cash. For private investors, it covers a range of activities amounting to a financial version of attention deficit hyperactivity disorder (ADHD):

a. Selling assets too soon—not recognizing when you are holding a good asset that has longer to run or not giving an asset time to deliver

b. Frequent switching in and out of assets, incurring high-transaction costs, and making record keeping hard

Impatience also causes many players to lose heart or become paralyzed by fear and stop saving money because the results don't seem worthwhile or are too slow coming; dig into capital to fund luxuries; go on a spending splurge; sell and abandon equities because they have lost money or because returns have not met their expectations; or get sidetracked by personal issues and forget to keep playing.

An impetuous player is likely to make rash, ill-considered decisions without carrying out proper investigations and due diligence into the asset or thinking through the consequences of buying it. You may buy a bad asset or one that doesn't suit you, or you may get your timing wrong, as in the following two cases:

a. Buying simply because you have the cash to spend, not because it is a good time to invest.

Occasionally, it's clear to most that there is more downside risk in a market than upside potential. The fuel driving price increases is running low or has run out, with momentum relying on a few last vapours. This is bubble territory, and investing heavily at such time is unwise. Mostly, the picture is clouded by various fuel sources on different time lines. Where there is considerable uncertainty (yet the markets remain buoyant), run a simple test before buying: Can you envisage the market rising or falling 10% or more in the next six to twelve months? If it's hard to see this level of upside but easy to see the downside, that tells you to exercise caution and wait to see what happens.

b. Buying too early in a downturn—This is a variation of the above. I saw many private investors buying bank shares and commercial property after the steep value falls of 2008, only to see them fall another 50–80% in value and stay there for years, while other assets prospered in the recovery.

Another particularly dangerous snare for the impatient is soundbite investing, as it offers apparent credibility and a shortcut basis for informed, sound decision making. Expertise, tips, and edges are ubiquitous and easy to collect, but most times, they are either as shallow as water on sand, which evaporates in the sun or soaks away, or are self-serving and designed for someone else's interests, not yours. Successful investing requires hard work and takes time.

3. Inertia
Ancient Jain statues depict naked men so detached from the physical that vines have begun to climb up their bodies. These individuals sought liberation through endless immobility and nonharm, and they maintained such respect for life-forms, whether animal or vegetable, that as death approached, some would practice starvation.

Most ordinary people don't set out to be inert; inertness just creeps up like ivy, which, unless cut off at the base or uprooted, slowly overcomes them. The result tends not to be spiritual enlightenment but gradual asphyxiation from within, as they fill up with every piece of physical and mental matter consumed and not released, growing heavier and more leaden, to the point of total immobility.

The wealth department is generally an early victim, thanks to its low chart position in the top-twenty things that matter to us. This is partly due to a poor internal PR function that delivers mixed messages and fails to properly explain and promote the benefits. So begins the universal habit of not getting around to doing things that are self-evidently in our best financial interests.

The only cure I know is activity, mental and physical, preferably with some routine built in. This shakes off torpor and promotes vitality and further productive activity, creating a virtuous circle. Taking medicine that generally appears much more unpleasant than it tastes requires self-discipline.

4. Being too disorganized and chaotic

"It's easy to be a busy fool," an old boss of mine frequently lectured us. It's the opposite problem to the last one but just as serious. Endless goals and initiatives collide with an inability to process them properly, which creates a frenzy of unproductiveness and exhaustion. Any genuinely worthwhile objectives on the shopping list are buried along with all the others, and despite a plainly evident lack of results, we are too busy, stubborn, or frightened to acknowledge them, and we drive on, consoled by the endeavour.

Economy of effort is an advantage in the wealth game. It allows you to complete more tasks well. If you are naturally disorganized or chaotic, not only are you slow to process things, but you'll also be a lousy delegator, and the only sensible answer is to take on fewer tasks. Those who are incisive and efficient can gain leverage through delegation and build systems capable of processing far more. This isn't a matter of sweat and hard work but skills—some of which can be learned, while others are beyond your capability—so it is as well to recognize your limitations and adapt to be most effective.

Happiness surveys consistently reveal that alongside financial worries, another perennial blight for adults is feeling out of control. Unsurprisingly, both contribute to each other.

5. Fear

The world is full of fear, and we each create our own "favourites" list from a very long drop-down menu. Like adrenaline and butterflies in the stomach, a certain amount is helpful. On one hand, it alerts you to danger; on the other, it spurs and excites you. Anyone who watches snowboard and ski racing, jumping, and tricks or ice sledding also witnesses the competitors' exhilaration alongside the danger and horrific-looking crashes. Too much fear paralyzes you and hampers productive activity.

In finance, where so much is seen as complex or in the hands of others, awareness of danger can work for the good, sharpening your senses and forcing you to confront and analyse risks. I have also seen many people let their imagination run unchecked, not informed by facts and evidence, and they conjure up such a dismal list of dangers that inaction is inevitable. Even the brightest can hide behind reason and analysis, manufacturing so many possible options that they become too mentally exhausted to make a decision or take action. For them, the intellectual process both masks and promotes their fears.

As discussed earlier, most ordinary people fear loss, failure, or just looking stupid, but oversensitivity to it bars many from playing the wealth game to their full potential. They lose confidence in their own capabilities and judgements, and do foolish things, like panic and sell at the bottom of markets, avoid sound investments, or trust no one for help—in short, they retreat into a shell.

I don't know what the cure is. My mother used to sprinkle "wolf powder" in my bedroom when I was terrified of being eaten as a little boy. That worked. Throughout the course of our marriage, Jessie has always dismissed my financial worries and preoccupations by saying, "What's the worst that can happen?" and telling me that we'd be "fine with a boiled egg." Even though things often looked pretty bad from where I was standing, this also helped. When I visualized life with no money or assets and was still able to see an existence offering happiness, fear receded. In fact, observing first hand people in some of the poorest and least developed parts of the world made me wonder whether I wasn't missing something.

Seeking refuge in the as-yet-undefined principles of the wealth game probably also helped. As long as I had a family to look after, surrender was never an option, and systematic attention to each element of the game kept me busy and distracted from difficulties.

6. Losing the joy
This is a big one—a monster, in fact—and the list of possible accusations is long. Here are a few contenders to start with:

> Where's the fun in the game?
> It's all about abstinence and deferred pleasure.
> Life spent trying to save money is dull.
> We have to wait years or decades for the rewards.
> I know it's the right thing to do, but it's just too dry.
> We need to keep a balance to make life manageable.

Unlike studying for exams or working long shifts, playing the wealth game is a long-term lifestyle choice, like staying healthy. The actions in our power that promote health include eating the right amounts of the right foods; avoiding toxins like chemical preservatives and additives, cigarette tar, nicotine, alcohol, and drugs; exercising regularly; managing stress; sleeping well; drinking clean water; keeping excess fat off; stimulating our brains; and staying connected socially.

Virtually every activity we undertake and choice we make has a direct or indirect effect on our health and, to a slightly lesser extent, on our wealth. They are all-encompassing subjects. We can ignore them, tune in occasionally as optional extras, or weave helpful behaviours into the fabric of our lives in a way that is sustainable and manageable. They can be adopted at general meeting into our constitution.

Elevating health or wealth to this level renders the question of whether or not they bring joy irrelevant. If you can't find pleasure and satisfaction in their everyday pursuit, you need to look elsewhere for your fix. It's as simple as that.

Reflecting on my own experience, I now see that without realizing it at the time, I followed a two-pronged strategy based on the principles of the wealth game: maximizing satisfaction on the one hand while minimizing my need for it on the other, and so creating a positive satisfaction-to-needs gap.

This involved eking every bit of pleasure possible from everywhere, however unlikely a source. Some things (but not everything) cost money, and a large part of the fun was finding great products or experiences for free or at a fraction of their high-street cost. Meals, clothes, holidays, socials, exercise, transport, books, boating, music, film, theatre—in fact, virtually any material or sense pleasure could be acquired for peanuts in a throwaway, thrift-shop, discount society fuelled by consumption. The pickings were easy and rich, and playing the role of Victorian urchin sat wonderfully in contrast to the social expectations of "someone in my position." It fed my inner rebel, providing deep and enduring contentment.

At the bleakest times, I'd revert to black humour. Some of my longest nights at work, most miserable journeys, and mind-numbingly dull or pointless projects have delivered classic comedy moments to cherish. In fact, the worse things were, the more preposterous the levity became, following great traditions of Monty Python, Tony Hancock, Spike Milligan, *Not the Nine O'Clock News* and Count Arthur Strong. This tended to kill any productivity or effectiveness, which made things even funnier. As for daily existence, I peppered in small treats that today seem pitifully insignificant, although at the time, they carried great weight—things like browsing in bookshops or a market, eating lunch on my own in a park, taking time out for a swim, staying up until the small hours, or going to bed at nine, driving at great speed, and every Friday, without fail, buying a raisin Danish.

The other side of the coin was to remember that I wasn't issued a promise at birth that everything would be fun or that contentment is a basic human right. I toned down my level of pleasure expectation and turned off the "indignation" and "bitterly disappointed" switches in favour of "pleasant surprise." It was a kind of self-preserving mental recalibration—not so much dumbing down and suppressing but reorienting away from the fuddle of craving and desire to a calmer place with silence, pure air, and clear light that offered space to properly see, enjoy things, and create efficiently.

Underneath it all was an unshakable belief that playing the wealth game to the utmost was the right thing to do, was wise and well founded, would work, and was already working. Here was a cause worth fighting and suffering for, and this alone gave great solace and fulfillment. Selfish? Yes and no. Yes to the extent that the goal was a personal wealth pot to meet personal needs, but no to the extent that personal needs could be managed down to a fraction of the pot, allowing provision for a wide range of family and other beneficiaries, and that it would contribute through taxes to a society and welfare system able to serve those in genuine need. Also, no inasmuch as O was only a staging post on the way, not a lifetime objective, so there would be plenty of time for reorienting further towards the greater good.

To know this was a defence against my own cravings and frailties as well as the many doubters and critics along the way who didn't quite get it. If they'd had their way, I would have spent most of my earnings on luxuries and consumables, and, like them, I would still be working for a living now, questioning the purpose of it all.

7. Other half not buying in
Somehow, it is your duty in the game to carry the debate. If there's no opposition, the arguments can be put to one side in favour of discussion about strategy, tactics, and planning. If there is, it needs to be flushed out into the open and dealt with.

Broad ground rules are better established before or in the early stages of serious relationship commitment, when the ground is rich with optimism. Anything is possible—no hurdle is too high, and no hardship is too hard. Goodwill and tolerance abound. This approach is far from fail-safe, but at least it anchors future debate. In practice, memories can fade fast, and good intentions give way to expediency, so, as with paying taxes, you're back to choosing one of the three universal options when faced with something you don't like: make a stand and fight it, join the other side, or ignore the issue completely.

Joining the other side is the financial equivalent of *Fear and Loathing in Las Vegas*, just slipping gently together into blissful inertia that marks the end of any serious chances you'll have in the wealth game. Ignoring the issue completely is even worse, as not only do you play the game, hopping on one leg with one arm tied behind your back and an eye patch, but any unity is shattered by inevitable division and resentment on both sides. The only logical solution is to face the problem and fight to eliminate unhelpful behaviours. Of course, fighting isn't conducive to harmonious relations, nor are pressure tactics, emotional blackmail, or incessant nagging. Gentle persuasion works better, but whatever the approach, reason with a touch of humility, plus compromise need to prevail.

Here are some examples: "You can go to the pub once a week with your friends but not daily," "We will get some part-time help at home but not a cleaner, cook, nanny, and gardener," "We will eat out occasionally but not every week," "Our next car doesn't need to be new or top of the range," "Just because things are on special offer doesn't mean you need to buy them," "Try alternating outfits rather than wearing a new one to each event," "How about spacing luxury holidays to keep them special?"

If the going gets really tough, you need to become an artist and paint large pictures of paradise after O.

8. Having too many children

To some, children are a blessing, and to others, they are an inconvenience, but to all, they are a financial cost. Whether they wear secondhand clothes or designer brands, eat bread and soup or five portions of fruit or vegetables a day, are left to run feral or are protected, or are sent to the local school or educated amongst the elite, they still cost. It's an unavoidable truth.

More children mean more time, more effort, and more cost. They can bring joy, but they don't bring money for a long time, if at all. I have already highlighted the timing effects on compounding; the issue here is quantum and how much you choose to spend on them beyond the bare minimum. These are personal decisions, and as always, my interest extends only as far as the effects they have on your chances of winning the wealth game. Loading yourselves with overheads before you have established the necessary income sources and wealth generation capacity simply isn't skillful play.

Fortunately, trying to create babies is generally optional, so it is something you can endeavour to manage.

CALAMITIES

Having pared away behaviours responsible for much of the self-inflicted damage to our wealth and net-assets-to-needs gap, it's time to mention some of the wildcard wealth disasters that are genuinely beyond our control.

No doubt you could dream up a very long list of bad-luck items that render you blameless in your poverty, but in my experience, there aren't so many, and fewer still in which we play no part in at all. It's impossible to shake off the fact that most of what happens to our finances arises, to some extent, from our own behaviours. It's time to step away from excuses and recognize that.

Here are ten of the worst personal poverty-causing events, aside from war and end of the world:

1. Death
2. Living too long
3. Chronic disablement or illness
4. Bankruptcy
5. Divorce or final separation
6. Redundancy
7. Unprotected asset failure
8. Uninsured asset loss
9. Market collapse
10. Long-term unemployment

I briefly added a successful claim by HMRC or other tax authority for unpaid taxes plus interest and penalties, an event that I have seen induce mental breakdown as well as inflict permanent damage to wealth, but then I remembered that paying taxes is within your control, so it doesn't count.

Which of the ten do you play absolutely no part in? Think about each for a moment. Whatever the cause, they serve as a reminder that wealth-damaging things will happen and as a prompt to press on with self-improvement in every department.

By their nature, calamities outside of your control tend to be unpredictable and hard to deal with. All you can do is to be as well prepared as possible to face them, and when they do arrive, deal with them as best you can and move on. If the cause of the wealth erosion is continuing, you first need to do what you can to neutralize it, or you will suffer more loss, and second, you need to manage the consequences. If the cause has run its course, only the consequences matter.

Without wishing to deny or trivialize any of these unpleasant occurrences, I offer a framework for their consideration:

1. Is the problem permanent, can you resolve it on your own or with help, or can time cure it?
2. What is the actual loss to your existing assets, not on paper but crystallized?
3. How much of your future income will you lose, best and worst cases?
4. How big is the impact? Can you bounce back over a few years or not?

A full ten years before my disc prolapse and lower-back trauma, I weathered another health event, this time a potentially lethal autoimmune attack. It was the centrepiece of three setbacks over two years that left me reeling and exhausted. Suddenly, I was no longer immortal and indestructible; something of my gung-ho spirit disappeared, and weariness crept in as I began the long slog back to health.

Systemic lupus erythematosus (SLE) was the title; it caused my immune system to attack and inflame healthy cells, tissues, and organs, triggering a cocktail of woes—painful and seized joints, nephritis, stomach ulcers, a blotchy leg condition called *erythema nodosum*, and overwhelming fatigue. Diagnosis was largely a process of elimination, and, like a piece of meat, I lay in London's St Thomas' Hospital, giving blood and tissue samples and smiling at student doctors and nurses invited to study this rare condition. We never knew for sure the cause, but I instinctively felt it was a physical response to relentless pressure and overwork.

The problem began when my department at work was closed down just before Christmas, and all ninety staff around Europe were let go. We were all called into a large room and told the news by an ashen-faced head; it was a scene of high drama, just the kind of roller-coaster excitement I craved after four turgid years in law. It didn't matter that my first banking job was finished after only eighteen months or that I hit the street as an economic recession was deepening.

By March, I was back in employment but also determined to build a parallel income as insurance. I invested £25,000 in a start-up recording studio and label in Tottenham, London, producing break-beat-drum-and-bass music, or jungle, which was showing signs of crossing over to mainstream. For a year, I spent almost every free weeknight, weekend, and holiday at the studio filled with clouds of smoke, bottles, and bodies, a far cry from the square mile.

This, of course, was unsustainable, and it ended badly. SLE took hold as the business folded; I lost the money, and was bedridden for two months, no good to anyone. My new boss brought a cheery deputation from work to my hospital bed, and I felt comforted to know that there was still a job to go back to.

I fought back gently with newfound respect for my body and a determination to avoid extravagant time wasting; my youth was over, and there would be no more indulgent and reckless wasting of these precious resources. This new cause was not about money but self-preservation, where focus and efficiency could create space for proper time off and relaxation.

Applying the four questions to your particular disaster is for you to do. Interestingly, market collapse scores very well, since the kind of established markets that ordinary people participate in tend to bounce back, and by holding on to assets like equities, bonds, and property, paper losses may never crystallize into actual ones. Dividend or rental income may be temporarily disrupted, but bond coupons stay the same, and normal service generally resumes before too long. For patient players, the overall effect is no more than a nasty shock.

The worst-scoring events are divorce or final separation and complete asset failure—for example, a business in liquidation, an investment Ponzi scheme, or a house that falls over a cliff and isn't insured for that risk. These events are final, do crystallize actual wealth loss, and will reduce future income, either from work or foregone potential returns from the assets lost. The only possible escape here is scale.

A final thought is that in finance, small problems often lead to bigger ones, and big problems can lead to catastrophes and meltdown. Never is this truer than when people are overindebted or short of cash. Normally manageable situations turn nasty, time seems to accelerate, and everything becomes harder to handle under the magnifying power of leverage and illiquidity.

PART SIX

THE END GAME

XVII

HAVE I WON?

To an extent, winning the wealth game is a state of mind; not only must you reach O but you must also realize and believe that you have. If you aren't sure where you are in the game or doubt your success, even if you have passed O, you won't collect the full prize.

The brief is as follows: identify a reliable shortcut method that you can easily apply to calculate your position in the wealth game, confirm whether or not you have passed O, and identify any shortfall or surplus between your net assets and needs.

Two expressions to highlight are "shortcut method" and "easily apply," as it is these qualities that make it usable and accessible to all. The long method of delivering these answers is to build a forward cash flow projection for all incomings and outgoings as they are expected to arise over the forecast period, factoring in assumptions for cost inflation and investment returns. Feeding into this is a projected balance sheet showing the value of net assets and taking account of gains and losses, additions, and any sales or liquidations to deliver cash for living. The cash flow can be measured weekly, monthly, quarterly, or annually. It is like treating you as a business enterprise and seeking to predict and quantify every activity and event that affects you financially for the rest of your life.

Unsurprisingly, this approach is fraught with difficulties: First, the granular and extensive detail of inputs and outputs promotes a sense of spurious accuracy—in other words, the exercise feels and looks scientific but isn't. Second, time horizons may be very long (fifty-plus years), making detailed annual forecasting meaningless. Third, results are highly sensitive to rates of future cost inflation and investment return, which are impossible to predict with certainty. Fourth, advanced financial modelling skills are needed. Fifth, if done properly, the exercise is extremely time consuming and complicated. Finally, answers are quickly out of date, as time elapses, and assumptions need to be revised.

Yes, you can take raw data and spend time with a financial planner or other expert refining it; have them input the numbers into their chosen model template, and play with different assumptions to provide answers. Current software packages used by financial advisers include Voyant, Truth, Moneyscope, Planlab, and Money Hub. This is a perfectly rational course, but it doesn't overcome the aforementioned principal difficulties and, if done thoroughly, will be expensive. And that expense will continue every time you want to revisit and update the model. Instead of offering you the chance to upgrade your own skills and learn to help yourself, this approach makes you reliant on others. People you pay to help you may or may not have the necessary skills, and none will be as interested in your finances as you should be. If, through outsourcing the exercise, you lose track of where numbers are from and how they are manipulated, you can't rely on the results with confidence.

There is a place for granular cash flow forecasting, particularly where forecast periods are short and cash flows are simple and easy to predict or where players can't manage without outside help. The rest should look elsewhere for a useful planning tool. There are various free systems available online, such as the independent www.retireeasy.co.uk and www.retiready.co.uk from Aegon, and it is worth looking at these.

THE NAN TEST

I propose a tool called the net-assets-to-needs, or NAN, test. It is a refinement of the net-worth-and-needs calculations and NAN gap exercise you have already done, adapted for prudence and greater accuracy. Textbook planners may wince at some of the liberties, but the basic structure is sound. It's free and straightforward to use and provides enough accuracy for planning and making decisions year after year. When the time comes to retire from paid work permanently, you may want to undertake a detailed cash flow modelling exercise with a financial planner to verify your own work and provide reassurance that you really have reached O.

The outputs are simple:

Table 17.1

Calculation of NAN surplus or shortfall, NAN ratio and net assets cover

	£000	£000	£000	£000	£000	£000
needs	1,000	1,000	1,000	1,000	1,000	1,000
net assets	0	250	500	750	1,000	1,250
NAN (shortfall)/surplus	(1,000)	(750)	(500)	(250)	0	250
NAN ratio (%)[1]	0	25	50	75	100	125
NA cover[2]	0	0.25x	0.5x	0.75x	1.0x	1.25x

Notes
1. Net assets / needs x 100.
2. How many times needs are covered by net assets.

In this example, needs are set at £1m and compared with a range of net asset numbers to produce NAN gap, NAN ratio, and net assets cover figures.

Before you can rely on these, your calculation of net assets needs to be amended and the effects of asset returns and cost inflation considered. For the NAN test, your task is to match your available productive assets with your needs, so the traditional net worth number must be shaved in certain areas to provide a more accurate number.

First, remove depreciators other than cash, bonds, and all consumables. In your personal net worth calculation, include all assets, whatever their classification. The NAN test measures only your total productive asset base, so appreciators, bonds, and cash. Other depreciators and all consumables are disregarded, as these wasting items don't appreciate and can't be relied on to service future needs.

You might think this harsh in the case of luxury items that you can live without and that have a genuine (albeit declining) sale value, such as boats and caravans. Again, it is up to you how prudent you want to be, but the NAN test is a shortcut founded on prudence, and it works properly only if the assets you count produce an income or will definitely appreciate in value over time.

Next, add today's value of guaranteed future income, including pensions. So far, you have included all existing asset pots in your net assets. Now, add in the after-tax value of any certain receipts in the future, as they will contribute to your needs. These might be maintenance settlements, fixed inheritances where the person has already died, or defined benefit and state pensions. Don't include inheritances that haven't crystallized, because they can't be guaranteed. Income from future work obviously doesn't count, as O assumes that no paid future work is necessary.

To convert future income receipts into a balance-sheet sum, add them up in today's value for all the years you expect them to continue, and then adjust for tax. A state pension of £6,000 per annum in today's money over twenty-three years, say from age sixty-seven to ninety, is £138,000 before tax. To be prudent, deduct tax at your expected marginal rate; after 20% basic-rate tax, £110,400 would be added to your net worth. Do the same for annuities, or, alternatively, include in your balance sheet a figure for the resale value of your annuity on the open market after tax. An inheritance of £50,000, after inheritance tax (if any) should be recorded at that level.

For private, defined contribution pensions, including SIPPs, work out the after-tax value of the pot after accounting for any reliefs and allowances and making reasonable provision for tax payable on withdrawals.

This is one area, along with home values and unlisted shares, where you'll need some expert help to arrive at a number that can be relied on, but for a working model, make your best guess, and carry on with the test without getting too caught up in detail and complexity.

At O, you are better off with no debt whatsoever, particularly if you plan to stop paid work. This makes life simpler, clearer, and a great deal safer. If you do carry debt, I recommend that you deduct from your net worth for the NAN test—not just the principal amount outstanding but also today's value of the interest due over the lifetime of the loan. It is a real cost that shouldn't be ignored. You should factor in the terms of your debt package, whether it is fixed or variable rate, and the effect of special deals ending to arrive at a prudent figure.

It is now time to factor in the effects of asset returns and cost inflation. You may recall that by capitalizing all numbers at today's values, you set aside the effects of time value of money on your assets and future needs. As things stand, your net-asset-and-needs totals can't be meaningfully compared until you have decided how each one will grow into the future. The cost of your chosen needs basket will rise or fall with market prices, and it's safe to assume that, overall, the direction will be upward. The question is, at what rate. Similarly, your assets should produce income or capital returns over time, but again, at what rate?

If both rates are the same and stay that way (so they rise or fall together), you reach O as soon as your net assets match your needs. If your needs are £1 million, and your net assets are also £1 million, you are over the finish line. It doesn't matter when your needs arise or in what quantities they are incurred, since you will have corresponding assets of the same value to match them.

In practice, the rates are likely to diverge; it is hard to construct an asset base that grows at the same rate as your needs over a long period, and when this happens, the relationship between net assets and needs changes either for better or worse. You will suddenly have a surplus or shortfall, and no longer are you are indifferent as to when your needs arise.

For your NAN test to stand up in real life, you must adjust the results to reflect your views on certain time value of money–related problems:

1. Likely differential between rates of asset return and cost inflation
The difficulty stems from the principle that £1 today is worth more than £1 tomorrow because today's £1 will have grown by tomorrow. In the NAN test, you value both needs and net assets in today's money value, but over the course of your forecast, these values will change. If as is most likely, they move out of line, one is going to grow faster than the other.

A solution to this problem is to build a spreadsheet that grows needs at one rate and net assets at another, and builds in a regular amortization of needs over the period. Take your total needs figure and divide it by the number of years in your forecast to produce an average annual needs number. This is your first year's payment. In the next year, it grows by whatever inflation rate you choose, and so on throughout the period.

The start net asset number necessary to meet these inflating needs in full varies depending on the rate of return on assets versus needs. Each year, your net assets number reduces by the amount of the needs payment for that year, and the balance earns a return at your chosen rate. Gradually, it erodes to zero. The object of the exercise is to find the starting net asset number that runs out at the end of the final year of your forecast. This can be trial and error or via a ready reckoner that runs the calculations for a range of starting numbers. The range in my ready reckoner runs from 300% of needs down to 50%.

I have run numbers for a range of scenarios, to offer a table you can make your own adjustment to needs, depending on your views on relative growth rates. The three forecast periods of thirty, forty, and fifty years are based on a current age of sixty, fifty, or forty and a life expectancy of ninety. It is for you to pick the period that most closely suits your own circumstances. If you're off the scale because you think you'll live for a shorter or longer period, at least the following results give you an idea of the direction of travel, so you can make a reasonable estimation. For an accurate picture, you can run the model yourself.

For each of these time periods, there are six rate scenarios. The first three assume that costs rise faster than asset returns by 1% to 3% per annum. The second set is reversed, showing asset returns beating cost inflation by 1% through to 3%.

The resulting numbers in the table show the required starting net assets as a percentage of today's needs total. Where growth rates are expected to be equal, starting net assets are 100% of needs whatever the period.

Table 17.2.1

Ready reckoner showing required net worth based on different assumptions for future cost inflation and investment returns

number of years to death	30 %	40 %	50 %
equal rates	100	100	100
different rates			
return v inflation (%)			
0 : 1	116	122	129
0 : 2	136	151	169
0 : 3	159	189	226
1 : 0	87	83	79
2 : 0	76	70	64
3 : 0	67	60	53

If your investment returns exceed needs inflation by 3% per annum over a fifty-year period, you only require net assets equal to 53% of your starting needs total while a reverse differential leaves you needing 226% of needs. This staggering difference is worth illustrating further.

Let's say that your needs are £1.5 million over fifty years, equivalent to a starting number of £30,000 per annum. On the +3% per annum scenario, you reach O when your net assets are £795,000, but at –3% per annum, you must accumulate £3,390,000 to finish the game!

Understanding how growth rates interact and choosing appropriate portfolio structures to suit is the key to stretching your assets further. The table shows that the difference in outcomes between managing your money and assets well or badly are huge. The ordinary person, weighed down with the challenges of earning, providing and saving, too often has little or no time to properly address this aspect. For all your laudable efforts, you might as well be peeing into a force ten gale. Somehow you need to turn around, face the other way and let the wind work for you.

2. Needs arising at different times and in different quantities
The problem here is an extension of the first. If the cost of your needs inflates at a different rate to your net assets, timing matters. Fortunately, the impact of this isn't great, and a tweak to your target NAN ratio deals with the issue.

Logic dictates that if your needs are inflating faster than your net assets, the sooner you incur them, the better, while if net assets are growing faster, deferring needs will enhance your wealth. The question is, "How big is the effect either way?"

As before, forecast periods are thirty, forty, and fifty years. In this case, instead of dividing your needs total equally between all years, the following table assumes that you spend an extra 30% of total needs in the first ten years, spread equally each year, and that the remaining 70% are spread equally between all years in the forecast. If your total needs are £1.5 million and time horizon forty years, the cost for the first ten years is £71,250 per annum and, for the remaining thirty years, is £26,250.*

*30% × £1,500,000 = £450,000 = £45,000 per annum over ten years
£1,500,000 – 450,000 = £1,050,000 = £26,250 per annum over forty years
£45,000+ £26,250 = £71,250

If you want to allocate your needs more scientifically, simply enter the relevant cost portion in the year it is expected to be spent, rather than averaging them as I have done. The following table is designed to illustrate the effects of early spending, so a broad assumption works fine. It shows how your required starting net assets figure changes versus the average annual cost basis example in Table 17.2.1. The numbers in brackets are the answers from that table.

Table 17.2.2

The effects of early needs spending on required net worth based on different assumptions for future cost inflation and investment returns

number of years to death early spend	30 %	40 %	50 %
equal rates	100	100	100
different rates			
return v inflation (%)			
0 : 1	113 (116)	117 (122)	122 (129)
0 : 2	128 (136)	139 (151)	152 (169)
0 : 3	146 (159)	167 (189)	193 (226)
1 : 0	90 (87)	87 (83)	85 (79)
2 : 0	81 (76)	77 (70)	73 (64)
3 : 0	74 (67)	69 (60)	64 (53)

The results show that outcomes are more sensitive to inflation and return rate differential than to time. When incurring your needs early, you must set aside more net assets to meet them if you think your asset returns will beat cost inflation, but can rely on lower starting assets if you expect your assets to underperform. I haven't modelled the reverse situation, where needs are weighted in the last ten years of the forecast period, partly because it is a less likely scenario for most people, but also because the direction of results can be deduced from the table.

You can also use the multipliers from Table 17.2.1 to calculate the effect of inflation on your needs total, its future value. This is useful if your assets are less than your needs, which by definition is the case until you reach O.

The following table illustrates how annual inflation of 2% and 3% affect needs of £30,000 per annum over thirty, forty, and fifty years, assuming you have no assets.

Table 17.3

Use of inflation multiplier to grow needs total

average annual needs (£)	30,000	30,000	30,000
forecast years (£)	30	40	50
needs in today's money (£)	900,000	1,200,000	1,500,000
2% inflation multiplier	1.4x	1.5x	1.7x
adjusted needs (£)	1,260,000	1,800,000	2,550,000
average annual earnings required (£)	42,000	45,000	51,000
3% inflation multiplier	1.6x	1.9x	2.3x
adjusted needs (£)	1,440,000	2,280,000	3,450,000
average annual earnings required (£)	48,000	57,000	69,000

Note that multipliers from table 17.2.1 are rounded.

Each year, your annual spending grows by the rate of inflation. Table 17.3 shows the adjusted total compared with today's value. Over fifty years of 3% per annum inflation, the £1.5 million total more than doubles to nearly £3.5 million, an effective cost of £69,000 per annum. Building a productive asset base to offset this effect is the only solution for avoiding this treadmill.

What does all this mean in practice? For my own planning, I assume that the after-tax return on my net assets will equal the cost inflation of my needs, in effect a 100% NAN ratio or 1× NA cover. This may sound undemanding, but remember that all tax is deducted from asset returns before comparing them with needs. Since giving up full-time work in 2009, my after-tax asset returns have beaten cost inflation each year. As I have not expanded my needs, the result is a stronger NAN ratio. The extra safety margin will be useful in a downturn.

WHAT IS THE RIGHT NAN RATIO?

Just as you set O by designing and managing your future needs, so you must also choose a NAN ratio that you trust and believe in. There is no universal answer.

It is time to account for downside risks. In capitalizing your future needs and taking a view on asset returns versus cost inflation, you are forecasting the future in a changing world. Not only must your NAN test calculations be correct but they must also be commercially sensible and prudent; make allowance for faulty assumptions. Only then can you believe beyond reasonable doubt that your chosen ratio will deliver enough to see you through, come what may. Set your target at a level that allows you to sleep at night. The more dispassionate may rest easily with zero surplus, a 100% NAN ratio, and a 1× NA cover, but fitful sleepers of a nervous disposition will need a greater comfort level.

The risks to your financial security have already been discussed but, in essence, amount to either underestimating your needs or the rate at which they'll inflate in the future, or overestimating your net assets or their future returns. This is very easy to do, and you should assume that all your calculations so far include a built-in bias towards the positive. O is too valuable a prize, and human nature is too predictable to deny the possibility of any fudging along the way. It is also impossible to rule out investment losses, tax rises, and unexpected mishaps or emergencies that will damage your finances. In fact, you should assume that these events will arise.

But how prudent should you be? It is easy to overdo the caution and provide for so many contingencies that running out is beyond imagination in all scenarios but Armageddon. This misses the point that your goal is to reach O in as short a time as you are able. Piling up material resources for a rainy day takes valuable time. Why choose to devote a minute longer than necessary to the pursuit of your own financial security when there is so much else to do? Caution is a natural defence against danger, but it stems from fear and promotes a mind-set of fear. It also reinforces the unhealthy habit of clinging to money and material possessions as if your life depends on them.

If you have mastered the art of needs management, your confidence will be great, and you can survive comfortably with a small safety buffer for overspending and rash actions. If you cannot control yourself, you should set a higher margin. You should also not underestimate the risks of investment losses and events beyond your control, and plan accordingly.

Before deciding on the size of your safety margin, it's worth recapping on some of the prudence and protections already contained in the NAN test.

Needs
The test encourages you to be prudent at every stage, to include your fullest possible needs in each category, and to avoid overly scientific attempts to allocate or reduce them. For example, assumptions that you will spend steadily on holidays and living expenses overlooks the fact that some time before reaching ninety, your appetite for travel and adventure will probably wane, and that household and dependants should cost less. In some years, you may not go away at all, and for a period, you may live on your own.

Further overestimates may include work-related costs—for example, my living costs have fallen considerably as a result of not working as I used to. I have no commuter travel or work-related accommodation costs, I don't wear a suit and tie or buy sandwiches for lunch, and I have replaced private gym membership with a community leisure centre. When I do go somewhere, I travel off-peak and take my time. This releases about £8,000 each year, equivalent to a pretax sum of £10,000 for a 20% taxpayer and £13,300 for a 40% taxpayer. Over forty years, the after-tax saving of this alone is £320,000 in today's money, and that's before the compounding benefit available by putting the savings to work. Some of this is offset by greater leisure spending, but a good surplus remains.

Any fixed-cost commitments, such as cash maintenance or legacies, are not index linked and won't grow with inflation. As your matching assets grow, the real value of these needs decreases.

The biggest inbuilt protection on the needs side is your ability to manage them down. Beyond subsistence and absolute necessities, every element can be reduced or eliminated, perhaps not instantly but certainly over time. As the architect of your needs, you have the power to decide your final home value, choice of schooling for your children, legacies, cars, holidays, lifestyle, care provision and so on, and you can change your mind on these as you go.

Net Assets
As the test includes only cash, bonds, or appreciators, proceeds of sale from any other depreciators or consumables is a positive and may offer some degree of protection, depending on how much of them you own.

The biggest inbuilt protection is that you record your assets at after-tax values, rather than gross, and then apply return assumptions to this lower figure. In practice, you earn returns on the gross figures—for example, rental yield on a property is set on its market value rather than after-tax value to you. If the return beats inflation, the positive effect is exaggerated further still.

Many will argue that capitalizing future interest payments on debt and adding them to your needs is unnecessarily tough. It assumes that all interest is due today, which it isn't, and that its current rate will go on rising with inflation each year of the forecast, which it won't. If you are one of these, why not include principal only and nudge up your target NAN ratio a few notches?

A problem with including loan principal only is that lenders set loan interest rates to exceed inflation so that they can make a profit. To stay level, therefore, that portion of your assets that matches your debt must deliver an after-tax return that matches. If loan interest is 7%, and you pay tax at 20%, these assets must deliver a pretax return of 8.75% per annum every year that you hold the debt. If you hold debt, a way to compensate for this demanding requirement is to add a factor to your target NAN ratio for the time value of money adjustment, say moving it from 100% to 105%.

As I have said before, the best protection here is to have no debt at O.

Another big positive factor is the effect of compounding returns on any net assets that exceed your needs. Assume that you hold net assets of £1.25 million against needs of £1 million (NAN cover of 1.25×). If after-tax returns on the first £1 million of your assets keep up with inflation of your needs, you'll have a "free" £250,000 to grow each year. Over five years at 5% per annum after taxes, this would be nearly £320,000,* almost £70,000 more. The protection itself adds more protection!

*£250,000 × $(1 + r^5)$ = £250,000 × (1.05^5) = £250,000 × 1.2763 = £319,070

Returning to the question of what is the right NAN ratio for you, it is fair to plan that after taxes, your assets will at least keep up with cost inflation, although this does require that you don't have a large portion of your assets in cash earning less than inflation. If you do and plan to stay this way for a while, it would be sensible to increase your starting NAN ratio target slightly, say to 1.05× or 1.1×.

Equally, it is prudent to assume that after-tax asset returns will not beat inflation, even if you think they will. To keep your whole pot up with inflation is an achievement after factoring in tax and underperforming cash, so why add pressure?

As to downside protection, I personally add 25% for investment losses and 15% for additional needs, making my NAN ratio target 140%, or 1.4×.

As long as my adjusted net assets are worth no less than 1.4× my needs, I can relax and carry on as I am. If the ratio falls, I may trim my needs slightly. Over time, I expect to operate with a lower ratio, because time equals risk, so less time left means less risk to protect against.

A ratio of 1.5× or more is strong, but you should question how necessary such a large comfort margin is; too high a ratio suggests that you have worked and accumulated for too long or have limited faith in your asset- or needs-management capabilities.

Let's say that you are fifty and have a needs total of £2 million composed of a final home value of £300,000, an after-tax subsistence income target of £25,000 per annum for forty years (so £1,000,000), £60,000 provision for children, £80,000 for another eight cars, luxuries of £12,000 per annum over thirty years until you are eighty (so £360,000), and five years of end-of-life care for two at £200,000.

Your chosen NAN ratio drives your required adjusted net worth. Here are three alternative approaches:

How chosen NAN ratio affects net worth target

neutral NAN ratio (%)	100	100	100
adjustment for different asset and needs inflation		5	-5
downside protection (%)			
investment losses (%)	25	15	15
additional needs (%)	15	10	10
NAN ratio (%)	140	130	120
NAN cover	1.4x	1.3x	1.2x
required net worth based on needs of £2.0m (£)	2.8m	2.6m	2.4m

A REALITY CHECK

Run the test now, however flimsy your numbers are. I promise that from the first minute, it will get to you. The best way to start is with rough (even fictional) numbers. Spending too long at this stage tailoring the inputs disrupts the flow. The trick is just to play with numbers to see how the outcomes change. The results can be surprising and horrific, and many of you will recheck the calculations and methodology, frequently in disbelief. Very large needs numbers can be produced without effort and before adding any safety margins.

At this stage, treat it as a toy, like an abacus with coloured balls that you can flick from end to end, making patterns and shapes. In time, it becomes a tool, like a calculator, and eventually, it will become a financial machine, like a computer, with wide capabilities and memory. You may put it away for long periods, but, once used, it can't be completely forgotten. It calls out to be played with.

It should also be clear by now that the NAN test is unorthodox and far from perfect. It is full of shortcuts and assumptions, and it is wholly reliant on human inputs, but somehow merely doing it is useful and rewarding. With practice and time, the results become clearer and more useful. The scales eventually tip when you have more behind you than ahead—more time, more earnings, more needs, and probably more wealth—and you are ready to take the test for real.

A variant on the exercise is to try to create the lowest set of needs you can imagine living with and cost that. In a developed Western country, it is quite a challenge to keep a forty-year needs total under £1.5 million. An after-tax income of £25,000 per annum—so just over £2,000 per month—amounts to £1 million on its own; adding a home at, say, £250,000 leaves only £250,000, or £6,250 per annum, for all holidays, cars, other luxuries, and emergencies, and that's before the costs of any children and end-of-life care.

For less of a hairshirted approach, unless you are single and childless, a forty-year needs total of £2 to 3 million is more realistic. If you apply my 40% safety factor, this raises the targets to £2.8–4.2 million.

HOW TO BE SURE

Numbers and targets are fine, but to use them for real, to rely on them being right for your future livelihood and financial well-being, is a big ask. No amount of testing against the bleakest scenarios alters the fact that they are only projections that will be wrong in some shape or form over time.

Real acceptance that you are safe comes only from your direct knowledge and experience, through actually living with financial security. The trick, therefore, is to do exactly that. As you approach the grey area that is O, start behaving as if you have reached it; monitor your investments and net worth as if they are all you have, refine your needs to the highest degree of accuracy possible, run the tests, and start to recognize the feelings associated with living without a wage. Why not siphon off all your earnings from work into a separate account as if they don't exist, and treat them as pure upside for another day? Carry on working anyway, and road test O to satisfy yourself that you are there and that you have enough of a safety margin for problems.

In my own case, there was no single flash of realization, because reaching O was a gradual process. Evidently, at a certain point in time, I reached the necessary NAN ratio, but objective clarity was still evolving, and it took a while for the truth to sink in and for me to accept beyond doubt that I had crossed the line. By this stage, I was hard at work planning next steps and too distracted to particularly notice. The celebrations did come, but in fits and starts—quietly to start with and then more confidently.

Nothing builds confidence like action. There is a huge amount you can do to strengthen your position and eliminate fears and doubts in the O phase, particularly if you plan to stop paid work. Here are just a few suggestions:

1. Asset spring-clean
As the precious commodities that will sustain you from now on, these should be in good order. Do you have the right ones in the right places? Are they owned in the most tax-efficient way? If they are physical assets, what condition are they in? Are any surplus to your requirements? The object is partly to avoid time wasting later, but it is mainly to nail down your projections and minimize uncertainty.

Beyond all else, is your home the one you want to live in for the next few years? If not, consider moving before you stop work. A wage cheque is a comforting insurance against unexpected outcomes. A swing of –10% on sale proceeds and +10% on a new purchase makes a big difference in outcome that is best factored in before resigning.

Investment properties should be brought up to scratch through catch-up repairs and maintenance in order to maximize renting appeal and avoid hassle with tenants and nasty cash outflows in the near future.

Costly depreciators, like cars, boats, and caravans, must be checked, serviced, and upgraded where necessary or sold if they are not being used sufficiently. Fuel efficiency and running costs matter so much for a car that, unless the current model is a top-quartile performer, there's a good case for trading it in for a more economic model. Too many people dread the frequency of stops to fill up with petrol and the scale of the cost when they do. Why put yourself through it?

Good housekeeping requires that your affairs and will should be up-to-date and in good order. Imagine that you were drop dead right now. Could your loved ones access the necessary accounts, funds, and other assets, and would they know what to do?

2. Tax clearout
Tax authorities have long memories and can reach into the heart of your affairs at any time. At the least, any outstanding questions should be answered, and you should be comfortable that your recent few years' filings are correct and that full disclosure has been made.

3. Needs test
Clearly, by now you have honed your needs calculations and should be very confident that your needs are not underestimated. I would still recommend another granular interrogation to double-check cash outgoings for the next two years. Timing of spending is not the issue here, because you should have more than enough set aside in cash, but overall amount matters.

4. Solvency plan
From the beginning, solvency has been paramount. It always will be. The difference now is that once you stop paid work, your pot isn't attached to a drip, injecting regular cash from outside. It is self-sustaining.

A common mantra in wealth books is that you are rich only when you can live purely on the investment returns from your assets without touching capital. Some even set the bar at living on the interest on the interest. This is macho talk and misses the point of the game, which is to generate enough and no more. To leave capital untouched and generate £100,000 per annum at 2% per annum return into perpetuity would require me to hold £5 million from today until I die, and that's before any tax and inflation. Not only is it impossible for most people to generate anywhere near this kind of capital, but the notion of holding on to it until death is misguided, because a large portion will go to the tax man.

In the wealth game, you generate enough money to cover your future needs with a margin for safety and then manage down the balance to your final home value plus fixed legacies and a small cash surplus by the time you die (but not before). By definition, this requires you to spend capital. Your cash inflows will be a mix of investment income, such as interest, dividends, and rents, plus other unearned money like maintenance settlements and pension annuities, plus periodic capital realizations.

This requires active management and some careful thought. You become a steward and asset manager rather than an earner and accumulator. Your assets must be put to work so that they grow and deliver healthy returns. Most importantly, you shouldn't lose them. You should aim to

- generate an after-tax and expenses return on your total net worth that beats inflation;
- match risk and return on specific asset classes and overall portfolio in line with your appetite and time frame;
- use attribution to match assets with specific needs; and
- maintain adequate levels of solvency at all times.

The notion of running capital down is alarming, and I haven't started doing it yet, even though on paper, the numbers support it. There is still too much time before my assumed drop-dead date, time for losses and mishaps. For now, until my needs have reduced and some years have passed, I want my net worth to grow (or at least not fall) each year. To help achieve this goal, I have adopted a further test to balance spending and asset returns:

Total spending in a year should not exceed half of the expected growth rate in net worth.

If your net worth is £1 million, and you expect to grow that figure by 5% after taxes over the year, spending should not exceed 2.5% of starting net worth (£25,000). In very rough terms, ignoring the detailed sources, uses, and timing, half the annual growth is spent, and half is retained. If you spend at a rate higher than that of your net asset growth, capital is eroded, and your net worth will fall over the year. This may be part of your asset rundown plan, but if it isn't, you should reduce spending over the next year to allow investment returns, gains, and other income to re-store your net worth to growth. It is worth keeping an eye on this.

Solvency margins are a personal choice, like NAN ratios. I have friends who hold ten years' cash and others who live from year to year. As a rule, I aim to hold at least eighteen to twenty-four months' worth of spending in cash. Quite separate is the cash margin in our investment portfolio to take advantage of market dips. This ranges from 5 to 40% of the pot size, depending on how I feel about values and position in the cycle.

If asset prices are high, I may cash in more than I need for solvency. If they are low, I will live with tighter solvency until they recover. In this way, cash acts as a type of buffer, meeting near-term needs as well as insu-lating us from the effects of market tumbles.

As for day-to-day practicality, life without a salary can be disconcert-ing in the early stages. You have relied on this for a long time, and it has dictated habits. From now on, unless you carry on working for money, the only cash entering your account will be interest added and what you direct into it from elsewhere. Some thought should be given as to how you'll work this.

Jessie and I have always held our own personal current accounts and debit and credit cards. She receives a monthly allowance direct from my account, from which she pays personal and household expenses and her credit card bill. I know exactly what is coming out of my account and have no interest in what she is spending unless she runs short and asks for more. I top up my current account about every three months from jointly held deposit accounts that, in turn, collect savings interest, rental income, and asset sale proceeds. It is a simple arrangement and works well. What was for years a monthly cycle has become a quarterly one.

5. Systems overhaul
Good systems reduce complexity, save time, and produce better outcomes. The problem is that we rarely set out to design them from the bottom up, partly because this takes precious spare time, but also because it is boring. Furthermore, our circumstances change frequently, which adds to the burden. As a result, any systems we have tend to develop piecemeal over time, often becoming unfit or outdated and rarely integrating with each other.

The result is a lot of reinventing the wheel, searching for missing items, and generally wasting time and being frustrated. Approaching O is a perfect time to put this right, but what do you need? Personal and household administration I'll leave to you, but the money side should, in my view, include at least the following:

- cash flow forecast spreadsheets (annual and short term)
- asset spreadsheets, particularly for shares, bonds, and funds
- a balance sheet
- a NAN test spreadsheet
- tax files
- files for all bank, credit card, and other financial statements

How often you tend to the spreadsheets is up to you. I run the NAN ratios and balance sheet once a year. Cash flows I look at two or three times a year (more if there is a big spending under way), and asset sheets, more often. Staying close to these helps me pick up issues and opportunities quickly, and it also highlights developing trends, which makes for more informed investing. Instead of relying on the reporting formats from fund managers, I create my own spreadsheets in a standard format for each pot. This delivers a built-in check and allows easy comparison.

6. Limited company

For anyone who intends to continue working for money in any shape or form, this is an excellent vehicle. Set one up well before leaving work so that it is fully functioning as soon as you need it. Bank accounts, mandates, and online access take time to set up, as do Companies House and HMRC requirements.

A good reason to do it is to capture all income generated from work-related activity. This makes for an extremely simple life and a very short answer to the tax man, should he inquire. Any paid work or projects can be undertaken through the company that contracts directly with clients and other counterparties. In simple terms, it provides a wall between earned and investment income. The former goes to the company; the latter to you personally. No confusion.

Another benefit is that you can save tax. Allowable expenses can be offset against this income in calculating corporation tax due. Certain work-related expenses, both income and capital equipment—which, as a salaried employee, you paid out of after tax earnings—can now be repaid to you by the company, with the cost offset against corporation tax. Sole traders (i.e., those trading as an individual or partnership) can also do this, but the scope for muddling private and business expenses is greater, and HMRC is aware of this. Money can be withdrawn from your company either as salary, dividends, or a capital repayment on liquidation. You can time these events to suit and dovetail with your private investment returns to gain maximum benefit from tax thresholds and reliefs.

Somehow, just having the company can stimulate a slightly different thought process. What will it do, what services will you contract through it, does it need a website, and who will be your fellow shareholders and directors, if any? It's like building a warehouse speculatively. You are more likely to get requests for storage once it is standing than you would if you were only thinking about building one.

Since O assumes no more paid work, any money accumulated in your company is an upside to the plan. This is important and opens all sorts of opportunities. You may want to hold the cash to beef up your NAN ratio for a rainy day, or you might treat it as separate and disposable. Some might be allocated as risk capital and used to fund a new venture, or a portion might be given away.

Buying an off-the-shelf, ready-made limited company or forming a new one is quick and cheap. Administration is surprisingly easy once you have mastered the online setups for HMRC and Companies House and have online banking. A simple means of recording invoices issued, expenses incurred, and cash balances makes annual filings straightforward.

7. Ground rules for avoiding pitfalls

If you elevate common sense practice to the status of a rule, it becomes part of your own operating system and becomes more readily accepted by others. To break it requires exceptional circumstances. An example is "I never drink alcohol on weekdays." By apparently removing any discretion in the matter, no one can be offended because you choose not to drink with them. Of course, it's a construct, but it does work, particularly if delivered as a straightforward fait accompli. It's like being labelled a vegetarian or a nonsmoker. People tend to just accept it.

What specific pitfalls tend to follow arrival at O? An obvious one is falling out with one's other half, who isn't used to seeing so much of you. If not rules, at least some principles should be discussed and agreed upon, covering such areas as division of labour, noninterference, and decision making. What is your joint philosophy regarding individual travel and activities? Some couples make strenuous efforts to do their own thing regularly, and there are no rules on time frames or destinations. Others take a different approach. I have a happily married friend who is barred from staying away for more than one night at a stretch, and even then, it's allowed only once or twice a year within a few miles' radius of home and certainly not outside cell-phone or Internet range. Because he knows the rule, he has stopped asking the question.

Another common problem is falling into a kind of malaise through inactivity. Too much rest and relaxation becomes habit forming and is ultimately unsatisfying. Inertia dulls the body and mind, saps energy, and stultifies. The answer is to set up sustainable, everyday routines—setting an alarm on weekdays and scheduling exercise days, activities, meditation time, TV nights, and so on. Such rules are highly effective and self-sustaining through the benefits of the positive activities they foster.

You should also set strict rules about money for friends and relatives, and investment 'opportunities' from others. Are you a lender or investor or not? Will you borrow from friends and relatives? You can avoid awkwardness by announcing policy on a matter, whoever asks. This is a very real situation for the newly retired or moneyed, and it is particularly dangerous for those not used to holding relatively large sums of cash. It can burn a hole in your pocket if you let it, and other players are quick to spot this.

XVIII

THE PARADOX

O marks the end of the wealth game. You cross the finish line and enter a new place, a vibrant ecosystem brimming with opportunity and deep, sustainable rewards. I think of it as a kind of paradise. Reaching this goal with life to spare is the financial equivalent of climbing Everest unaided; it's an extraordinary feat. But here, unlike at the mountain summit, the air is rich and easy to breathe, and the routes ahead are not all downhill. It marks the end of the beginning and the start of a life potentially richer in every department. You have won the freedom to choose how to spend your time—on grand schemes, idleness, or both. The prize is there to be enjoyed. Why not claim it?

But a primary motivator has gone. In reaching O, you accept that you don't need to work for money again, so whatever your reasons are for carrying on work, they don't include that one. I believe that a human's drive for financial self-sufficiency is primordial, a modern-day version of the quest for shelter, food, clothing, warmth, and safety. In today's survival stakes, it ranks second only to personal security. If this is right, achievement of such a fundamental goal leaves a gap and raises the obvious question: What do I replace it with?

It is easy to underestimate the effects of such a powerful motivator on our actions and thoughts and, therefore, the consequences of losing it. I have seen people in the run-up to O deliberately create new needs or effectively raise their target NAN ratios to delay arrival at this position. The extra house, extension, car, or cash safety buffer may be necessary for you to reach O, but it may not be, and where do you draw the line? By exercising this kind of self-trickery, it's possible to stave off reaching O indefinitely.

The mind is too smart to be completely fooled by this. Somewhere deep within is the knowledge that the delay is contrived and that your precious primary motivator, once pure and authentic, is now manufactured and artificial. Its real purpose is missing; the whole exercise becomes hollow. Doubt creeps in, as do the questions of why you are still doing what you're doing. What was once simple to answer is no longer, and change is upon you.

From the moment you enter the no-man's-land between thinking you are at O and knowing you are there, change begins to arrive, imperceptibly at first. More of a general feeling than describable or tangible elements, it gathers speed as you accept your position, eliminate doubts, and celebrate your arrival. In a short time, the welter of changes become tangible and starts to flood like a tsunami. I have seen talented, successful players swept off their feet and washed into a maelstrom of swirling emotions, self-doubt, and restlessness—at least five high-achieving friends of mine are taking antidepressants and having counselling. Some have yet to reach O, but all are firmly in the grip of personal crises of confidence, feeling anxious, overwhelmed, and unable to see clear, positive outcomes.

The problem has been described by one friend as a perfect storm, where a small number of changes (or a single change) could be managed, but because these are compounded simultaneously with so many others, the situation becomes chaotic and untenable, like a violent weather system combining with a seabed earthquake, a continental shelf, and the meeting of opposing ocean currents at a headland. In my friend's case, the difficulty is exacerbated by high intellect and a brain that operates unusually fast but has no off switch. High-speed processing and analysis generates multiple options and solutions that themselves are dissected and evaluated, taking him to a point far from the original question and unable to retrace all the steps. The same exercise is replicated for other changes, problems, and questions.

Of course, for anyone who reaches O, life is as simple or as complicated as you make it. Long ago, the underlying causes of suffering were prescribed by the Buddha: craving, aversion, and attachment. Deal with these, and you minimize suffering.

In conversation with Anathapindika, a great banker of his time, the sage also described four kinds of happiness for the layman who leads an ordinary family life: first, enjoy economic security or sufficient wealth acquired by just and righteous means; second, spend that wealth liberally on yourself, your family, your friends, your relatives, and meritorious deeds; third, be free from debts; and fourth, live a faultless and pure life without committing evil in thought, word, or deed. Buddha reminded the banker that the first three are economic and that material happiness is "not worth one-sixteenth part" of the spiritual happiness arising out of a faultless and good life.*

*Walpola Sri Rahula, *What the Buddha Taught* (Gordon Fraser, 1978). Derived from Anguttara Nikaya II.

I intend to grab my freedom with both hands, do my best to upgrade every item in the personal-qualities prize, and pursue a range of spending suggestions. Here are my top ten:

1. Develop greater loving kindness, compassion and altruistic joy— actions as well as words
2. Tend to my body—healthy eating, exercise, and sleep

3. Purify and train my mind—virtue, mindfulness, inquiry, and meditation
4. Investigate and learn—study and practice to improve knowledge and capabilities
5. Socialize—physically connect person to person and with the community
6. Play—games, sports, and other activities, and generally rediscover being a child
7. Travel—independently explore the globe and meet its inhabitants
8. Build something (anything) creative—a book, garden, orchard, house, boat, wine cellar, or business
9. Idle and contemplate—savour the moment, enjoy space, and let time pass without anxiety
10. Give away—the acid test of letting go is releasing time, effort, money, and possessions.

Just writing this is sobering, as each activity is a multilayered world in itself. None of them is new, yet they look new. They have been released from the shadows of the previous number one on the list, "provide for the family," which dominated for so long. The mountain has gone, and the occupants of the valley can at last see the sun, the sky, and an endless horizon.

This brings me to the end, which is where I began. The original title for this book was *Travelling Light*, and my intent was to extol and flesh out the benefits of unencumbrance. It quickly became clear that this appealing philosophy didn't answer the bigger questions of how to become financially self-sufficient and know whether you've arrived.

The book runs two seemingly opposing themes: the first is an ordinary working person's fastest route to wealth; the second is the weight of wealth and materialism and the imperative to detach from them. Surprisingly, the two coexist perfectly: acknowledging the second helps you achieve the first, which in turn helps you understand the second better still, and so on. They are linked. It's a game.

Herein lies the paradox. Self-sufficiency requires financial independence, which requires wealth generation, which requires saving and investing, which requires working for money and not wasting what you earn. You work better and save more when travelling light, consuming and accumulating less. The lighter you are, the faster and farther you travel.

You generate more wealth the less you need, and less wealth the more you need.

By definition, any need counts against net worth, so a player in any given situation will be wealthier by having needs of £1 compared with needs of £2. Neediness erodes wealth.

And what of contentment? It has been said that adults are ready to marry only when they realize they can be fulfilled on their own. Subsistence requirements aside, I would argue the same for wealth—that you are best suited to money when you clearly see its challenges and limitations but can be detached from it without suffering. In other words, when you realize that you don't need it to be happy.

By learning to live with less than you thought you needed or wanted and discovering that instead of being dreadful, life offers an inexhaustible supply of pleasures, small and large, you can hone your ability to find contentment. Perhaps even this goal will become blurred and lose significance. What value is happiness tethered to suffering compared with wisdom, compassion, and equanimity born of detachment? The scope to discover such a prize is tantalizing.

THE END

GLOSSARY

All terms are defined as used in the wealth game. Those marked with an asterisk(*) are original words or concepts.

actively managed fund. A collection of investments managed by an individual or group, selected, bought, and sold to achieve a particular goal, such as income generation, capital growth, or a certain level of overall return.

anicca. One of the three basic characteristics of existence from the Buddhist Canon, this is the Pali word for impermanence and the ever-changing nature of all things. The other two characteristics are dukha (suffering) and anatta (no permanent self or soul).

appreciator.* An asset that will typically increase in value over time, despite short-term fluctuations, such as a collection of good-quality company shares or desirable property.

asset. An item with realizable financial value.

attribution. The action of setting aside particular assets to meet particular needs.

balance sheet. The value of your total assets less debts and other liabilities at a point in time. See also *net worth* and *net assets.*

beginner phase.* The period in the game from the time a person first adopts wealth generation as a goal through to the time that person has at least two meaningful platforms for wealth creation, such as a pension or an interest in residential property, and generates sufficient surplus cash to make further investment choices.

bond. A debt in which an investor lends money to an entity, usually a company or government, for a finite period of time at a fixed or variable interest rate.

buy and hold. A wealth-generating strategy whereby a person or entity acquires an asset and, instead of selling it to finance the purchase of a different asset, continues to hold it, often as security against new borrowings. As these borrowings are repaid and/or the underlying asset values rises, further asset purchases are possible, and the process can be repeated indefinitely.

capital-asset pricing model (CAPM). A model for calculating the rate of return on a particular investment that a rational investor should demand, given the riskiness of that investment.

capital return. The return generated on an investment through its change in value.

capitalize or **capitalization.** An accounting method of converting future income and outgoings into balance-sheet figures for easy comparison at a point in time.

carry trade. Borrowing in a country with a low interest rate in order to relend to another with a higher rate.

cash flow. A fluid and constantly moving element, like water, this is the difference between cash income and outgoings over a period of time.

cash-interest cover. See also *interest cover.* A comparison between available cash flow and the interest cost for a loan, generally expressed as a ratio or multiple.

central phase.* The period in the game between the end of the beginner phase and the point at which O is clearly reachable within five to ten years.

closed-end fund. A vehicle for holding investments, such as an investment trust, that has a fixed number of shares and doesn't issue new shares or cancel existing ones daily as demand from investors rises or falls.

commercial nous. A most valuable skill in the game, this means to understand value, price, financial risk and return, the financial effect of actions, the purpose of an exercise and the quickest means of achieving a financial goal.

compound annual growth rate (CAGR). The growth rate that gets you from a starting investment value to an ending one if you assume that the investment has been compounding over that period. The formula is as follows:

$$CAGR = (\text{ending value} / \text{starting value})^{(1/t)} - 1,$$
$$\text{where } t \text{ is the time period in years.}$$

compound interest. Interest earned on the principal or face value of an investment as well as on its previously received interest.

compound return. The absolute amount of income and capital value generated on an investment through compounding.

compounding. The exponential increase in value of an investment by earning income and capital returns on the principal or face value of an investment as well as on its previously earned income and capital returns.

compounding escalator.* An imaginary conveyor that moves players closer to O.

consumable.* An asset that doesn't survive long enough to justify inclusion in a player's personal balance sheet and has no meaningful resale value, such as food, clothes, or fuel for vehicles.

consumer prices index (CPI). A measure of price change for a basket of seven hundred goods and services using geometric mean. Currently it is the United Kingdom's official measure of inflation/deflation. It tends to be lower than the retail prices index, which is calculated using arithmetic average and, unlike CPI, includes mortgage interest payments and council tax.

contrarian investing. An investor strategy of going against the herd, which means buying when others are selling and selling when others are buying. It extends beyond timing to choice of investment, so the contrarian investor will seek unloved or overlooked opportunities with unrealized value potential.

convertible security or **convertible.** An investment instrument, such as a share or bond, that carries the right to switch partially or completely into another type of instrument in the issuer's balance sheet, usually at the holder's option. Common examples are convertible preference shares, loan stock, or *bonds*, which may be converted into *ordinary shares*.

cost of capital. The cost of money used for any purchase. If the money is borrowed, it is the *cost of debt*, which is interest and associated loan charges. If the money is from the investor's own savings, it is the *cost of equity* or *opportunity cost*; that is, the best available rate of return that could be earned from a similarly risky asset or portfolio of securities and is also known as *required* or *expected return*. Where the money is a mix of borrowings and savings, a weighted average of the costs of each is used. See also *weighted average cost of capital (WACC)*. The *capital asset pricing model (CAPM)* is commonly used by professional investors to determine the cost of capital.

cost of debt. The interest charge, arrangement fee, and any other costs applying to a loan.

cost of equity. The opportunity cost. See also *cost of capital.*

coupon. The nominal (money value) interest payable on a loan investment, typically expressed as a percentage of the principal amount of the loan when it is also known as *current yield.*

credit risk. The risk of a borrower having insufficient funds to repay a loan in full.

credit scoring. A process for assigning scores to borrowers based on the risk of their not repaying the loan in full.

creditor. The entity entitled to collect a debt.

current yield. Coupon expressed as a percentage. Also known as *running yield.*

curse of comparison.* An obstacle in the game where a player is distracted by the activities of other players and loses sight of his or her own path to O.

debenture. A loan instrument or bond.

debt-to-equity ratio. Total debt / total equity often expressed as a percentage also known as *leverage* and *gearing.* It is a measure of the financial risk added to an investment through its means of funding.

debtor. The entity that owes a debt.

default risk. The risk of a borrower not repaying a loan in full. It includes *credit risk* but also the chance that a borrower may challenge the validity of the amount owing or simply choose not to pay.

depreciation. Wastage in value of an asset over time.

depreciator. An asset whose value inexorably wastes over time to zero or a negative number if it costs more to keep than it is worth. Examples include most cars, boats, caravans, computers, mobile phones, and other electrical equipment.

discount factor. The multiplier that converts a *future value* to a *present value*. It is the inverse of the *discount rate*.

discount rate. The rate of return used to calculate the *present value* of future cash flows. It is typically used to value an asset, and the rate adopted is the *cost of debt* or *cost of equity* or *WACC*, depending on how the asset purchase is being financed. See also *cost of capital* and *required* or *expected return*.

discounted cash flow (DCF). A method of valuing future cash flows recognizing the time value of money, the riskiness of those cash flows, and the investor's own cost of capital. *Future values* are multiplied by *discount factors* for each period to obtain *present value*.

discretionary fund manager (DFM) or **wealth manager.** A person or team that manages an investor's money in line with preagreed risk and return targets.

disguised borrowing. Spending money out of income or savings whilst a debt of some kind, such as a mortgage or personal loan, is still outstanding. By choosing to spend the money instead of repaying the loan, the player is effectively using borrowed money for the spend. If the spend is for an *appreciator*, that's return is higher than the player's *cost of debt*, wealth is created but if the return is lower or it is used for a *depreciator* or *consumable*, wealth is lost. The borrowing is "disguised," because it is compartmentalized in the mind of the player as being associated only with a specific asset or need, such as a home purchase, car, or washing machine, rather just a debt obstacle in the path to reaching O.

dividend. A distribution of profits by a company to its shareholders.

dividend cover. A company's profits or earnings after tax / the dividend it pays. A high level of cover indicates that the company can comfortably pay its dividend and vice versa. Investors use it to assess the income return potential of companies.

dividend per share (DPS). Total dividend paid by a company / total number of shares in issue.

dividend yield. *Dividend per share (DPS)* / share price, generally expressed as a percentage.

earnings. Company profits after all costs and tax, also known as *profit after tax (PAT)* or bottom-line profit. This is the profit available to shareholders.

earnings before interest, tax, depreciation, and amortization (EBITDA). Company profits after deduction of costs of sales and administrative costs but before costs relating to debt finance and accounting costs for depreciation of assets and apportionment of goodwill, an intangible asset on the balance sheet. Also known as *operating profit*, this is a measure of the profitability of the company purely from its business operations rather than from its financing. It is the profit available to all finance providers.

earnings multiple. The valuation multiplier applied to a company's earnings to calculate value. It is the reciprocal of the investor's required rate of return for that investment, so a required return of 12.5% per annum is equivalent to an 8× multiplier (1/0.125). See also *price earnings ratio*. A high multiple indicates that investors value each pound of company earnings highly, perhaps because it has strong growth prospects or reliable profits.

earnings per share. Earnings or profit after tax / total number of shares in issue.

enterprise value (EV) or **total enterprise value (TEV).** The total value of a company's shares and debt less any cash held. From another angle, it is the total value of the assets and operations of the business before taking account of financing. This makes it a cleaner figure than *equity value*, which is distorted by the debt structure of the particular entity. It is the most commonly used expression of value for a business.

enterprise-value-to-EBITDA ratio or **multiple (EV/EBITDA).** A useful price-comparison tool when assessing different companies. It can also be used to calculate value where only an *EBITDA* figure is available.

equity. Ownership share of an asset after all debt has been deducted. *Equity* in an owned home is the value of the property on the open market less any mortgage debt. Applies equally to a company and *an equity* is also a term used to describe a company share.

equity risk premium. The historic additional return for a company share with average risk versus the return for a risk-free investment, such as a government bond or gilt. It has been calculated by academics at 7.3% per annum. This is adjusted for the riskiness of the particular investment being considered and added to the applicable gilt rate to give the *cost of equity*. An equity risk premium of 8% and a 2% risk-free rate produces a 10% *cost of equity* or *required return on equity* or *hurdle rate*. See also *risk premium*.

equity value. See also *equity*. The same meaning as *market capitalization* when applied to a company listed on a stock market. Unlike *enterprise value*, this is the value available to the owner or shareholders after all lenders have been repaid.

execution only. A security-dealing service where no advice is given.

exchange-traded fund (ETF). A security designed to track a stock market index.

expected return. Either the financial return an investor *hopes* to get from an investment or that which he or she *demands*. The latter is also known as *required return*.

final home value.* The value of a home in *today's money* that a player expects to hold at death.

final phase.* The period of the game between the end of the *central phase* and arrival at *O*.

financial asset. Money in its various forms and contracts entitling the holder to money, such as bank deposits, shares, bonds, and other securities.

financial risk. The risk imposed by debt.

fixed-interest security. A financial instrument that pays the holder a predetermined set rate of interest. Examples are *gilts* and corporate *bonds*.

future value (FV). The value of an asset at a specific date in the future, reflecting the time value of money. Future value (FV) of £1 = £1 × $(1 + r)^t$, where r is the annual rate of return earned over the period, and t is the number of years between now and the date of measurement.

gearing. (1) **financial gearing** is the ratio of debt to equity, typically calculated as debt minus cash balances / net assets. It is a measure of financial riskiness, so a high gearing level indicates greater risk. Also known as *leverage*. (2) **operational gearing** is the ratio of fixed costs to sales. Like debt, fixed costs are fixed rather than variable, so they add business risk since they do not fall in line with a tail off in sales. On the other hand, they do not increase with sales, allowing greater profit potential in a growing business.

gilt-edged security (gilt). Fixed-interest UK government bond traded on the London Stock Exchange.

goodwill. An intangible asset in a company's balance sheet, representing brand recognition, people skills, and know-how. When a company buys another business, the difference between the price it pays and the value of the target's net assets is recorded in the acquirer's balance sheet as goodwill. This *purchased goodwill* is generally written off (amortized) over a period of years as the acquired business becomes more valuable.

gross domestic product (GDP). The total value of all goods produced and services delivered by a country, typically measured over a year. It is the principal indicator of economic growth or decline.

gross dividend yield. See also *dividend yield*. It is calculated using the gross dividend per share, before tax has been deducted.

gross redemption yield. See also *redemption yield*.

growth platform.* A temporary home for your cash in which additional value will automatically accrue by virtue of someone else's efforts or market forces. In the wealth game, these are the foundations for personal wealth generation. They include *appreciators* and *productive depreciators* if their cash generation exceeds their depreciation. They do not include *depreciators* and *consumables.* Growth platforms can be a single asset or a grouping of assets, such as rental properties or financial securities. The more effective the growth platform and the more surplus cash a player allocates to it, the faster the player's asset base will grow.

growth stock. A company that generates a higher earnings per share than average and is expected to continue doing so for the foreseeable future. Also associated with low dividend payout, as profits are retained to fuel growth.

HMRC. Her Majesty's Revenue and Customs, a UK government department responsible for collecting taxes.

impermanence. See also *anicca.* A Buddhist concept that all things are impermanent and subject to constant flux and change. It follows that to try to anchor yourself to anything, to cling to it, or to become overly attached will lead to disappointment. Similarly, craving and aversion are misguided, as in each case, the object in question has no permanent substance.

income return. The return generated on an investment through the income it generates.

income stock. A company that generates a higher dividend yield than average and is expected to continue to do so for the foreseeable future.

independent financial adviser (IFA). A person authorized by the financial regulator to provide financial advice. IFAs should offer impartial, expert advice suited to the client's circumstances and in the client's best interest.

index linked. In theory, anything that has a fixed price relationship with a specific index. Most commonly used as a tie to inflation (either *CPI* or *RPI*) for rental property and bonds.

index tracker. A fund that is designed to replicate a particular stock market index, also known as a *tracker fund*. See also *ETF*.

inflation. An average increase in prices and corresponding reduction in the purchasing power of money. Causes include *demand-pull*, where demand outstrips supply; *cost-push*, where raw-material costs rise; or a weak exchange rate that causes the cost of imports to rise. *Money supply*, both quantum and rate of spending versus saving, also fuels price increases.

interest cover. Cash available to service interest/interest cost. Applicable to any entity that takes on debt and a primary test of affordability, solvency, and financial risk.

internal rate of return (IRR). The discount rate at which an investment has a present value of zero.

individual savings account (ISA). UK tax-free savings account that can be invested in stocks and shares or held as cash on deposit.

investment trust. A closed-end fund, usually listed on the London Stock Market, which holds a wide range of financial assets. Investors buy and sell shares in the trust between each other like any public listed company. Unlike open-end funds, they have permanent fixed capital and do not need to sell underlying assets when investors sell shares. They can also borrow to enhance returns on equity.

lagom. A Swedish concept of "just enough," "not too much or too little," "enough to go round," "fair share," or "just right." It indicates balance, not perfection, and reflects the country's cultural and social ideals of equality and fairness.

leverage. See also *financial gearing*. A measure of the level of debt relative to asset value, high leverage equates to the possibility of high returns on equity and also high risk of insolvency.

liquidity. The measure of cash strength and an ability to pay near-term outgoings as they fall due without having to sell assets in a hurry or borrow. *Solvency* is a broader test over the longer term.

liquidity ratio. There are several tests under this heading. Common is the *quick ratio*, also known as the *acid test*: cash and cash equivalents + money due in shortly / current liabilities (due within one year).

listed company. A company whose shares are listed on the London Stock Exchange. Also known as quoted company. Whilst not technically "listed" under UK regulations, the reference also includes companies on other exchanges, such as the Alternative Investment Market (AIM) and international exchanges. Shares are freely tradable on the relevant market, and prices are constantly updated and published.

loan to value. The ratio of debt to asset value, also known as *debt / total assets ratio*. Can be calculated using gross debt or net debt after deduction of cash balances. Differs from *gearing*, which is typically a debt/equity ratio. This is another form of solvency ratio, typically used in property purchases.

London Inter-Bank Offered Rate (LIBOR) or **International Continental Exchange LIBOR (ICE LIBOR).** The rate of interest offered for fixed-length, short-term loans to highly rated, low-risk banks in the London interbank market. It is used as a reference point for loans worldwide.

managed fund. See *actively managed fund*.

mark to market. Revaluation of an asset in line with the currently realizable price in the market.

market capitalization or **market capital.** See also *equity value*. For listed companies, this is share price × number of shares in issue.

maturity date. The point at which a debt security is redeemed and the par value paid to the lender. It also refers to the final repayment date in a loan agreement.

mental contrasting. A process of allying goals with potential obstacles to their realization, promoting realism and solution-oriented behaviours.

monetary policy. A tool to control the volume of money in circulation in an economy, typically wielded by a country's central bank. Key component is interest rates, which affect the demand for money and inflation. Low rates promote economic growth and inflation and vice versa. Governments and financial regulators also engage indirectly through setting minimum solvency and capital-adequacy ratios for banks, which affect their ability to lend.

money supply. Various measures exist for the total money in circulation in an economy. M0 and M1 (Narrow money) = notes and coins + other money equivalents easily convertible into cash; M2 = M1 + short-term deposits in banks and twenty-four-hour money-market funds; M3 = M2 + longer-term deposits.

NAN value.* *Net assets* compared with *needs*.

NAN gap.* The monetary difference between *net assets* and *needs*.

NAN ratio.* *Net assets* / *needs*.

NAN test.* An diagnostic exercise in the wealth game to determine a player's *NAN gap* and *NAN ratio* and their position relative to *O*—in other words, where they are in the game.

needs.* Today's money value of all future needs added together *(capitalized)*. For the purposes of the *NAN test*, *needs* include all those chosen by the player, whether essential subsistence needs or luxuries.

needs architecture.* The philosophical and practical framework for consumption, designed by a player, either consciously or by default.

negative equity. A position where debt exceeds equity.

net assets or **net asset value (NAV).** Total assets minus all liabilities. Also known as *net worth*, *personal net assets*, or *personal net worth* if referring to an individual. In personal finance, the term should not be confused with *wealth*, as NAV is an absolute number, and *wealth* is a relative concept.

net gearing. A measure of *gearing* in which cash balances are offset against total debt before performing the *gearing* calculation.

nominal rate. A rate expressed in money terms, taking no account of the eroding effect of inflation. Examples include a nominal interest rate paid on a loan, a nominal interest rate received on a cash deposit, or a nominal return on an investment. The inflation-adjusted equivalent is a *real rate*.

nominal value or **par value.** The face value of a debt security, loan, or share. Also known as *principal*. It bears no relationship to the market value or price of the asset.

O.* The ultimate objective in the wealth game: "I can live the life I want without needing to work for money again." Players can measure their financial position against O by running the *NAN test*.

open-end fund. A vehicle for holding investments, such as a unit trust, that issues new shares or cancels existing ones daily as demand from investors rises or falls.

operating profit. See also *earnings before interest, tax, depreciation and amortization (EBITDA)*.

operating profit margin. *EBITDA* / sales, usually expressed as a percentage.

opportunity cost. In microeconomic theory, the opportunity cost of a choice is the value of the best alternative foregone where a choice needs to be made between several mutually exclusive alternatives and where you have limited resources. It lies at the heart of *commercial nous* and rational behaviour in personal finance, and it forms the basis of a sound financial strategy. In simple terms, can you spend your money more effectively in the quest to reach O?

ordinary share. A unit of ownership in a company entitling the holder to participate in any distributions of profit (dividends) or returns of capital.

preference share. A unit of ownership in a company with special rights, such as a guaranteed dividend or enhanced voting rights, and that ranks ahead of ordinary shares on a capital return, such as a winding up of the company.

present value. The discounted value of future cash flows. Also *today's money value*. Present value (PV) = future value (FV)/$(1 + r)^t$, where r is the annual *discount rate* over the period, and t is the number of years.

price. Material or monetary payment for sale and purchase of an asset, often the outcome of a negotiation between buyer and seller. A buyer asks,

"What can I get it for?" and a seller asks, "What can I get for it?" Asking price may differ from final agreed price. It is quite distinct from *value*.

price-earnings ratio (PE ratio) or **price-earnings multiple (PE multiple).** Share price / *earnings per share (EPS)*. See also *earnings multiple*.

price versus value. The difference between price and value represents a wealth gain or loss. Price greater than value equals wealth gain for the seller and loss for the buyer, and value higher than price equals wealth loss for the seller and gain for the buyer.

principal. See *nominal value*.

primary utility value. The benefit an asset confers to its holder.

private equity. An asset class of shares and debt mainly in private companies. Specialist investment managers select and buy stakes ranging from minority to majority in companies and oversee or direct management and operations. Equity returns are boosted by often high levels of debt (*gearing* or *leverage*). Hold periods are, on average, three to five years, at which point the business is sold or floated on a stock market. In some cases, private-equity managers can recover their initial equity investment and more by refinancing the company with new debt and withdrawing some of it.

productive appreciator.* An *appreciator* that produces or is capable of producing income, such as a share that delivers a dividend or a property that has rental potential.

profit after tax (PAT). See *earnings*.

profit before tax (PBT). Profit after all costs except tax.

profit margin. Profit / sales. See also *operating profit margin*.

quantitative easing. An unconventional form of monetary policy used in emergencies or economic depression, where a central bank creates new money electronically to buy financial assets, like government bonds, from institutional investors, such as banks and pension firms. The "new" money adds liquidity to the financial system, whilst the assets acquired by the central bank increase the size of its balance sheet. The central bank continues to collect interest payable on the assets it has acquired, which adds to state coffers. In due course, theoretically (because at the time of writing, this hasn't happened), the central bank sells the financial assets back to institutional investors and cancels the proceeds electronically, thereby managing down the money supply.

rate of return. The income and capital return on an investment expressed as a percentage.

real asset. A physical or tangible asset that has value due to its substance and properties, such as precious metals, commodities, oil and gas, land, and property. Distinct from a financial asset.

real rate. An inflation adjusted rate. Examples include a *real* interest rate paid on a loan, a *real* interest rate received on a cash deposit, or a *real* return on an investment. The non–inflation adjusted equivalent is *nominal rate*. A *nominal* rate of 5% per annum becomes a *real rate* of 3% per annum if inflation is 2% per annum.

redemption yield or **yield to redemption** or **yield to maturity (YTM).** A measure for comparing bond returns, which combines current or running yield with any theoretical capital gain or loss arising from the difference between the purchase price of the bond and its *nominal* or *par value*. In technical speak, it is the *discount rate* at which the sum of all future cash flows from the bond (income and capital) is equal to the current price of the bond. See the section on *bonds* for a worked example.

required return. The financial return an investor demands to compensate for the risk of a particular investment.

retail prices index. A measure of the price change of goods and services using the arithmetic average. It tends to be higher than the *consumer prices index* and, unlike *CPI*, includes mortgage interest payments and council tax.

return on investment. There are many ways of measuring this. For example, do you want to measure (1) *income return, capital return*, or income and capital combined (*total return*); (2) a pretax or post tax return; (3) return against the total cost of the investment (*return on capital*) or just your equity contribution (*return on equity*); and (4) the *annual return* or that over the entire hold period. A prudent approach in personal finance is to use (income after tax and any expenses + capital gain after tax and selling expenses) / original cost of investment. Divide the answer by the original cost of the investment and multiply by 100 to produce the *rate of return* over the period you have chosen.

risk. (1)Wider geographic/natural, political, economic or market risk (*systemic*);(2) asset specific, *credit*, or *default* risk (*unsystemic*); and (3) personal circumstances risk around age, health, behaviour, home setup, job, relationships, and so on.

risk and return. The finance concept that a rational investor should try as far as possible to measure the risks and return of any investment and balance the two when pricing it. The *yield equation* and its various forms are useful pricing and comparison tools.

risk-free return (RFR). The return available on a risk-free investment, such as a gilt issued by a financially strong nation.

risk premium. The required additional return for making a risky investment rather than a safe one. See also *equity risk premium.*

running yield. See *current yield.*

security. (1) Another name for a share, bond, or other financial instrument. (2) An asset available to a lender in the event of a loan default.

self-invested personal pension (SIPP). A UK tax-efficient private pension plan managed by its holder, who can, within limits, choose contribution levels and asset allocation.

share. A unit of ownership in a company. See also *ordinary share* and *preference share.*

shareholders' funds. The portion of a company's balance sheet that belongs to shareholders or the *equity* in the balance sheet. Calculated as *net assets* after deduction of all short- and long-term liabilities and minority interests.

simple interest. Interest earned only on the principal or face value of an investment. Contrast with *compound interest.*

skimming.* An activity that, instead of adding to the overall wealth of an economy, redirects existing wealth to the entity or person doing the skimming. Examples of this capture of wealth include buying and holding *appreciators* or acting as an agent or broker. Appropriation of state assets has, throughout history, been a way of *skimming* wealth.

solvency. The measure of financial strength and an ability to pay near- and long-term outgoings as they fall due without having to sell assets in a hurry or borrow. See also *liquidity.*

solvency ratio. See *liquidity ratio.*

subordinated interest. A right that ranks behind that of another in order of priority. Examples include an unsecured overdraft or personal loan, which ranks behind a mortgage, or an ordinary share, which ranks behind a preference share, which, in turn, ranks behind debt in a company.

surplus cash flow. Cash flow after tax and expenses but before spending on *net worth*. It is the cash available to fund *growth platforms*. In calculating it, exclude money allocated to savings and the purchase or funding of growth platforms. This is the fuel for wealth generation.

tax allowance or **relief.** A sum that can be deducted from gross income in arriving at taxable income.

term loan. A loan of a fixed amount for an agreed time and on specific terms. Most commonly requires payment of interest and partial repayments of principal at periodic intervals throughout. It may be secured or unsecured.

time value of money (TVM). A pound today is worth more than a pound received tomorrow, because the pound today can earn interest between now and tomorrow.

today's money value. See *present value*.

total enterprise value (TEV). See *enterprise value*.

TEV/EBITDA multiple. See *enterprise-value-to-EBITDA ratio* or *multiple*.

total return. *Income return + capital return.*

total yield. Total return / cost or value of investment expressed as a percentage.

tracker fund. See *index tracker*.

unit trust. A type of *open-end fund*.

unsecured. No collateral or charge over assets available.

value. The monetary worth of an asset. See also *present value*. A different concept from *price*.

value versus price. See *price versus value*.

vicious circle or **spiral.** A sequence of reciprocal cause and effect in which two or more elements intensify and aggravate each other, leading to a worsening of the situation—a domino effect of damage.

virtuous circle. A recurring cycle of behaviours or events, the result of each one being to promote more and increase the beneficial effect of the next—one good thing leads to another.

way-of-the-wealth game.* Incorporation of the philosophy and methods set out in this book into your own being and life so that they become second nature.

wealth. Measure of *net worth* against *needs* A player with *net worth* greater than *needs* is wealthy, but one with *needs* greater than *net worth* is not.

wealth game.* The challenge of reaching *O* in the shortest time possible. It is just one of many distinct life challenges or games.

wealth-game paradox.* The seemingly contradictory (but actually true) statement that you generate more wealth the less you need and less wealth the more you need. By definition, any need counts against *net worth*, so a player in any given situation will be wealthier by having *needs* of £1 compared with *needs* of £2. Neediness erodes wealth.

wealthy. See *wealth*.

weighted average cost of capital (WACC). The *(cost of debt* × ratio of debt to overall capital) + *(cost of equity* × ratio of equity to overall capital). It forms the basis of the *required return* on an investment.

yield. Return (income, capital, or both) / price, usually expressed as a percentage. See also *current, dividend, gross dividend, redemption, running,* and *total yield*.

yield to maturity (YTM). See *redemption yield*.

zero-sum game. A concept in *game theory* and economics that each participant's gain (or loss) is matched exactly by the loss (or gain) of other participants. It contrasts with a win-win scenario in which new value overall is created, allowing all participants to improve their positions, or a lose-lose scenario in which overall value is destroyed, and all participants can suffer loss.

ABOUT THE AUTHOR

Peter Alcaraz is a qualified lawyer who practiced company law before moving into corporate finance, where he spent twenty years advising small and medium companies on take-overs, acquisitions, disposals, and fundraisings. He is married with two teenage daughters.

Printed in Great Britain
by Amazon.co.uk, Ltd.,
Marston Gate.